The Dalai Lamas
The Institution and Its History

Emerging Perceptions in Buddhist Studies (ISSN 0971-9512)

1-2. An Encyclopaedia of Buddhist Deities, Demigods, Godlings, Saints & Demons — with Special Focus on Iconographic Attributes; by Fredrick W. Bunce. 2 Vols. (ISBN 81-246-0020-1; set)

3. Buddhism in Karnataka; byR.C. Hiremath; with a foreword by H.H. the Dalai Lama (ISBN 81-246-0013-9)

4-5. Pāli Language and Literature: A Systematic Survey and Historical Study; by Kanai Lal Hazra. 2 Vols. (ISBN 81-246-0004-X; set)

6. Maṇḍala and Landscape; by A.W. Macdonald (ISBN 81-246-0060-0)

7. The Future Buddha Maitreya: An Iconological Study; by Inchang Kim (ISBN 81-246-0082-1)

8. Absence of the Buddha Image in Early Buddhist Art; by Kanoko Tanaka (ISBN 81-246-0090-2)

9. A Few Facts About Buddhism; by Gunnar Gällmo (ISBN 81-246-0099-6)

10. Buddhist Theory of Meaning and Literary Analysis; by Rajnish K. Mishra (ISBN 81-246-0118-6)

11. Buddhism as/in Performance; Analysis of Meditation and Theatrical Practice; by David E.R. George (ISBN 81-246-0123-2)

12. Buddhist Tantra and Buddhist Art; by T.N. Mishra (ISBN 81-246-0141-0)

13. Buddhist Art in India and Sri Lanka: 3rd Century BC to 6th Century AD — A Critical Study; by Virender Kumar Dabral (ISBN 81-246-0162-3)

14. The Tibetan Iconography of Buddhas, Bodhisattvas and Other Deities — A Unique Pantheon; by Lokesh Chandra & Fredrick W. Bunce (ISBN 81-246-0178-X)

Observations

"Ardy Verhaegen's *The Dalai Lamas: The Institution and Its History* is an excellent introduction to the history of Tibet, focusing on the personal contributions of the Fourteen Dalai Lamas to Tibet's unique spiritual culture during the past six centuries of the Tibetans' careful preservation and strenuous practice of the Buddhist arts and sciences. It gives the reader a good overview of the current plight of Tibet, and the present Dalai Lama's central role in seeking relief for his oppressed and endangered people. It is clearly written, displays sound scholarship, and glows with the author's honest appreciation for Tibet, its leader and its people. I highly recommend this book."

— **Robert A. F. Thurman**, Ph.D., Jey Tsong Khapa Professor of Indo-Tibetan Studies and Chair, Department of Religion, Columbia University, author of *Essential Tibetan Buddhism*

"What is a truly spiritual person like? In answer to this question, countless people in the West as well as in the East will name His Holiness the Fourteenth Dalai Lama. Only a few of them, however, will know anything about his thirteen predecessors and their role in history. Ardy Verhaegen's inspiring account fills this intellectual gap; but it does more. It points to an urgent task: Tibet must be preserved for the spiritual life of the world."

— **Brother David Steindl-Rast**, O.S.B., co-author with Robert Aitken Roshi of *The Ground We Share;* www.gratefulnes.org

"Tibet and its Vajrayana tradition of Buddhism, with His Holiness the Dalai Lama, Tenzin Gyatso, have captured the attention of the world. The Dalai Lama, in his being, presence and teaching, emanates an eminently human face, the face of loving compassion and kindness in an institution, but he is himself the incarnation of the truth and spirit of this unique office. There is considerable interest in and curiosity about the Dalai Lama as a person, and the institutional lineage he represents. Ardy Verhaegen contributes his scholarship and dedication in producing a very precious book that is much needed in shedding historical light on this increasingly important spiritual tradition that, through the Fourteenth Dalai Lama, is giving significant spiritual leadership in a very troubled, confused world. I see great longevity for this book."

— **Wayne Teasdale**, author of *The Mystic Heart*

"As a long-time supporter of refugee Tibetan Buddhist nuns, I welcome Verhaegen's tribute to the present Dalai Lama, born of a long line of Dalai Lamas, and hope that it stimulates an ever-widening awareness of the spiritual riches of this venerable tradition as well as of the plight of the Tibetan expatriates. To have in one place the complete history of the Dalai Lama line in a popularly accessible form, is to have a resource for which we in the interfaith world are rightly grateful."

— **Beatrice Bruteau**, Ph.D., author of *What We Can Learn from the East* (Crossroad)

"The Dalai Lamas is an important, even monumental work, what must be for generations to come a source book on the history of Tibet's most important religious institution. This scholarly, most readable text, due to the painstaking research and fine literary skills of the author, has been endorsed by the Fourteenth Dalai Lama, who recognizes its importance for keeping alive awareness of the plight of the Tibetan refugees. Verhaegen has succeeded in writing a classic in the field of Tibetan studies."

— **James M. Somerville**, Professor of Philosophy Emeritus, Xavier University, Cincinnati, author of *The Mystical Sense of the Gospels* (Crossroad)

Emerging Perceptions in Buddhist Studies, no. 15

The Dalai Lamas

The Institution and Its History

Ardy Verhaegen

D.K. Printworld (P) Ltd.
New Delhi

Cataloging in Publication Data — DK

Verhaegen, Ardy, 1946–
The Dalai lamas.
(Emerging perceptions in Buddhist studies, no. 15).
Includes bibliographical references (p.).
Includes index.

1. Dalai lamas—Biography. 2. Dalai lamas—History.
I. Title. II. Series: (Emerging perceptions in Buddhist studies no. 15).

ISBN 81-246-0202-6

First Published in India in 2002

Published and printed by:
D.K. Printworld (P) Ltd.
Regd. office : '*Sri Kunj*', F-52, Bali Nagar
New Delhi - 110 015
Phones : (011) 545-3975; 546-6019; *Fax* : (011) 546-5926
E-mail: dkprintworld@vsnl.net

Foreword

by **His Holiness the Dalai Lama**

HISTORICALLY the Dalai Lamas as individuals and as an institution have been closely concerned with the welfare of Tibet, her people and their culture. Of course, when we think of Tibetan culture, we generally mean Buddhist culture, because of the profound and pervasive effect that Buddhism has had on so much of the Tibetan way of life. It was Buddhism, with its poweful central message of compassion that transformed Tibetans from the powerful warlike nation that dominated Central Asia in the seventh century to the more peaceful and religious people they are today. Buddhism, with its fundamental humane values of compassion and wisdom, provided the inspiration for art and literature and the widespread establishment of monasteries and nunneries that became the major source of education.

And, of course, it is within the context of Buddhism that the Dalai Lamas came to prominence. The early Dalai Lamas excelled as spiritual teachers and practitioners. They were truly great. Their influence steadily increased and extended, each in a different area, so the Great Fifth Dalai Lama's emergence, not only as a widely regarded spiritual leader, but also as the country's ruler seems a natural consequence. His impact was so deep that the government he established has continued to command popular confidence up to recent times, even when the person of the Dalai Lama was absent or unable to be effective.

As I have already indicated, I have great admiration for my predecessors. The First, Second, and Third Dalai Lamas in particular were highly accomplished in spiritual and scholarly matters, whereas the Fifth and Thirteenth Dalai Lamas were in addition politically adept.

I believe they were each able to make a significant contribution to improving the lives of the Tibetan people as a whole. Nevertheless, I imagine that for all their greatness, each of them found themselves in a situation similar to my own.

As a Buddhist monk I live the life of a religious person. As a Tibetan and as Dalai Lama, I have a special responsibility towards Tibet and its people. Because the people of Tibet have placed their trust and hope in me, I have a moral responsibility to speak up for them. In this capacity I try to raise public awareness of the real situation inside Tibet and the true nature of our freedom struggle. It is in this context that I welcome this book that succinctly tells the story of each of the Dalai Lamas and their contribution as human beings to Tibet's destiny.

The continued occupation of Tibet today poses an increasing threat to the very existence of a distinct Tibetan national and cultural identity. Therefore, I consider that my primary responsibility is to take whatever steps I must to save my people and their unique heritage from total annihilation. This is not a struggle to preserve old institutions, such as the institution of Dalai Lama. It is a struggle for national survival and the preservation of Tibetan culture that has some potential to serve humanity and to keep the peace in the part of the world in which we live.

As Dalai Lama myself, I do not claim to have high realisations or any other quality, but there is something within me, as I believe there was within each of my predecessors, that is the result of certain karmic formations and prayers made over many lives. Because of this I was born at this critical juncture when we Tibetans are facing great trouble. In the more than four decades since we lost our freedom, I think we have made some contribution to keeping the Tibetan spirit and a sense of hope alive. However, it is now clear that these efforts alone are not sufficient to bring about a positive solution. Therefore, I appeal to everyone who reads this book to support the Tibetan people in whatever way you can, as human beings who are presently prevented from exercising the rights and freedoms that many of us take for granted.

November 16, 2001

Tenzin Gyatso, the Fourteenth Dalai Lama

Preface

SINCE his flight from Tibet to India in 1959, His Holiness the Dalai Lama has emerged as perhaps the most widely respected and popular religious leader in the world. His popularity exceeds that of the approximately one hundred and forty thousand Tibetans in exile whose spiritual and political head he is. Although the Dalai Lama has no formal status in other Buddhist communities, he is popularly, though mistakenly, regarded as the "pope of Buddhism". During his time in exile in Dharamsala in north India, he has attempted to preserve Tibetan culture by establishing institutions such as TIPA, the Tibetan Institute for the Performing Arts, to reform the political constitution of Tibet through the Tibetan Government in Exile, to restore the great monasteries of Tibet in India. Sera Monastery, one of the largest monasteries of Tibet and the world, with over 5,000 monks, has been re-established in Bylakuppe in south India and now has nearly 5000 monks and students. He has also sought to engage other religious and secular traditions in dialogue and worked tirelessly to present the teachings of Tibetan Buddhism in numerous books and addresses around the world. In 1989, he received the Nobel Peace Prize. He has become, as Verhaegen notes, "a global figure". Yet few know that His Holiness Tenzin Gyatso is the *Fourteenth* Dalai Lama. And that "Dalai Lama" is not his personal name, but "the name of an office" that is currently held by "a human being . . . who chooses to be a Buddhist monk," as Tenzin Gyatso explains in his *Freedom in Exile, The Autobiography of the Dalai Lama*. It is the merit of this important study by Ardy Verhaegen that he helps us to understand the *institution* of the Dalai Lama and its history.

This study was initially undertaken as an Independent Study project at the University of Waterloo and has since been revised for publication. It is divided into four parts. Part 1 sets the stage for the emergence of the Dalai Lamas of Tibet. Part 2 takes us through the history of the Dalai Lamas from their beginnings in the 1400s down to the present.

Part 3 focusses on the workings of the institution of the Dalai Lama, and Part 4 explores the situation of the current Dalai Lama since 1959. What is especially important about this study is that it documents the emergence of the institution or office of the Dalai Lama and gives us a coherent history of the fourteen holders of this office. Thus it moves us beyond the more anecdotal 1984 study by Inder Malik of the *Dalai Lamas of Tibet*. Although Verhaegen does not know Tibetan and thus did not have access to Tibetan sources, he has reviewed virtually all the English-language sources to put together this account of the Dalai Lamas. His documentation is extensive and impressive, and his footnotes, liberally laced with comments, are an important review of the English-language sources for the study of Tibetan Buddhism and its central institution.

Verhaegen's interpretation of the institution of the Dalai Lama is plausible and grounded in the historical emergence of the office. He is a sympathetic reader of his sources, and what emerges is a portrait of the institution and history of the Dalai Lamas that clarifies and enlightens.

Dr. M. Darrol Bryant
Dean & Professor of Religion and Culture
Renison College, University of Waterloo
Waterloo, Ontario, Canada

Contents

Introduction

THIS study presents a history and description of the institution of the Dalai Lama in Tibetan society from its inception to the present. Since the rapid growth and acceptance of Tibetan Buddhism in the West[1] and since the personality and status of the current Dalai Lama are of topical interest[2] such a study seems timely.

The introductory section is a survey of early Tibetan history up to the time of the appearance of the Dalai Lamas. Central to this survey will be an overview of the tenets and structure of Buddhism, particularly Tibetan Buddhism, its introduction and spread throughout Tibet, and its development into different schools or sects. In my approach to Tibetan history I agree with Klieger who states,

> Indigenous Tibetan history is not a secular history — the chronicles of important people and events cannot be readily interpreted without an implicit understanding of the Buddhist ideological framework in which they were written.[3]

---

1. One need only refer to such directories as, Graham Coleman, editor, *A Handbook of Tibetan Culture*, 1994 or, Don Morreale, editor, *Buddhist America*, 1998 to find a large number of teaching centres, academic institutions and publications throughout the Western world dedicated to Tibetan Buddhism. The following quote referring to the recent enthronement ceremony in Nepal of the reincarnation of Dilgo Khentse Rinpoche is instructive. "A total of about 15,000 people from all over the world attended . . ." See, *Snow Lion Newsletter*, vol. 13, no.1, Winter 1998, p. 1.
2. With the awarding of the Nobel Peace Prize in 1989 to His Holiness The Dalai Lama, the institution of the same name came to worldwide attention. See, Huston Smith, *The World's Religions*, 1991, p. 143.
3. P. Christiaan Klieger, "The Institution of the Dalai Lama as a Symbolic Matrix," *The Tibetan Journal*, vol. XVI, no. 1, Spring 1991, p. 96.

Part two, the major portion of this study, explores the history of the Dalai Lamas. Each of the Dalai Lamas is profiled within the context of historical events of the times. Once again I have followed Klieger when he states, "Since Shakabpa's seminal study, other scholars have interpreted the institution of the Dalai Lama within the context of Buddhist understanding".[4] The section following this historical survey examines the structure and workings of the institution itself within the greater context of Tibetan culture and civilization. The final section looks at the current status of the institution of the Dalai Lama and the Dalai Lama himself within the Tibetan community and the world at large. Throughout each of these sections such issues as the relationship between the secular and spiritual roles of the Dalai Lamas, the relationship between the Dalai Lamas and the people of Tibet as well as to other spiritual and secular leaders, and the role of the Dalai Lamas in preserving Tibetan cultural and spiritual values are addressed.

The sources used are almost all written by Western scholars, though most of them combine Tibetan and Western sources in their writings. The problem presented by these sources is that those of Tibetan origin tend to be concerned with history from a particular religious point of view, while earlier Western sources are focussed on the secular aspects of Tibetan history. Scholars such as Klieger, in his reference to Shakabpa, have addressed this problem in recent decades. It should be noted, however, that just as Tibetan works understandably had a strong pro-Buddhist bias, some of the earlier Western observers, such as Waddell, portrayed "a skeptical image of Tibetan spiritual life".[5]

---

4. Klieger, "The Institution of the Dalai Lama as a Symbolic Matrix", p. 96.
5. Glenn Mullin, *Mystical Verses of a Mad Dalai Lama*, 1994, pp. 256-7. Mullin says "that Tibetan religions and historical writings tend to gloss over . . . much of the negative . . ." while recording "the good things, the "enlightenment activities"," which means that in order to find out the extent of conflicts or persecutions one must read between the lines, p. 264. Also, David Snellgrove & Hugh Richardson, *A Cultural History of Tibet*, 1967, who state that Tibetan writers of history see everything from "a rather special Tibetan Buddhist point of view". If "it furthers the interests of their religion in general and their own religious order and monastery in particular, it is good, in so far as it works against their religion, their order and their monastery it is evil", p. 175.

In order to strike a balance between these polarities the example of more recent scholars such as Snellgrove, Richardson, Shakabpa, Mullin, Michael and Smith Jr. has been followed. These writers seem to have a good understanding of both the Western and Tibetan points of view. Another important matter is the usage of Tibetan words. The text follows the examples of Mullin, Stein, Michael, Smith Jr., Shen & Liu and Shakabpa, using the common phonetic system of transliteration of Tibetan names and terms. Even amongst the sources just cited there are differences as to correct phonetic renderings, but this is a minor problem. One final note: since this book is a general introduction to the institution and history of the Dalai Lamas the extensive use of annotation is deliberate, intended to provide the serious student with as broad a reference base as possible.

I am indebted to Professor Darrol Bryant of the University of Waterloo whose depth of knowledge, consistent support and gentle encouragement were instrumental to the development of my research and manuscript. Professor Robert Litke of Wilfred Laurier University gave invaluable advice regarding the preparation of my manuscript and the broad perspective necessary to keep me in touch with my wider objectives. Dr. James Somerville, Professor of Philosophy, Emeritus, Xavier University, Cincinnati, and Ruth Sutter, historian and independent scholar, both graciously and generously reviewed my manuscript, providing insightful suggestions and editorial commentary. The kind advice of Dr. Al Evans of the University of Waterloo was instrumental in my initiating this project and helpful throughout its duration. Deserving of special thanks is the Independent Studies Program at the University of Waterloo, within which the spirit of individualized scholarship is encouraged and nurtured.

Venerable Bhikshuni Tenzin Kalsang, the founder and spiritual director of Tengye Ling Tibetan Buddhist Temple in Toronto, was generous with her library and advice. Much gratitude is due to Diane Edgerton for her professional editing of the manuscript. Kim Elliott, my long time friend, patiently provided technical expertise. Particular appreciation goes to my wife, Maureen Kennedy, who performed the always under-appreciated task of typing the manuscript. Her continuous encouragement and occasional prodding helped to keep me on track. To these and the many others especially Heidi Ponzo, who provided support, suggestions, and materials I offer my gratitude.

His Holiness the Dalai Lama is deserving of special thanks for taking the time out of his ever-busy schedule to prepare the foreword to this volume. His tireless support of scholarship in the area of Tibetan culture, which, as he states, is generally synonymous with Buddhist culture, is but one facet of a life dedicated to the service of humanity in general and the Tibetan people in particular. His life is an example to those who work for peace in the world and for those who seek peace of mind. It is my belief that Tenzin Gyatso will be regarded as one of the greatest, if not the greatest Dalai Lama.

Finally, I would like to dedicate this book to the people of Tibet, possessors of one of the great wisdom traditions bequeathed to mankind. Their stories and culture have fascinated and inspired me. Their courage, determination, and dignity in the face of grave and dangerous circumstances cannot but move one to admiration and appreciation. May their struggle for self-determination be met with sympathy and understanding. It is my hope that this book will play some small role in furthering that process.

1

Developments in Tibet
up to the Advent of the Dalai Lamas

IN the mid-1970s His Holiness, Tenzin Gyatso, The Fourteenth Dalai Lama, told a Polish newspaper that he thought he would be the last Dalai Lama. In a later interview published in the English language press he stated "The Dalai Lama office was an institution created to benefit others. It is possible that it will soon have outlived its usefulness".[1] These statements caused a furor amongst Tibetans in India. Many could not believe that such an option could even be considered. It was further felt that it was not the Dalai Lama's decision to reincarnate. Rather, they felt that since the Dalai Lama is a national institution it was up to the people of Tibet to decide whether or not the Dalai Lama should reincarnate.

The institution of the Dalai Lama has become, over the centuries, a central focus of Tibetan cultural identity; "a symbolic embodiment of the Tibetan national character".[2] Today, to those Tibetans inside Tibet, living under a harsh Communist Chinese rule, and to the many thousands of Tibetans who were able to escape the Chinese takeover in the 1950s, the Dalai Lama and the office of the Dalai Lama have become focal points in their struggle towards independence and, more urgently, cultural survival. The Dalai Lama is regarded as the principal incarnation of Chenrezig (referred to as Avalokiteshvara in India), the *bodhisattva* of compassion and patron deity of Tibet.[3] In

1. Glenn Mullin, "Faces of the Dalai Lama: Reflections on the Man and the Tradition", *Quest*, vol. 6, no. 3, Autumn 1993, p. 80.
2. Mullin, "Faces of the Dalai Lama . . . . ," p. 27.
3. Franz Michael, *Rule by Incarnation*, 1982, p. 16. See, Coleman, *A Handbook of Tibetan Culture*, *op. cit.*, who defines *bodhisattva* as one who has attained the altruistic aspiration towards enlightenment for the benefit of all sentient beings, p. 285.

that role the Dalai Lama has chosen to use peace and compassion in his treatment of his own people and his oppressors. In this sense the Dalai Lama is the embodiment of an ideal of Tibetan values and a cornerstone of Tibetan identity and culture.

The Dalai Lamas have also functioned as the principal spiritual guide to many Himalayan kingdoms bordering Tibet, as well as western China, Mongolia and Ladakh. The literary works of the Dalai Lamas have, over the centuries, inspired more than fifty million people in these regions. Those writings, reflecting the fusion of Buddhist philosophy embodied in Tibetan Buddhism, have become one of the world's great repositories of spiritual thought.[4]

The land and people

It is important to understand that the institution of the Dalai Lama is central to Tibetan cultural, religious, and political life. Placing the institution of the Dalai Lama within the context in which it developed facilitates this understanding. A brief look at the geography and climate of Tibet as well as the origins of its peoples and their basic nature presents us with the physical milieu within which this development took place.

Tibet is, arguably, one of the most remote and inaccessible countries in the world.[5] It is ringed on three sides by some of the world's highest mountains: to the south and west the majestic Himalaya stretches for fifteen hundred miles, the forbidding Karakoram, Pamir and Ladakh Mountains lie to the west, and to the north the Kuen Tun and Tang La ranges along with the Chang Tang and Takla Makan deserts create a formidable barrier.[6] The open plains to the east are divided by the almost impenetrable, deep river gorges of the Huang Ho (Yellow), Yangtse, Mekong and Salween rivers with mountainous highlands in between.[7] It is only towards the Kokonor region in the north-eastern sector of the country that there is relatively unimpeded access. But nearly a thousand miles of wasteland, poor pasturage,

4. Glenn Mullin, *Selected Works of the Dalai Lama II*, 1985, pp. 7-8.
5. Snellgrove & Richardson, *A Cultural History of Tibet*, p. 19.
6. H.E. Richardson, *Tibet and Its History*, 1962, p. 3. See, Warren Smith Jr., *Tibetan Nation*, 1996, p. xxi.
7. Michael, *Rule by Incarnation*, p. 6.

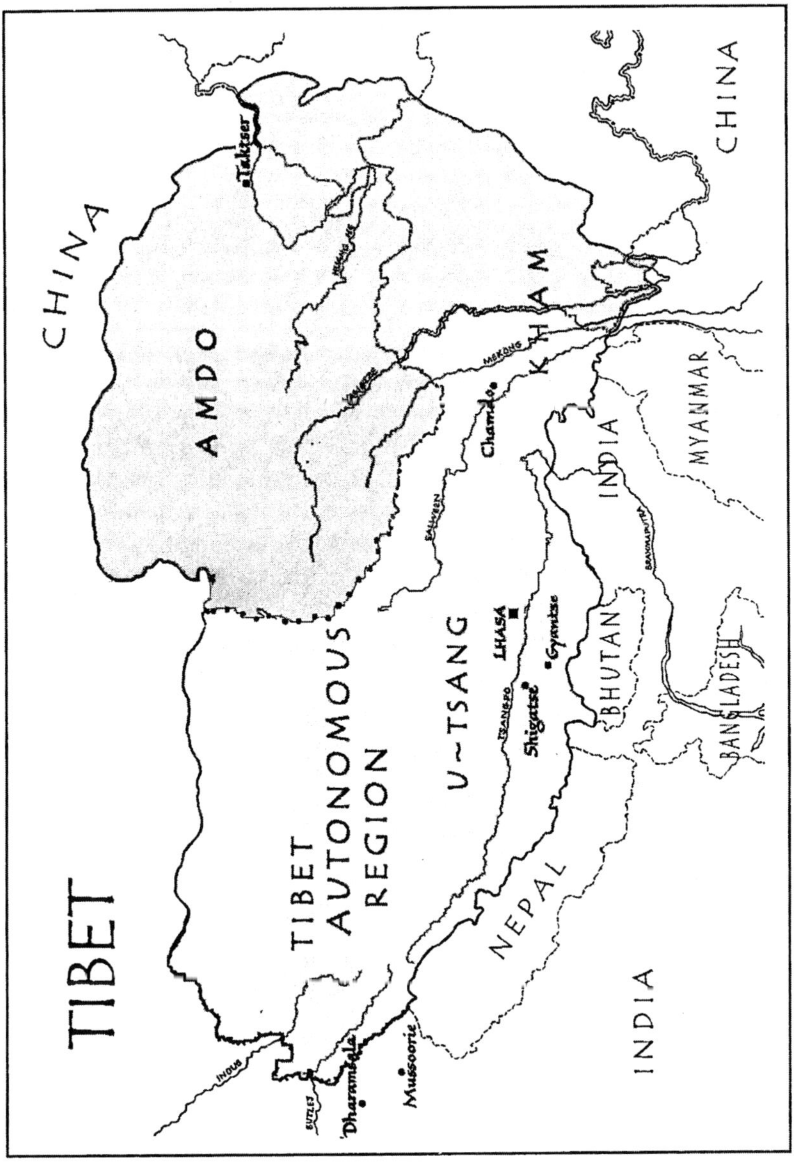

Map of Tibet[8]

8. As prepared by author.

and severe weather isolate the central parts of Tibet from frontier China and beyond that, Mongolia. In fact, up until the mid-1900s the trip from Lhasa to Beijing took upwards of eight months to complete.[9] Tibet was never on the migratory trade routes. Marco Polo does not mention the country in his writings nor did the earlier Chinese pilgrims of the fifth and sixth centuries pass through Tibet on their way to and from India.[10] Tibet was never a through route for migratory peoples or armies on the move, and the difficulty of communication with neighbouring countries tended to preserve the seclusion, conservatism, independence, and national homogeneity of the Tibetans.[11]

Very few Tibetans lived in the northern 75 per cent of the country, those areas being primarily frozen wastes, crisscrossed by mountain ranges all over 16000 feet, and suitable only to the nomadic way of life traditional to much of Tibet. The only fertile agricultural lands lay in the valleys to the south (which are, incidentally, on the same latitude as Cairo) between elevations of 15000 to 19000 feet. This is where Tibetan culture developed and flourished, and the bulk of the population was to be found.[12]

The origin of the Tibetan people is generally found amongst the nomadic, non-Chinese Ch'iang tribes of east-central Asia.[13] Shakabpa writes that modern anthropologists regard Tibetans as belonging to the Mongoloid race.[14] This is a view shared by Bell who notes that Tibetans and Mongols are physically and mentally alike[15] but very

---

9. Snellgrove & Richardson, *A Cultural History . . .*, p. 19.
10. Sir Charles Bell, *The Religion of Tibet*, 1968, p. 3.
11. Richardson, *Tibet and Its History*, p. 4. Richardson goes on to say "the rule of religion led to a determined conservatism and dislike of change of any sort", p. 13.
12. It should be noted that cultural or ethnographic Tibet historically included Ladakh, Lahul and Spiti in India, Dolpo and Mustang in Nepal, and the countries of Sikkim and Bhutan. See, Snellgrove & Richardson, *A Cultural History . . .*, pp. 20-1. See, Smith Jr., *Tibetan Nation*, who notes the climate of the Tibetan plateau was sub-tropical before the rising Himalaya range blocked the flow of warm air masses from the south, p. xx.
13. Snellgrove & Richardson, *A Cultural History . . .*, p. 21. In a later work Snellgrove asserts that Tibetans did not develop from a single racial stock. See, David Snellgrove, *Indo-Tibetan Buddhism*, 1987, p.386.
14. W.O. Shakabpa, *Tibet: A Political History*, 1967, pp. 5-6.
15. Bell, *The Religion of Tibet*, p. 9.

distinguishable from the Chinese.[16] The Fourteenth Dalai Lama asserted in 1962 that Tibetans are a distinct and separate race with no ethnological connection to anyone else in Asia and with a distinct language and culture.[17] In a later book he makes brief mention of the fact that that Tibetans and Chinese are ethnically and racially distinct.[18] Chinese authors Wang Furen and Suo Wenqing seem to concur with Snellgrove and Richardson, asserting

> the major section of Tibetan nationality is descendant of the ancient Xiquiangs (Quiang or Ch'iang), whereas the Hans and other people who were assimilated in the long course of history constituted merely a tiny portion.[19]

Michael says that the racial origins of Tibetans are uncertain but appear to be of two types. There is a shorter round-headed people who predominate in the agricultural valleys of central and western Tibet while a taller, long-headed type originates in the north and east and eventually came to dominate Tibetan society.[20] At the very least, it would appear most experts agree that the Tibetan people have nothing in common with Han Chinese racial origins, culture, and language, a matter of some importance to the Tibetan people and their government.

Over time there was a gradual movement of rival clans from the north-east to the southern valleys.[21] They took up agricultural ways of living, with rival chiefs establishing fortified strongholds in the central and eastern tributaries of the T'sangpo (Bhramaputra) river.[22] The people of the northern- and eastern-most reaches meanwhile remained nomads, herders, and traders, the latter an occupation followed to some extent by most Tibetans.[23]

16. Bell, *The Religion of Tibet*, p. 4.
17. The Fourteenth Dalai Lama, *My Land and My People*, 1962, p. 59.
18. The Fourteenth Dalai Lama, *Freedom in Exile*, 1990, p. 63.
19. Wang Furen and Suo Wenqing, *Highlights of Tibetan History*, 1984, p. 13.
20. Michael, *Rule by Incarnation*, pp. 9-11.
21. Snellgrove & Richardson, *A Cultural History . . .*, p. 20.
22. *Ibid.*, p. 22.
23. Richardson, *Tibet and Its History*, p. 7.

The Tibetan people were friendly, hospitable, independent, and, until the coming of Buddhism, expressed their courage and determination through warlike activities, even to the point of great conquest.[24] Over the centuries Buddhism has tempered the Tibetans who, taking their religion very seriously, have become a compassionate, forbearing people.[25] Buddhism has so permeated Tibetan culture and society that it is worth examining Buddhism's basic tenets and its development in Tibet. That development spawned a religiously oriented culture out of which evolved the institution of the Dalai Lama. This unique institution developed in a land physically isolated from the countries and cultures around it. The people, descending primarily from Mongoloid racial origins, according to most observers, either became nomadic herders or settled in the central and south-eastern areas of Tibet most suited to agriculture. While courageous and given to inter-clan rivalries the people were also friendly and hospitable. In spite of their reluctance to change, the people of Tibet were about to embark on a wholesale transformation of their culture with the embracing of Buddhism.

Buddhism

In order to understand the context in which Tibetan society and culture, including the institution of the Dalai Lama, developed, it is useful to survey Buddhism's basic precepts. Tibet adopted, assimilated, and adapted Buddhism, creating a vibrant Buddhist centered culture, which survives to this day. Before proceeding to a historical overview of Buddhism's development within Tibet, it is useful to outline the major themes of Buddhism.

Buddhism starts with Shakyamuni, who became the Buddha, the enlightened or awakened one. Shakyamuni Buddha (silent sage of the Shakya clan) had been the prince Siddhartha Gautama. He was born in 563 BC in Lumbini, which was then in northern India, now in Nepal. He was "a man who woke up" and became enlightened through

---

24. Bell, *The Religion of Tibet*, p. 7.

25. *Ibid.*, p. 7. (It should be noted, however, that while generally a peaceful, non-violent people the Tibetans, nevertheless, continued to show their ancient warrior ways through involvement in internecine struggles between rival families or monastic institutions to which they were loyal. In the historical survey to follow this becomes quite apparent.)

a long search for the meaning of life.[26] Upon attaining enlightenment he taught the basic precepts of what was to become one of the great world religions, a religion which eventually divided itself into many schools which, according to Dorjee, "differ from one another largely in terms of how they present the philosophy of final reality".[27]

The foundation of Buddhist teachings are the Four Noble Truths: (1.) life is full of suffering (*dukkha*); (2.) desire (*tanha*) is the cause of suffering; (3.) the end of suffering is the cessation of *tanha* or clinging; (4.) the way to let go of desire is through following the Eightfold Path.[28] The Eightfold Path is training in a way of life. It calls one to seek and practice: (1.) right views, (2.) right aspiration (intent), (3.) right speech, (4.) right conduct (which includes the five precepts of not killing, not stealing, not lying, not being sexually immoral and not indulging in alcohol or drugs), (5.) right occupation or livelihood, (6.) right effort, (7.) right attention and, (8.) right concentration (quieting the mind). The Eightfold Path is also referred to as the Middle Way, which is a life of calm detachment through which the wise avoid the extremes of austerity and self-indulgence.[29] This path, Buddhists believe, can lift us out of the endless cycle of birth and rebirth dictated by our karmic tendencies.

Price writes that "*Karma* is the force or energy created by human thoughts, words and deeds",[30] a law of action and reaction, of cause and effect which shapes our destiny in terms of future lives. Buddhists believe that the attitudes and patterns of this life determine our next life. Cessation of this continuous cycle leads to *nirvana*, which, according to Smith, is an extinction of the boundaries of the finite self or, more literally, a going out of the fires.[31] The Buddha regarded *nirvana* as the highest destiny of the human spirit, and referred to it as bliss, a bliss that is incomprehensible and indescribable. Those

---

26. Huston Smith, *The World's Religions*, 1991, pp. 82, 92.
27. Lotswana Tenzin Dorjee, "The Experience of Buddhism", *White Lotus: An Introduction to Tibetan Culture*, 1990, p. 102.
28. Smith, *The World's Religions*, pp. 99-103.
29. Joan Price, "The Life and Teachings of the Buddha", *Quest*, vol. 8, no. 1. Spring, 1995, pp. 54-5.
30. *Ibid.*, p. 55.
31. Smith, *The World's Religions*, p. 113.

who find *nirvana* find peace within themselves and the world, the end of suffering, freedom from future rebirth.[32]

All Buddhist adherents take refuge in the three jewels: the Buddha, the Dharma (the teachings), and the Sangha (the community of followers).[33] The Sangha, especially the monks and nuns, soon split into two differing schools of Buddhism. The Theravada (Way of the Elders) school emphasizes individual self-liberation through rigorous self-discipline without supernatural aid. Wisdom and constant commitment, primarily for monks and nuns, to a path of meditation, devoid of much ritual or metaphysics, are also emphasized. The Buddha is regarded as a man, a saint, and a supreme teacher. Theravada was also called Hinayana (the lesser vehicle) by the Mahayana (great vehicle) school to which a majority of Buddhists belong. (Hinayana is considered a derogatory term by Theravada Buddhists.) Mahayana Buddhists regard the Buddha as a saviour who, through divine power and grace, supports human aspirations towards the *bodhisattva* ideal of a compassionate commitment to the eventual liberation of all sentient beings. Religious practice, which elaborates metaphysics and ritual, includes petitionary prayer and is relevant to life in the world — to laypeople as well as monks and nuns. Out of the Mahayana tradition a number of schools developed; the principal ones include *Ch'an* (*Zen*), *Pure Land* and Tibetan Buddhism.[34]

Tibetan Buddhism is often referred to as Vajrayana (The Diamond Way), "the way of strength and lucidity to realize the Buddha's vision of luminous compassion".[35] A direct path of sacred formulas and *mantras*,[36] it is distinctive enough to be considered the third way, or *yana*. Its roots are in Indian Mahayana Buddhism.

Tibetan Buddhism was also referred to as *Lamaism* by Western scholars such as Waddell, Hoffmann and David-Neel and the term is still sometimes used in some general reference works.[37] The Tibetans prefer not to use the term since they find it misleading. The Dalai Lama commenting on this point states:

---

32. Price, "The Life and Teachings . . . ," p. 56.
33. Giuseppi Tucci, *The Religions of Tibet*, 1988, pp. 48-9.
34. Smith, *The World's Religions*, pp. 126-8.
35. *Ibid.*, pp. 139-40.
36. Helmet Hoffmann, *The Religions of Tibet*, 1961, p. 33.
37. See, for example, *Guide to Places of the World*, 1987, p. 154.

> . . . those who, noticing the slight differences with Indian Buddhism due to locality, time, or external conditions, identify Tibetan Buddhism as 'Lamaism' specifically in the sense of its being a transformation of Buddhism are completely wrong.[38]

He goes on to point out how modern scholars often have to refer to the Tibetan translations of original Indian texts, written many centuries ago, to uncover the entire and original meaning of doctrinal passages. Many scholars generally confirm this.[39] Guenther concurs with the Dalai Lama, calling Lamaism a "misleading and inappropriate designation".[40] He notes the word derives from *bla-ma*, meaning a potency of highest significance corresponding to the Indian notion of *guru,* or spiritual preceptor, but also to a spiritual friend or teacher. Nevertheless, most scholars agree that Tibetan Buddhism does incorporate the Indian Mahayana Buddhism of the eighth and ninth centuries, which at its heart was Tantric Buddhism (see footnote 51), and Tibet's pre-Buddhist *Bon* deities.

The original Bon religion was a quasi-national Tibetan form of an old animist-shamanist religion widespread in Siberia, inner Asia, Turkestan, Mongolia, Manchuria, the Tibetan plateau, and even western China. It incorporated a highly ritualistic system of propitiation of deities, both good and evil, for the purposes of smoothing life's rocky road.[41] This form of Bon was later influential in shaping the development of Buddhism in Tibet. Bon itself was later systematized, primarily in Western Tibet, the former kingdom of Zhangzhung, under the influence of Buddhism and likely Persian and Manichaean

---

38. The Fourteenth Dalai Lama (tr. & ed. Jeffrey Hopkins), *The Buddhism of Tibet*, 1987, p. 22.
39. Bell, *The Religion of Tibet*, p. 45. See also, Snellgrove & Richardson, *A Cultural History . . .*, p. 76.
40. H.V. Guenther, *Tibetan Buddhism in Western Perspective*, 1977, pp. 178-86. Also, Giuseppi Tucci, *Tibet: Land of Snows*, 1967, states Tibetan Buddhism is dubbed *Lamaism* due to the importance *Lamas* have in it, but *Lama* only means teacher or master. Not every monk is a master (in the sense of spiritual guide), p. 68. See also, Heinrich Harrer, *Seven Years in Tibet*, 1957, who says the term lama is only applied to incarnations and a few other monks distinguished by their ascetic lives or by the miracles they have performed, p. 148.
41. Hoffmann, *The Religions of Tibet*, pp. 14-24.

teachings, into a syncretistic system with a developed doctrine and a sacred literature.[42] In this form Bon operated on the fringes of Tibetan culture and still survives today within Tibetan society.[43] In its contemporary form it is sometimes difficult to distinguish Bon from Tibetan Buddhism.[44]

The Emperor Asoka, who had converted to Buddhism, propagated Indian Mahayana Buddhism in the third century BC almost to the point of its becoming a world religion.[45] He became, in a way, the prototype of the priest-king within Buddhism. Claiming the divine right to rule he called himself "Blessed of the Gods".[46] About this time Buddhism spread into north-western India from where it naturally migrated via trade routes to central Asia and China.[47] By the seventh century all of Tibet's neighbours except those further west of Tibet had received Buddhism. Tibet remained hostile to Buddhism but eventually that situation was reversed to where, today, Tibetan culture has become the principal inheritor and progenitor of Indian Buddhism.[48] In India, Buddhism had declined almost to the point of extinction after AD 1200 with the Muslim conquest. In many respects, Buddhism in India merged back into the Hinduism from which it had sprung.[49]

In India, Buddhism, like all successful religions, came to terms with the world on which it depended for support. The need to preserve oral traditions fostered academic and literary pursuits. To meet the needs of lay supporters, local divinities were incorporated and monks became priests. Around the beginning of the Christian era the

---

42. Hoffmann, *The Religions of Tibet*, p. 84. *Webster's Dictionary*, 1957 defines Manichaean as pertaining to the religious philosophy of the Persian Manes, or Manichaeus, which combined Zoroastrian, Gnomic, Christian and Pagan elements. See, Smith Jr., *Tibetan Nation*, p. 15.
43. Graham Coleman, (ed.), *A Handbook of Tibetan Culture*, 1984, pp. 12-16.
44. Per Kvaerne, "Bon", *The Encyclopedia of Religion*, vol. 2, Mircea Eliade, editor-in-chief, 1987, p. 277.
45. Smith, *The World's Religions*, p. 126.
46. L.A. Waddell, Tibetan *Buddhism*, 1972, p. xxxi.
47. Snellgrove & Richardson, *A Cultural History . . .*, p. 26.
48. *Ibid.*, p. 66.
49. Smith, *The World's Religions*, p. 148.

southern, more contemplative form of Buddhism became referred to, by Mahayana Buddhists, as Hinayana or the lesser way, since it was primarily concerned with personal salvation. Followers of the new great way, Mahayana, strove to become Buddhas, "enlightened ones", *bodhisattvas* who worked for the enlightenment of all through a universal compassion.[50] By the seventh century Mahayana Buddhism had already developed the concept of the perfected teacher, the *guru*. The *guru* was often a great scholar but also possibly a *yogin* (spiritual master) not associated with any monastery who was adept in the practices of tantra.[51] He took the place, in the eye of the devotee, of the Buddha because he or she had become a Buddha, an awakened one.[52] Virtuous laypersons could now also take the *bodhisattva* vow and aspire to enlightenment, for the goal was open to all. This practice is quite different from the Hinayana tradition, where only the *arhat*, or one who had attained freedom from the cycle of existence, and who also came from the ranks of the monks, could aspire to Buddhahood.[53] A principle means to that end of enlightenment was the practice of deity yoga — visualizing, then merging with the deity being visualized to appropriate that deity's

---

50. Snellgrove & Richardson, *A Cultural History* . . . , pp. 66-7.

51. Smith, *The World's Religions*, says tantras are texts founded on the interrelatedness of all things, all phenomena and are practices which utilize all energies latent in the human make up, the body included, in the service of the spiritual quest. These practices which channel physical energies "into currents that can carry the spirit forward rather than derail it", include *mantras* (holy formulas), *mudras* (hand gestures and sacred dance) and *mandalas* (icons representing the sacred), pp. 140-2.

    Andrew Harvey, *A Journey in Ladakh*, 1983, quoting the Ladakhi scholar Nawang Tsering of Leh, says "The Way of Tantric Buddhism is the Way of Acceptance, the way of working with all the energies and powers of living, refusing and denying none of them; but using all of them, transforming all of them into wisdom . . . . It is the hardest way . . . because it is the most dangerous; because it has so many temptations — to hedonism, to the relish of worldly power. It is also the most effective way. The man who can travel it successfully, we believe, can attain Enlightenment in one lifetime", p. 159.

52. Andrew Harvey, *A Journey in Ladakh*, again quoting Nawang Tsering says "When you have met the guru everything shines with his wisdom and his beauty; you see him in everything; you feel him in everything that happens to you", p. 107.

53. Herbert Guenther, "Buddhism in Tibet", *The Encyclopedia of Religions*, vol. 2, Mircea Eliade, editor, 1987, p. 406.

powers and virtues. These visualization practices were, according to Huston Smith, "designed to modulate the human spirit to the wave lengths of the tutelary deities that are invoked".[54]

One of Buddhism's great strengths was in its monasteries. Great monastic universities in India and Nepal became sources for Tibetan Buddhist and cultural development through the use of Indian and Nepalese teachers. The presence of Indian and Nepalese teachers in Tibet eventually led to the assembling of a great canon of Buddhist scripture during the thirteenth century. Snellgrove and Richardson consider the Tibetan canon the most "composite in its extraordinary range of teachings that any group of Buddhists had produced".[55] This created a historical irony in that Tibetans were virtually the sole inheritors of the Indian Buddhist tradition. This inheritance included forms of Buddhist practices that interested no one else in Asia except for the Mongols and the Chinese court, who were usually interested for political reasons.[56]

From about 500 BC Buddhism developed into a world religion, first in India, then spreading throughout Asia. Central to Buddhism are the basic tenets of the Four Noble Truths, the Eightfold Path, the concept of *nirvana* and taking refuge in the three jewels of the Buddha, the Dharma and the Sangha. Three major schools or *yanas* developed: Theravada (Hinayana), Mahayana and Vajrayana (Tibetan Buddhism). Tibetan Buddhism was an amalgam of Indian Mahayana Buddhism, which, in itself, was an expansion of Hinayana precepts and Bon, the indigenous religion of much of Tibet. One of its principal and most distinctive features was the inclusion of tantra, a highly important development of late Indian Buddhism,[57] which was an esoteric

---

54. Smith, *The World's Religions*, p. 143. To put the foregoing into a broader perspective it is useful to consider what Lama Anagarika Govinda has to say. "Prayers in the Buddhist sense are not requests to a power outside ourselves and for personal advantages but the calling up of forces that dwell within ourselves and that can only be effective if we are free from selfish desires. . . . Buddhists do not put their faith in the power of gods, residing in some heavens beyond, but they believe in the power of motive and the purity of faith (or purity of intention)." See, Lama Anagarika Govinda, *The Way of the White Clouds*, 1970, p. 22.
55. Snellgrove & Richardson, *A Cultural History . . .* , p. 72.
56. *Ibid.*
57. Donald S. Topaz Jr., "Mahayana Buddhism: Theory and Practice", *White Lotus . . .* , p. 106.

approach to Mahayana Buddhism. The current Dalai Lama sums it up well,

> there is within Tibetan Buddhism the complete practice of all Buddhism . . . explained as externally maintaining a Low *Vehicle* [yana or way] system of ethics, internally maintaining the *Sutra* Great Vehicle generation of altruism, love and compassion, and secretly maintaining the practice of the Mantra Vehicle.[58]

Other important developments were the concept of the perfected teacher or *guru*, its availability to the layperson, and the continuation and strengthening of the monastic tradition with its great emphasis on scholarship that led to the preservation of the Buddhist canon.

The spread and development of Buddhism in Tibet

The introduction and spread of Buddhism occurred during reigns of the early kings of Tibet (618 to 838), predominantly the three religious kings, Songtsen Gampo, Trisong Detsen, and Trisung Detsen (Ralpachen). This was a period when Tibet was at the height of its influence in Central Asia and beyond. With expansionism and subsequent contacts with surrounding countries came foreign influences and ideas. One of the more significant influences was Buddhism, which came primarily from India and to a certain extent, from China.

According to Snellgrove and Richardson, the first book of Buddhist scripture was introduced into Tibet in AD 233. It was called *Nyenpo Sangwa* (The Secret) but since no one could read Sanskrit it remained true to its namesake until translated by Thonmi Sambhota, who was sent to India by Songtsen Gampo (617-49). Sambhota used the *Gupta* alphabet of northern India to devise a Tibetan script.[59] This was the beginning of a long, prolific, and successful literary venture in the field of Buddhism.[60]

Songtsen Gampo's father, Namri Songtsen, had united Tibet under his rule. His son continued the tradition, subjugating the tribes of the Kokonor region bordering China. He also conquered parts of

58. The Fourteenth Dalai Lama (tr. & ed. Jeffrey Hopkins), *Kindness, Clarity, and Insight*, 1985, pp. 51-4.
59. Shakabpa, *Tibet: A Political History . . .*, pp. 24-5.
60. Snellgrove & Richardson, *A Cultural History . . .*, p. 75.

Burma (now Myanmar) and occupied Nepal and the north-western regions of China resulting in political marriages to princesses from both Nepal and China. The princesses were Buddhist and as part of their dowries brought images of Akshobhya and Shakyamuni Buddhas respectively, both of which were said, according to legend, to have been blessed by Lord Buddha himself. The temples erected to house these images included the Jokang, the foremost cathedral in Tibet.[61]

Due to Tibet's incursions into foreign lands, Buddhist influences were entering Tibet, primarily from India, to which the Tibetans turned for spiritual direction. China was the teacher in matters such as treaties, social behaviour, and technology.[62] Buddhism in Tibet at this stage was still primarily a court religion and not practiced widely by the populace.[63] Nevertheless, it was during the reign of Songtsen Gampo that Buddhism was firmly established in Tibet and future pathways of influence and teaching were opened with China and India.

The second great religious king, Trisong Detsen (755-97) used Buddhism as a means to establish an absolutist regime in his struggles with the aristocracy who saw the native Bon religion as its ally in the struggle for power.[64] It was during his reign that Buddhism was imported in a wholesale manner from India. Bell notes that Tibet looked to India rather than China since relations with China were strained after the sacking of the Chinese capital Ch'ang-an (Xian) in 763 by Tibetan forces. A more fundamental reason was that Indian Tantric Buddhism had a greater appeal to Tibetan sensibilities.[65]

King Trisong Detsen invited the great Buddhist sage Shantirakshita, who was representative of the conventional academic and monastic tradition in India, to teach in Tibet.[66] His initial preaching

61. Shakabpa, *Tibet: A Political History . . .* , pp. 25-7. See also, Rato Khyongla Nawang Losang, *My Life and Lives*, 1977, p. 43.
62. Hoffmann, *The Religions of Tibet*, pp. 36-9.
63. *Ibid.*, p. 39.
64. *Ibid.*, p. 44.
65. Bell, *The Religion of Tibet*, p. 37. See also, Shakabpa, *Tibet: A Political History . . .* , p. 39, who speaks of Tibetan forces installing a new Emperor and exacting annual tribute payments from China. See also, Dawa Norbu, *Tibet: The Road Ahead*, 1997, p. 368.
66. Snellgrove & Richardson, *A Cultural History . . .* , p. 78.

met with little success. The people felt he had angered the Bon spirits of the country who brought down storms, lightning and floods. Sensing the time was not ripe, Shantirakshita suggested that the Indian Tantric master, Padmasambhava, be invited. Padmasambhava is credited with subduing the Bon spirits with rituals and formulas more acceptable to the Tibetan people. Many of these spirits were subsequently absorbed into the Buddhist pantheon.[67] Under Shantirakshita's guidance, on a site selected by Padmasambhava, the first monastery in Tibet, Samye, was built. Here Hinayana monks from India came, and from Samye the first Tibetan monks were ordained. These, along with the Chinese monks now present in Tibet promoted an alternative to the rapidly growing sect of Padmasambhava's Tantric Buddhism.[68] The king eventually chose as his model for Tibetan Buddhism, the more doctrinally pure teachings of Shantirakshita over those of Padmasambhava. The reason, Bell speculates, was because Shantirakshita was favoured by the upper class. This is the view also taken by Hoffmann who asserts that the nobles forced the king to give up his support of tantric ways. But Tantrism appealed to the masses of Tibetans who were more predisposed to it through their long association with Bon. It was from this sect that the majority of priests were later to come.[69] Padmasambhava himself is considered one of the patron saints of Tibet[70] by most Tibetans and held in the

---

67. Shakabpa, *Tibet: A Political History . . .* , p. 36. That a powerful shaman such as Padmasambhava could "subdue malevolent spirits" and the elements may be regarded as a serious statement, since not only the Tibetans held such matters to be possible. Ken Wilber, *Up from Eden*, 1983, pp. 52-6, citing the work of Eliade and Levi-Strauss in discussing the "reality of extrasensory capacities and paranormal powers ascribed to shamans and medicine men", says, "a fairly large number of ethnographic documents has put the authenticity of such phenomena beyond doubt", pp. 52-6. See also, Erlender Haraldsson, *Modern Miracles: An Investigative Report on Psychic Phenomena Associated with Sathya Sai Baba*, 1987, pp. 84, 153, 162, 233, in which he relates accounts of Sai Baba stopping heavy rains. (This is a phenomenon, which I, along with thousands there at the time, have witnessed on two occasions.) See also, Pradyumna Karan, *The Changing Face of Tibet*, 1976, pp. 67-8.
68. Hoffmann, *The Religions of Tibet*, pp. 47-9.
69. *Ibid.*, p. 70. Also, Bell, *The Religion of Tibet*, p. 38.
70. Sir Charles Bell, *Tibet: Past and Present*, 1968, p. 26.

highest esteem by all, who refer to him as Guru Rinpoche (Precious Master).[71]

This was also a time when many sacred texts were translated from Indian and Chinese sources. As doctrinal matters gained in importance it became necessary to choose between the two schools. The Indian school espoused a gradual, moralistic course towards Buddhahood involving several lives of gaining knowledge and collecting merit. The Chinese school argued the absolute nature of Buddhahood, which could be realized, even in a single lifetime, by any practitioner who established a state of complete repose; its teachings were derived from the Perfection of Wisdom doctrine. The deciding debate was held from 792-4. Shantirakshita's disciple, the Indian sage Kamalashila, won it over the Chinese led by the monk Hoshang Mahayana. However, the reasons may have been more political than doctrinal since Tibet and China were often at war.[72] Actually, the Chinese philosophy was attractive to many Tibetans then interested in Buddhism, since it was not inconsistent with Mahayana and Tantrism.[73] Nevertheless, the final outcome was the expulsion of the Chinese monks and the turning towards India for spiritual guidance.

Trisung Detsen (Ralpachen) (805-36), the grandson of Trisong Detsen was the third of the religious kings. Buddhism had by this time gained in strength especially since it had become the official orthodox faith[74] after the great debate at Samye in 792-4. Ralpachen, a Buddhist, superseded his older brother Lang Dharma, a Bonist, to become king and went on to champion Buddhism. He also secured the last great Tibetan military victories over China. Ralpachen also had the Tibetan language standardized for purposes of translation and supported the revival of *Sarvastivadin* (Hinayana) teaching. At the same time he humbled himself before the new Buddhist priesthood.

---

71. Snellgrove & Richardson, *A Cultural History . . .* , p. 78. See also, Michael Goodman, *The Last Dalai Lama*, 1987, p. 47.

72. Snellgrove & Richardson, *A Cultural History . . .* , The authors go on to mention that the Chinese view of "contemplation for contemplation's sake", leading to spontaneous realization without the need of moral and intellectual efforts, remains one of the main streams of Tibetan religious life from the eighth century to the present, p. 79.

73. R.A. Stein, *Tibetan Civilization*, 1972, pp. 67-8

74. Shakabpa, *Tibet: A Political History . . .* , p. 38.

Many of the people whose leanings were towards Mahayana Buddhism, as well as some pro-Bon government ministers, who opposed Buddhism, resented this gesture. Ralpachen was eventually killed by a conspiracy of pro-Bon ministers and his brother, Lang Dharma, was returned to the throne.[75] The subsequent suppression of Buddhism by Lang Dharma threw the country into turmoil and after his assassination at the hands of a Buddhist monk the country descended into internecine struggle between rival families for control of the country, since no successful candidate for king could be found. The new religion had thrown the divine status of the king into question, and with the end of the royal line Buddhism was eclipsed in central Tibet for the next 120 years.[76] Authority in Tibet remained decentralized from 842 to 1247.[77]

The first diffusion of Buddhism took place during a time of expansion unparalleled in Tibet's entire history when Tibet was one of the great military powers in Asia.[78] Buddhism was well received by the governing and educated classes, needing official patronage in order to become established.[79] With several Buddhist schools (Hinayana, Indian tantric, and Chinese Mahayana) as well as the indigenous Bon religion finding favour amongst various clans and factions, Buddhism became involved in political activities from its very beginning. This eventually led to Tibet becoming an "ecclesiastical state operating on two levels, that of the central government and that of the more or less independent local states",[80] a situation which evolved after the disintegration of the royal line.

The second diffusion of Buddhism and founding of the religious schools

After a period of collapse (842 to 978), both culturally and religiously, during which Buddhism and Bon struggled for survival,[81] power slowly

75. Bell, *The Religion of Tibet*, pp. 43-5.
76. Snellgrove & Richardson, *A Cultural History . . .*, p. 94.
77. Shakabpa, *Tibet: A Political History . . .*, p. 54.
78. Bell, *Tibet: Past and Present*, p. 20.
79. Guenther, "Buddhism in Tibet", *Encyclopedia of Religion*, vol. 2, p. 406.
80. *Ibid.*, p. 406.
81. Hoffmann, *The Religions of Tibet*, p. 83.

coalesced in the various regions of Tibet. While Bon never fully recovered, Buddhism regrouped steadily and irreversibly, thus establishing itself as the foundation of Tibetan culture. Tibetan Buddhism soon took on a distinct appearance within Buddhism and over time divided itself into various schools or sects.

Monks, who has escaped the persecution of Lang Dharma, kept Buddhism alive in eastern and western Tibet. A new dynasty arose in western Tibet and at the invitation of the king-turned-monk, Lama Yeshe Od, monks from India arrived in 978. This was the beginning of the renaissance of Buddhism in Tibet.[82] At the king's urging the great monk/scholar Atisha Dipamkara (982-1054) came to western Tibet in 1038, from the great monastic university of Vikramashila in India and proceeded to teach, reform and elucidate points of doctrine.[83] He is credited with the founding of the Kadam school (literally — bound by command)[84] which became the forerunner or parent of the Gelug (Virtuous Order) school out of which the institution of the Dalai Lamas arose. Atisha's disciple Dromton became the actual founder and first head of the Kadampa order. The Kadam school featured the three vows (i.e., Theravada, Mahayana, and Vajrayana) and a reform of relationships, which emphasized celibacy and high morality while maintaining tantric practices and meditation.[85] The unreformed monks, the followers of the Padmasambhava doctrines, became known as the Nyingmapa (The Ancient Ones)[86] and thus, the oldest school of Tibetan Buddhism. The Nyingmapa closed ranks around their special brand of Buddhism, an amalgam of early Indian, Bon and tantric teachings. Authority rested in the person of Padmasambhava to whom were ascribed the extraordinarily miraculous powers of a second Buddha.[87] In addition to philosophical, metaphysical, and psychological studies as well as meditation

---

82. Shakabpa, *Tibet: A Political History . . .* , p. 56.
83. *Ibid.*, pp. 56-8.
84. Snellgrove & Richardson, *A Cultural History . . .* , p. 131. *Note*: The term school also means a tradition or lineage in this particular context.
85. Michael, *Rule by Incarnation*, p. 20.
86. Tulku Thondup Rinpoche, *Buddhist Civilization in Tibet*, 1987, p. 31. *Note*: When the suffix *pa* is added it denotes a follower of that tradition, the order, or the sect itself.
87. Snellgrove, *Indo-Tibetan Buddhism*, p 397.

practices, elaborate magic rites, spells, and *mantras* were emphasized, often to serve the laity or provide mystical experiences. In some cases disciplinary vows, celibacy, and alcohol prohibition were ignored for reasons of religion.[88] Excesses in these latter areas were instrumental in bringing about reforms.

Shortly thereafter the Kagyud school (*kagu*: transmission of oral teachings) was founded. Its beginning can be traced to Marpa Lotsawa (1012-99), a great *yogi* and tantric master, through his disciple Milarepa (1040-1123), one of Tibet's most beloved saints, a great poet and ascetic, to the actual founder Gampopa (1079-1153), who combined the teachings of Milarepa and the Kadam school.[89] Many subsects developed, the most prominent being the *Karma Kagyud* or *Karmapa* founded by Karmapa Tusum Khyenpa. His reincarnation, Karmapa Pakshi (1206-83) was the first recognized incarnation, or *tulku*, in Tibet.[90] The *Gyalwa Karmapa*, the head of the Karmapa sect, is generally considered head of the whole Kagyud lineage.[91] This sect was to play a considerable role in power struggles amongst the various sects, especially with the Gelugpa since the Gyalwa Karmapa and the Dalai Lama were both considered incarnations of Chenrezig.[92]

The Sakya school (Grey Earth) began with the building of the Sakya monastery (named for the place it was built) in 1073 by Konchog Gyalpo, on his ancestral lands.[93] One of its primary features was a hereditary passing of the mantle of power. Its monks were able to marry and carry on a secular life as well. One of its most prominent scholars and head of the lineage was Sakya Pandita (1182-1251) who was invited to the Mongol court by the emperor Gotan, a grandson

---

88. Michael, *Rule by Incarnation*, pp. 19-20.

89. Thondup Rinpoche, *Buddhist Civilization in Tibet*, pp. 49-50. Also, Thomas Merton, *The Asian Journal of Thomas Merton*, 1975, who says *Kagyudpa* literally means "the upholder of esoteric transmission", p. 43.

90. This concept of reincarnation was quickly adopted by all the other sects and soon led to the transfer of authority from the religious families to the monastic establishment. See, Michael, *Rule by Incarnation*, p. 21.

91. Thondup Rinpoche, *Buddhist Civilization in Tibet*, p. 50.

92. Michael, *Rule by Incarnation*, p. 21.

93. Thondup Rinpoche, *Buddhist Civilization in Tibet*, p. 57. Also, Michael, *Rule by Incarnation*, p. 22.

of Ghengis Khan, and rose to be the supreme teacher of the emperor.[94] Phagpa (1235-80), the grandson of Sakya Pandita, was made preceptor to the imperial court in 1254 and was given temporal authority over Tibet by the emperor Kublai Khan, whom Phagpa had converted to Buddhism.[95]

This event marked the beginning of the lama or priest-patron relationship (*Cho-Yon*) between the supreme lamas of Tibet and the emperors of China — first the Mongol (*Yuan*), then the *Ming*, and finally the *Manchu* (*Ch'ing*) emperors — a relationship which endured in some form until 1911.[96] The emperor bestowed his patronage and support on the high lamas who, in exchange, became spiritual preceptors to the imperial court and were very influential in keeping peace in Tibetan controlled territories. This was at best a tenuous relationship as Mongol armies regularly invaded Tibet to quell internecine struggles amongst the various noble families. The Sakya hierarchy lasted only seventy-five years, ending in 1345 due to internal disputes.[97] The *Phamo Drukpa* (*Phagmotru*) family soon replaced the Sakya family, but it was not long before the concept of a leader from amongst the monks reincarnating to assume authority shifted from the leading families to the religious schools. The unique religio-political order of Tibet, rule by incarnation, was thus established.[98]

The last school to gain prominence was the Gelug, founded by Tsongkhapa (1357-1419), who along with Padmasambhava and Atisha is considered one of the founding religious figures of Tibet. All three are renowned and venerated by the Tibetan people.[99] Tsongkhapa's reformation stressed a return to strict monastic discipline, celibacy, a moral life, and a gradual path to enlightenment for all.[100] The Gelugpa,

---

94. Thondup Rinpoche, *Buddhist Civilization in Tibet*, p. 57.
95. Shakabpa, *Tibet: A Political History . . .*, p. 65. According to Snellgrove & Richardson, *A Cultural History . . .*, this event took place in 1260, p. 149. Bell, *The Religion of Tibet*, places the year as 1270, p. 67.
96. Shakabpa, *Tibet: A Political History . . .*, p. 71. Also, Smith Jr., *Tibetan Nation*,
97. Bell, *The Religion of Tibet*, p. 69.
98. Michael, *Rule By Incarnation*, p. 22.
99. R.P. Anuruddha, *An Introduction Into Lamaism*, 1975, p. 43. See also, Robert Thurman, *Essential Tibetan Buddhism*, 1997, p. 1.
100. Michael, *Rule By Incarnation*, p. 23.

or the Virtuous Order,[101] took as their model the Kadampa order. Their appeal was immediate and the Gelugpa order grew rapidly. Tsongkhapa and his disciples founded the three monasteries of Ganden (1409), Drepung (1416) and Sera (1419), all near Lhasa and soon to become the leading monasteries and teaching institutes of the country.[102] Another important monastery, that of Tashi Lhunpo, was founded by Tsongkhapa's disciple Gedun Drupa (1391-1474), who was installed as the third grand lama of the Gelugpa order and later came to be regarded as the First Dalai Lama.[103]

---

101. Anuruddha, *An Introduction Into Lamaism*, p. 46.

102. Michael, *Rule By Incarnation*, p. 23.

103. Anuruddha, *An Introduction into Lamaism*, claims Gedun Drupa was the first disciple of Tsongkhapa to succeed him as abbot of Ganden, the official hierarch of the Gelugpa order, p. 47. In reality he was the third to do so. More on this in note # 20 in chapter 2. It is also interesting to note that Anuruddha claims the First Dalai Lama was a nephew of Tsongkhapa, p. 47. Glenn Mullin, *Mystical Verses of a Mad Dalai Lama*, 1994, states this is a historical error perpetrated by Waddell and constantly repeated by Western writers, p. 255. Snellgrove & Richardson, *A Cultural History . . .*, use the phrase "said to be Tsongkhapa's nephew", p. 182. However, in his earlier book, Richardson, *Tibet and Its History*, clearly refers to Gedun Drupa as Tsongkhapa's nephew, p. 40. Michael, *Rule By Incarnation*, does likewise, p. 40, as does Hoffmann, *The Religions of Tibet*, p. 167. An interesting twist to this comes from Alexandra David Neel, *Initiates and Initiations in Tibet*, 1975, who states Tsongkhapa's nephew was Khasgrub, his successor as abbot of Ganden, p. 115. (Most authorities place Khasgrub as the second successor to the Gelugpa hierarchy.)

2

A History of the Dalai Lamas

Within the Context of Their Times

THE spiritual and temporal authority of the Dalai Lamas grew in significance during a period of adjustment between Tibet's Buddhist hierarchy and lay nobility, which lasted from the mid-thirteenth to mid-seventeenth centuries.[1] Buddhism had become firmly established as the basis for Tibetan cultural life[2] and was increasingly part of the collective life of the Tibetan people. The various schools of Buddhism spawned a number of monastic institutions out of which a great deal of scholarship, teachings, and translation emerged, as well as bitter philosophical battles between the various sects.[3] Being politically involved from its very beginnings in Tibet, Tibetan Buddhism's various schools and sub-sects, in order to further their own interests, had become allied with the hereditary nobility. The aristocratic families, seeking power, influence, and support, increasingly became the secular arms of the monasteries and sects they supported. In time, as the monasteries became increasingly economic and political entities, their power often eclipsed that of their patrons.[4]

The Mongols, who had conquered both countries, had reestablished the connection between Tibet and China, beginning in 1207 with Tibet's formal submission to Ghengis Khan in order to avoid invasion. As time passed the Mongols became less cohesive as the various Mongol tribes manoeuvered for power and influence

---

1. R. Rahul, "The Institution of Dalai Lama", *International Studies*, vol. 10, no. 4, April 1967, p. 495.
2. Snellgrove & Richardson, *A Cultural History* . . . , p. 177.
3. *Ibid.*, pp. 178-80.
4. Giuseppe Tucci, *The Religions of Tibet*, 1988, p. 40.

amongst themselves, generally in support of the ambitions of one prince or another. This lack of cohesion resulted, in 1368, with the collapse of the Yuan (Mongol) dynasty as rulers of China. (The collapse of the dynasty was due to their taste for the pleasures of courtly life as well as to their unpopular adulation of the Buddhist priesthood[5].)

Tibet had also regained much of its independence through the efforts of the monk and noble, Changchub Gyaltsen. He was of the Phagmotru family, which was initially allied with the Kagyupa sect. Consolidating his personal power, he took over many influential positions, disregarding the imperial and Sakya authorities, so that by 1350 he was *de facto* ruler of most of Tibet.[6] During the Phagmotru rule, the state was reorganized, security was increased, and the infrastructure and agriculture were improved as were the justice system and the general standard of living.[7] Though the Yuan dynasty fell, diplomatic ties to the Mongols were maintained.

China, having also achieved its independence from the Mongols did not attempt to retake Mongolian or Tibetan territories.[8] Thus, there seems to be "no substance in the claim of some Chinese writers that Tibet was in unbroken subordination to China from the time of the Yuan dynasty".[9] In fact, relations with China were cordial. The Ming emperors invited the famous lamas of all sects, some of whom, such as Tsongkhapa, instead sent disciples to visit China. Many of these were accorded special treatment and titles. Shakabpa claims this indicated that "the Ming emperors viewed Tibet as an independent 'Kingdom of the West'".[10] The official Chinese view was that these visits by lamas were tribute missions, which some modern Chinese writers regard as evidence that Chinese suzerainty was maintained over Tibet during the Ming dynasty. Wylie discounts this view citing a study by Fairbanks and Teng as well as the writings of Li Tieh-tseng.[11]

---

5. Richardson, *Tibet and Its History*, pp. 33-5.
6. *Ibid.*, p. 35.
7. Shakabpa, *Tibet: A Political History . . .* , pp. 81-2.
8. Richardson, *Tibet and Its History*, p. 36. Also, Turrell Wylie, "Lama Tribute In The Ming Dynasty", *Tibetan Studies In Honour of Hugh Richardson*, Michael Aris & Aung San Suu Kyi, editors, 1980, p. 338.
9. Richardson, *Tibet and Its History*, p. 36.
10. Shakabpa, *A Political History. . .* , pp. 83-5.
11. Turrell Wylie, "Lama Tribute. . . ," p. 335.

These visiting lamas, while influential, could not speak for Tibet as a whole for there were many noble families who, along with their ecclesiastical allies, vied for temporal control of the country. Tibet was primarily ruled by the Phagmotru family until 1481: the Rinpung family ruled until 1565, and the princes of Tsang after that (the latter two supported by the Karmapa order). The Tsang leadership lost power during the time of the Fifth Dalai Lama to the Mongol-backed Gelugpa sect.

The Gelugpa ironically owed much of their initial success to their lack of political affiliation and their unworldliness.[12] This soon changed, as Tsongkhapa's disciples were not only gifted spiritually but also ambitious to promote the growth of their religious ideology. Their growing political power owes much to the generally accepted view of all Tibetans that human activity was to be subordinated to religious concerns.[13] The enmity generated by their quick rise resulted in alliances against them between various monasteries of the Nyingmapa, the Kagyudpa and of its powerful subsect, the Karmapa, whose power base was in the province of Tsang, somewhat south-west of the province of U or central Tibet. These alliances were largely unsuccessful against the superior and more centrally organised Gelugpa. Out of mutual concern the Gelugpa soon found themselves allied with the ruling Phagmotru family in central Tibet. Power struggles between U and Tsang were finally resolved when the Fifth Dalai Lama consolidated temporal authority in Tibet.

In the midst of all this seeming turmoil, genuine religious and spiritual development did occur. Tsongkhapa's reforms and his personal spiritual legacy were a sound basis on which to build a new religious movement. A principal element in that movement was the perfected teacher coming again and again to teach, inspire, and lead the community of adherents. Many such teachers appeared, as they had for centuries, not only among the Gelugpa, but also among all the various Tibetan Buddhist sects. However, it was within the Gelugpa reformation that a lineage appeared that, due to spiritual excellence, administrative acumen, political circumstance, and above all the admiration of its followers, was to play a preeminent role in

---

12. Snellgrove & Richardson, *A Cultural History . . .*, p. 181.
13. Giuseppe Tucci, *Tibet Land of Snows*, 1967, p. 37.

the spiritual and temporal affairs of Tibet.[14] That was the lineage of the Dalai Lamas.

As previously mentioned Tsongkhapa's reforms struck a receptive chord amongst religious and lay Tibetans. Tsongkhapa was born Lobsang Drukpa[15] in the Tsong ka pa (land of Onions) region of the province of Amdo. Following in the spiritual footsteps of Atisha he proved his brilliance early, studying with the best teachers from all sects. In 1403 he composed his two famous syntheses of Buddhism, the *Lam rim* and the *Ngag rim*,[16] following which he set about implementing his reforms within the general framework of the Kadam tradition. To distinguish his schools from the Nyingmapa and Karma Kagyud, some of whom wore the red hat, the Gelugpa wore the yellow hat and were later so named.[17] In actuality, Tsongkhapa's followers were first called Galdanpa after Galden (Ganden) monastery, established by Tsonkhapa near Lhasa in 1409.[18] Along with the Sera

---

14. Janice D. Willis, writing in the foreword to Glenn Mullin, *Selected Works of the Dalai Lama I*, 1985, states "the Dalai Lama is revered by Tibetans primarily owing to the fact he is a lama, par excellence", p. 18.

15. Helmut Hoffmann, *The Religions of Tibet*, says Tsongkhapa's monastic name was Sumatikiri and that he was simply and reverentially called "Je Rinpoche" by his followers, p. 160. See, Snellgrove & Richardson, *A Cultural History. . .* , who translate Je Rinpoche to mean 'Precious Lord', p. 176, while Bell, *The Religion of Tibet*, translates it as 'The Chief of Great Price', p. 97.

16. R.A. Stein, *Tibetan Civilization*, 1972, p. 80. See, Hoffmann, *The Religions of Tibet*, who translates *Ngag rim* as 'great Stage Way To The Occult Sciences' and *Lam rim* as 'Steps to Enlightenment,' p. 164. The latter is referred to as "The Great Exposition of the Stage on the Path" by Guenther, "Buddhism in Tibet", *The Encyclopedia of Religion*, vol. 2, p. 411. The same work is referred to as "full account of the doctrine" by Snellgrove & Richardson, *A Cultural History. . .* , p. 181.

17. Snellgrove & Richardson, *A Cultural History. . .* , point out the term Yellow Hats was applied by Western scholars to the Gelugpa and Red Hats to all other orders rather indiscriminately, for the Tibetans only refer to one Karmapa school as Red Hat, the others as Black Hat, p. 181. See, Burman Bina Roy, *Religion and Politics in Tibet*, 1979, who says, "The older unreformed sects were known as Red Hats", p. 8. Also, Pradyumna Karan, *The Changing Face of Tibet*, 1976, notes the "common western usage" is to refer to the three earlier sects as red and Gelugpa as yellow, p. 68.

18. Snellgrove & Richardson, *A Cultural History. . .* , p. 181.

and Drepung monasteries, Ganden became the power base for the Gelugpa and helped reestablish Lhasa as a centre of influence. Whoever became abbot at Ganden, following in Tsongkhapa's footsteps, also became official head of the entire Gelugpa order. Tsongkhapa's illustrious disciple Gedun Truppa, posthumously regarded as the First Dalai Lama,[19] not only filled that role[20] but quite another as his lineage was to become the single most important within the Buddhist hierarchy of Tibet.

Dalai Lama I

Gedun Truppa (also written Gendun Drub, Gendun Druppa and Gedun Drupa) lived from 1391 to 1475.[21] He was born of nomadic herdsmen, who had moved from eastern Tibet to the western plateaus of the country.[22] They were then settled on a small farm at Shabtod in the Srad valley near Shigatse and not far from Sakya Monastery.[23] According to Tibetan chronicles the child was born in a cowshed where the family had taken shelter from attacking bandits. The family fled leaving the baby wrapped in blankets, hidden behind some rocks. Returning the next morning the herders saw, to their wonder, the child unharmed and a large crow or raven guarding him from the threats of other crows, vultures, and wild dogs. Later divinations stated the crow was a manifestation of Mahakala, the wrathful protective

---

19. Inder Malik, *Dalai Lamas of Tibet*, 1984, refers to Gedun Truppa as Tsongkhapa's "chief disciple", p. 5.
20. Snellgrove & Richardson, *A Cultural History. . .* , state that Gedun Truppa was the third abbot of Galden, p. 182. See, Hoffmann, *The Religions of Tibet*, who concurs, noting Gedun Truppa assumed the abbot's chair in 1438, succeeding Khasgrub (Khadrub), who was said to almost equal Tsongkhapa in scholarship, and before him Gyaltsen Dharma Rinchen (Gyal Tsab), pp. 167-8. See also, Thubten Jigme Norbu & Colin Turnbull, *Tibet*, 1968, who state Gendun Drub succeeded Khasgrub, who had been "given the job of teaching the great reformer's youngest disciple", p. 215.
21. The spellings of the First Dalai Lama's names employed at various points in the text reflect the spellings in the sources being cited.
22. Malik, *Dalai Lamas of Tibet*, p. 13. See also, Bell, *The Religion of Tibet*, p. 101.
23. Luciano Petech, "The Dalai Lamas and Regents of Tibet: A Chronological Study", *T'oung Pao*, no. 47, 1959, p. 370.

form of Chenrezig, the Buddha of Compassion, and that Mahakala would protect the boy throughout his life.[24]

As a young child the boy showed religious inclinations by carving *mantras* and prayers on rocks whilst tending the herds. He stated (at the age of five) that he did so to benefit "all sentient beings, each of whom had been a parent to me in some past life".[25] At age seven, upon his father's death, his mother placed him in Nartang, a Kadampa monastery, as a servant under the guardianship of his uncle, Geshe Chosey, to receive a classical education. He received the name Padme Dorje, "Thunderbolt Lotus", and studied under several teachers.[26] Showing promise, he was soon given every opportunity for study. The abbot, Drubpa Sherab, a renowned master, took the young novice under his wing and from him the boy received many important teachings and initiations. He was ordained at all three levels of monastic ordination, taking the monastic name of Gendun Drub, and even receiving material assistance, as he was very poor.[27] By age twenty-five, a fully ordained monk, Gendun Drub or Gendun Truppa, "The Perfecter of Those Who Yearn for Virtue", had studied under forty to fifty lamas and was already highly regarded for his writings and scholarship.[28]

Gendun Truppa left Nartang for central Tibet where he pursued further studies at several monastic colleges. In all he studied under more than sixty teachers, three in particular being highly instrumental in his development. The first was Drubpa Sherab, the second Tsongkhapa, and lastly the sage Sherab Sengge. Upon meeting Tsongkhapa in 1415, the great reformer tore a piece from his robe and gave it to Gedun Truppa, prophesising his future success in establishing and preserving "the purity of Tibet's tradition of Sangha,

---

24. Mullin, *Mystical Verses. . .*, p. 8. See also, Mullin, *Selected Works . . . I*, p. 23, and Norbu & Turnbull, *Tibet*, p. 215.
25. Mullin, *Selected Works. . . I*, p. 24.
26. Mullin, *Mystical Verses. . .*, p. 8. Mullin goes on to suggest the confusion around Tsongkhapa being the First Dalai Lama's uncle likely originates with his real uncle at Narthang monastery, p. 255. See also, Mullin, *Selected Works. . . I*, p. 24, and Bell, *The Religion of Tibet*, p. 102.
27. Mullin, *Selected Works. . . I*, p. 260.
28. Bell, *The Religion of Tibet*, p. 102.

or monastic community".[29] From Tsongkhapa and, later, his disciple Khadrub (Khasgrub) he received further training in Atisha's Kadam lineage, becoming in the process one of the master's chief disciples. In all Gedun Truppa stayed twelve years in central Tibet in meditation, retreat, and study, eventually ascending to the abbot's throne at Ganden and thereby assuming the leadership of the Gelugpa order.

While studying at Padme Choling Monastery, Gedun Truppa received the honorific title *Tamche Khyenpa*, or 'Omniscient One'. Mullin notes that this title became attached to all subsequent Dalai Lamas and was more likely to be used in Tibetan circles than Dalai, which was used more by foreigners,[30] possibly because the title Dalai was initially conferred by a foreigner (see p. 52). One of Gedun Truppa's Tibetan biographies notes that he was especially known for maintaining the Three Levels of Precepts, that is, the *pratimoksha* (Hinayana disciplines) of the monk, the Mahayana *bodhisattva* precepts, and the Vajrayana precepts.[31] He also received and mastered the Tara and Kalachakra Tantra *lineages* (lines of teaching) amongst others. According to Mullin, "each of the Dalai Lamas have devoted tremendous energy" to the preservation and dissemination of these lineages.[32] All in all he proved himself a model Buddhist monk who

29. Mullin, *Mystical Verses. . .*, p. 9. See also, Bell, *The Religion of Tibet*, p. 102, and Mullin, *Selected Works . . . I*, pp. 25, 207, who also mentions a previous vision of Gendun Drub's first *guru*, Drubpa Sherab, that his disciple would achieve great success, p. 24.

30. Mullin, *Selected Works . . . I*, adds that Tibetans will often refer to the Dalai Lama as Kundun, "Fulfiller of Wishes", pp. 38, 40, 261. See also, Harrer, *Seven Years in Tibet*, who translates Kundun as "Presence", pp. 146-7, a view shared by Rahul, "The Institution of Dalai Lama", who translates it as "Presence of Chenrezig". He lists several other names used by Tibetans for the Dalai Lama, the most commonly used being Gyalwa Rinpoche or "Precious Sovereign", p. 497. Norbu & Turnbull, *Tibet*, use this term throughout their book reflecting the viewpoint of its principle author, the elder brother of the present Dalai Lama.

31. Kunga Gyaltsen, *The Twelve Wondrous Deeds in the Life of Omniscient Gendun Drub*, in and translated by Mullin, *Selected Works . . . I*, p. 208. It is instructive to refer back to the Fourteenth Dalai Lama's summation of Tibetan Buddhism as "the complete practice of all Buddhism", on p. 17 of my introduction. See also note # 58 in Chapter 1.

32. Mullin, *Selected Works . . . I*, pp. 38-9. For more on the significance of these tantras see, Lama Tubten Yeshe's preface to this book, pp. 14-15. See also, China Galland, *Longing for Darkness: Tara and the Black Madonna*, 1990, who notes that Tara is regarded as a Buddha by Tibetans and also as a goddess or a *bodhisattva*, p. 158.

first, through study, contemplation, and meditation attained realization and then dedicated his life to teaching, writing, and the building of spiritual centres.[33]

As a teacher Gedun Truppa seemed to be of the highest caliber. A master of dialectics he was able to use his command of the subject to detect errors in arguments presented to him while forcefully presenting his own arguments using logical inquiry and analysis. These qualities he brought to teaching, never claiming the exclusive authority for views that seemed to naturally emanate from him. He was considered to have severed his attachment to worldly concerns as well as to possess *bodhicitta*, which aspires to enlightenment, and the middle view of *emptiness*. He was regarded as a great teacher who could lead his disciples to a true understanding and realization.[34]

Gedun Truppa left for posterity a vast corpus of writings, his collected works, or *sung bum*, containing seven volumes with several hundred titles included therein.[35] Some, such as his commentaries on *vinaya* and *abhidharma*[36] are over a thousand pages long. In addition to writing much poetry, a serious subject amongst Tibetans,[37] and many essays, his writings on Atisha's "Direct Methods for Training the Mind", or *lojong* method of spiritual training became one of his greatest legacies.[38] This method is quite important to all sects of Tibetan Buddhism, and it spread to the point that most schools of Buddhism in central Asia incorporated it. Because of his fame and the fact that he was a Kadampa monk, his writings and teachings had a profound and wide-reaching impact. His writing style, being concise, to the point, and very clear in revealing fundamental meanings, yet

33. Mullin, *Selected Works. . . I*, p. 27.

34. *Ibid.*, pp. 215-18.

35. *Ibid.*, p. 27.

36. Thondup Rinpoche, *Buddhist Civilization in Tibet*, in his glossary defines *abhidharma*, one of three collections of Buddhist canonical writing, as the Buddha's teachings on metaphysics. *Vinaya* is the Buddha's teachings on proper moral conduct. According to Mullin, *Selected Works. . . I*, three of the First Dalai Lama's works on *vinaya* remain amongst the most important and widely studied on the subject to this day, p. 25.

37. Shakabpa, *Tibet: A Political History*, says an inability to understand poetry was "considered a serious defect in educated persons", p. 97.

38. Gyalwa Gendun Druppa, the First Dalai Lama (tr. Glen Mullin), *Training the Mind in the Great Way*, 1993, p. 17.

humble in its demeanour, added to the popularity of his writings, particularly his commentaries on the *shastras*, which are commentaries on the Buddha's teachings.[39]

As a builder Gedun Truppa is best known for building Tashi Lhunpo Monastery "Mount of Blessing", in Tsang near Shigatse, as a memorial to his deceased *guru* Khasgrub. It was to become one of the great Gelugpa institutions and the eventual home of the *Panchen Lamas* who became second only to the Dalai Lamas in overall prestige.[40] Starting in 1447 he personally supervised the entire task of building Tashi Lhunpo Monastery, later becoming its first abbot and maintaining it as his principal seat for the rest of his life. His efforts also included the collection of funds, materials, and craftspersons. Renaissance man that he was, he even crafted several of the images within the temples himself.[41] He apparently had a hand in building other temples and is even credited by one authority with the building of Drepung Monastery.[42]

It would seem Gedun Truppa was able to accomplish so much through sheer force of personality, will, and determination. Bell refers to him as being high spirited from babyhood, taking "his own line regardless of what others said about him".[43] His Tibetan biographer emphasises his even mindedness, calmness of demeanour, humility, complete lack of both jealousy and competition, and avoidance of self-praise and the belittling of others.[44] Hoffmann paints a less flattering picture when, in a rather disparaging tone, he refers to him as "an intriguer and a somewhat arrogant personality who did everything possible to consolidate the hierarchical system of the Yellow Church".[45] This does not accord with the assessment of the present

39. Mullin, *Selected Works... I*, pp. 29-33.
40. Bell, *The Religion of Tibet*, p. 104. See also, Mullin, *Selected Works... I*, p. 26.
41. Malik, *Dalai Lamas of Tibet*, p. 14. See also, Mullin, *Selected Works... I*, pp. 26, 223.
42. Bell, *The Religion of Tibet*, p. 102. See also, Hoffmann, *The Religions of Tibet*, who points out another error in some European sources (Grunwedel, *Mythologie*, p. 76, and Schulemann, *Geschichte der Dalailamas*, p. 91) of placing Khasgrub as the first abbot of Tashi Lhunpo, p. 169.
43. Bell, *The Religion of Tibet*, pp. 103-7.
44. Mullin, *Selected Works... I*, pp. 26, 223.
45. Hoffmann, *The Religions of Tibet*, p. 168.

Dalai Lama who describes the First Dalai Lama as a quiet, introverted, and humble person.[46] Clearly, some early Western viewpoints regarding Gedun Truppa's personality differed from the Tibetan view.

Gedun Truppa passed away in 1475 in a manner of his own choosing. In his eighty-fourth year and having been in poor health for sometime, he told his monks that he was about to die and gave them some final instructions and advice. After telling them to always remember and meditate upon the teachings of the Buddha he entered into tantric meditation upon the *completion stage yogas*: techniques for "controlling the winds and seminal fluids within the energy channels of the yogin's transmuted body".[47] It is said his body began "to transform from that of an old man into that of a youth and shone with such brilliance few could bear even to look at it".[48] He remained thus for forty-nine days neither breathing nor with heart beat "seated in *tukdam*, a mystical state between life and death, wherein consciousness is withdrawn to the heart and the body is preserved intact by the powers of meditation".[49]

The First Dalai Lama carried on the work begun by Tsongkhapa with great success. As noted, he was a model Buddhist whose efforts towards realising the *bodhisattva* ideal were held in high esteem. His prodigious writings set a standard for subsequent Dalai Lamas to follow, as did his work as a teacher. He was especially noted for his

---

46. Mullin, *Mystical Verses. . .* , from the foreword, p. xv.
47. Coleman, ed., *A Handbook of Tibetan Culture*, p. 294.
48. Mullin, *Selected Works. . . I*, takes this account from Yeshe Tsemo's biography of Gedun Drub, "*A Rosary of Gems*", p. 27. "*The Twelve Wondrous Deeds in the Life of Omniscient Gendun Drub*", adds that many miraculous events occurred in the vicinity to demonstrate "the passing of a sage who had achieved the highest knowledge", p. 247. See also, Malik, *Dalai Lamas of Tibet*, p. 15.
49. Mullin, *Mystical Verses. . .* , p. 10. See also, Mullin, *Selected Works . . . I*, who says manifesting *tukdam* is a great accomplishment and of great inspiration to disciples. In modern times Kyabje Ling Rinpoche, the late Senior *guru* to the present Dalai Lama, sat in tukdam for fifteen days after passing away in December of 1983. His heart and breathing stopped but no other signs of death manifested, p. 275. For more on the Tibetan teachings of the intermediate stage between life and death, the *bardo* plane, see, W. Y. Evans–Wentz, *The Tibetan Book of the Dead*, 1960. Also, John Blofeld, *The Tantric Mysticism of Tibet*, 1970, pp. 233-4.

efforts to uphold the monastic precepts and discipline, thereby strengthening the emerging Gelugpa movement. His building of temples and monasteries, especially that of Tashi Lhunpo, and his creation of sacred images furthered that growth. While apparently an able administrator his primary focus was as a spiritual leader. His example set the tone for subsequent incarnations to emulate. This, above all, raised the prestige of his lineage to one of great prominence.

Reincarnation of the Dalai Lamas

Legend has it, according to the biography by Yangpa Chojey and also the account of the young Second Dalai Lama, that Gedun Truppa projected his consciousness, after passing away, to *Tushita Pure Land*.[50] There he consulted with Maitreya Buddha (the Buddha to come), Atisha, and Tsongkhapa as to where he should reincarnate. Tsonghkapa threw a white lotus flower and two hailstones to earth, saying he would appear where the flower landed. Tibetan mystical writings interpret this to mean there were three reincarnations of Gedun Truppa, the flower incarnation being the actual new Dalai Lama, the other two working "incognito" to carry on the First Dalai Lama's purposes.[51]

Mullin speculates that Gendun Drub was perhaps the most important Dalai Lama, being first in the line of incarnations, for his life 'set the stage for the success of the later incarnations in the lineage'.[52] This principle of reincarnation as mentioned earlier had

---

50. Thondup Rinpoche, *Buddhist Civilization in Tibet*, describes *Pure Land* as "naturally resplendent lands in which completely Enlightened Buddhas continuously teach for the benefit of all sentient beings", p. 106.

51. Mullin, *Mystical Verses. . .* , pp. 10-11. Also, Glenn Mullin, *Selected Works of the Dalai Lama II*, 1985, pp. 203-4.

52. Mullin, *Selected Works. . . I*, p. 39. Malik, *Dalai Lamas of Tibet*, makes the very significant claim that with Gendun Drub's reincarnation as Gedun Gyatso it was the first time the concept of *bodhisattva* was employed in conjunction with the reincarnation of a high lama. This greatly transformed Tibetan thinking and paved the way for the establishment of the institution of the Dalai Lama as a preeminent lineage in the eyes of the people, pp. 15-16. (Such a development, if true, would certainly explain much of the subsequent success of the Dalai Lamas and with them the fortunes of the Gelugpa.)

been adopted first by the Karmapa "Black Hat" order as a means of perpetuating the lineage of a highly advanced spiritual leader.[53] The Gelugpa, seeking to do the same, followed this example. It would appear, according to some Western authorities, that it was some years after Gendun Drub's death that the system was actually put into place.[54] Tibetan writers claim the First Dalai Lama chose his rebirth in accordance with a prophesy of Tsongkhapa that Gendun Drub would be reborn in successive incarnations.[55]

One of the more plausible accounts given is by Thubten Jigme Norbu, elder brother of the present Dalai Lama and an incarnate lama (*tulku*) himself, in his book *Tibet*, written in collaboration with Colin Turnbull. In his view, it was because Gendun Drub had successfully continued Tsongkhapa's work that the Gelugpa were a threat to those seeking secular power. The Phagmotru family was disintegrating due to infighting, with one of their leaders taking control of Shigatse and establishing the anti-Gelugpa Tsangpa dynasty. Because of this hostility the Gelugpa had to remain united and ensure an orderly succession of leadership. Hereditary succession, as with the Sakya was impossible as the Gelugpa maintained a strict celibacy. Nor was the Kargyupa (Kagyud) method of passing secret teachings from master to disciple appropriate, as the Gelugpa doctrines were not secret. The answer was reincarnation, not a new notion in the Buddhist world or in Tibet, where the system was already in use. The succession of Gendun Drub by Gendun Gyatso was at a purely human level in that Gendun Gyatso was returning to continue the work of his predecessor as a lama and a teacher. Thus the new incarnation was accorded the loyalty and devotion shown Gendun Drub, and the Gelugpa remained united.[56]

At this juncture it seems appropriate to discuss the important fact that each Dalai Lama is considered an incarnation of Tibet's

---

53. Turrell Wylie, "Dalai Lama", *The Encyclopedia of Religion*, vol. 4, p. 200.

54. Sarat Chandra Das, *Tibetan Studies*, 1984, p. 248. See also, Hoffmann, *The Religions of Tibet*, p. 168, and Bell, *The Religion of Tibet*, p. 109.

55. Hoffmann, *The Religions of Tibet*, p. 168. See also, Malik, *Dalai Lamas of Tibet*, who claims Gedun Truppa prophesized his own reincarnation, p. 15.

56. Norbu & Turnbull, *Tibet*, pp. 215-16.

patron deity Chenrezig or Avalokiteshvara, the *bodhisattva* of compassion. Most references credit the Fifth Dalai Lama with the beginnings of this association, which Mullin considers an error begun by Waddell and perpetuated by subsequent writers.[57] The prevailing view is that the Fifth Dalai Lama took advantage of the centuries old faith of the Tibetans in the *bodhisattva* Avalokiteshvara, proclaiming himself and previous Dalai Lamas as the reincarnation of this *bodhisattva*. The basis of the claim was a previously unknown, rediscovered text called a *terma*, "treasure" in the Nyingmapa tradition, which revealed the prophesy of this incarnation in the Dalai Lama lineage.[58] Mullin states the Fifth Dalai Lama did not invent this myth but rather he inherited it. According to the early Dalai Lama biographical literature it would seem Atisha always referred to his disciple Lama Drom (Dromton) as an incarnation of Avalokiteshvara. The First Dalai Lama came to be regarded as the reincarnation of Lama Drom, thus inheriting the mythology, which then followed the office of the Dalai Lama from that time forwards. Avalokiteshvara, regarded as a progenitor of the Tibetan race, was incarnated as the great kings, Songtsen Gampo, and Trisong Detsun, who brought Buddhism to Tibet, and then as Lama Drom who completed Atisha's work on entrenching the Dharma in Tibet. It is no wonder his incarnation as the Dalai Lama lineage added immense prestige to that line.[59]

Dalai Lama II

The white lotus that Tsongkhapa threw to earth landed on a hermitage at Tanak Dorjeden in the province of Tsang. The Second Dalai Lama, Gendun Gyatso (1475-1542)[60] was born into a family of *yogis*. His father, Kunga Gyaltsen, was a renowned lama and lineage holder from the Shangpa Kargyu, Shijey and Nyingma schools. He had received many teachings from the First Dalai Lama, as had his wife,

---

57. Mullin, *Mystical Verses. . .*, p. 17.
58. Hoffmann, *The Religions of Tibet,* pp. 175-6. See also, Malik, *Dalai Lamas of Tibet,* p. 24. Also, Wylie, "Dalai Lama", *Encyclopedia. . .*, p. 200, and Per Kvaerne, "Tibetan Religions: An Overview", *The Encyclopedia of Religion*, 1987, vol. 14, p. 500.
59. Mullin, *Mystical Verses. . .*, pp. 17-20.
60. Petech, "The Dalai Lamas and Regents. . .," p. 271. See also, Malik, *Dalai Lamas of Tibet,* p. 16.

the *yogini* Kunga Palmo. She was a recognised female incarnation of the thirteenth-century *yogini* Drowai Zangmo and adept in many tantric practices. One of the Second Dalai Lama's biographies suggests the First Dalai Lama was inspired to choose these disciples of his as parents for his rebirth.[61] The father and mother both had significant dreams foretelling the birth of a special child; the father was visited by Gendun Drub in his dream and the mother by a *bodhisattva* in hers, who advised her to name the child Sangye Pel, "He Expanded To Buddhahood". According to Tibetan accounts, the child's body was clear and radiant with light at birth. Within moments it turned its head towards Tashi Lhunpo Monastery, folded its hands in prayer and recited the Tara *mantra*.[62]

The young Sangye Pel very early on gave indications that he was an incarnation of Gendun Drub. At age three he told his father the story of how, after passing away in his previous incarnation, he went to Tushita Pure Land (the celestial realm of Buddha Maitreya) where, upon meeting Guru Tsongkhapa, his next birthplace was decided (see above). He also, on one occasion when scolded by his mother, told her he would soon leave this home for Tashi Lhunpo where he had "a home far pleasanter than this".[63] Because of these and other signs the search committee from Tashi Lhunpo, seeking the reincarnation of Gendun Drub, was directed to the home of Sangye Pel, and from there the family went to Tashi Lhunpo. The boy essentially proclaimed himself the reincarnation of his predecessor. He called by name several monks who were there during the time of Gendun Drub and recognized many personal articles from his former life. He also reportedly ran to the abbot's throne declaring it was his.[64] At the age of four, without a formal process of recognition, the boy Sangye Pel was simply accepted as the reincarnation of Gendun Drub. He would later become known as the Second Dalai Lama.[65]

His early training was with his father from whom he received many important lineages from a number of traditions, primarily

61. Mullin, *Mystical Verses. . .* , pp. 42-4.
62. Mullin, *Selected Works. . . II*, pp. 16, 202-3.
63. *Ibid.*, pp. 203-4.
64. Mullin, *Mystical Verses. . .* , p. 11. See also, Mullin, *Selected Works . . . II*, pp. 16, 204. See also, Das, *Tibetan Studies*, p. 248.
65. Mullin, *Mystical Verses. . .* , from the foreword by H.H. the Fourteenth Dalai Lama, p. xvi. See also, Mullin, *Selected Works . . . II*, p. 16.

Nyingmapa and tantric teachings.[66] The two became very close and in later life the Second Dalai Lama composed a long devotional poem in memory of his father. For his part Kunga Gyaltsen treated his son as more of an equal.[67] In due course, at age eleven and with great regalia the young Dalai Lama took up his place in Tashi Lhunpo. He took the pre-novice, or *upaseka* vows and was given the monastic name Gendun Gyatso.[68] This was followed by a long period of intense training and meditation practices. Much of his instruction came from the abbot, Panchen Yeshey Tsemo, who had been a close disciple of the First Dalai Lama.[69] It is said that during this period, while doing the White Manjushri retreat at age sixteen, the young Dalai Lama's memory was so enhanced that he was able to recall his previous lives and became able "to memorise a hundred lines of scripture in the time of a single tea break".[70] By his late teens the young prodigy, responding to many invitations, embarked upon a teaching tour of the various nearby hermitages and monasteries where his predecessor had taught. During his absence, jealousies arose within the Tashi Lhunpo administration, which led to Gendun Gyatso's forced departure from his monastery in 1494. Tibetan chronicles credit the mystical intervention of his guru Yeshey Tsemo, who wished to push his disciple out of a comfortable life at Tashi Lhunpo towards a greater destiny, for this development.[71]

Having been invited to Drepung, the foremost Gelugpa monastery, the young lama proceeded to study there for the next three years, under the tutelage of Lamyang Tekpa Chojoi, hardly leaving the precincts of the monastery. At the minimum age of twenty-

---

66. Mullin, *Selected Works... II*, pp. 204-5.
67. Mullin, *Mystical Verses...*, p. 58.
68. *Ibid.*, p. 62. See also, Mullin, *Selected Works... II*, pp. 161, 205-6.
69. Mullin, *Mystical Verses...*, p. 66. As will be seen later, the process of the disciple of the previous incarnation teaching the new incarnation is a continuing feature in the education of the Dalai Lamas. This takes on some significance in the relationships between the Panchen and Dalai Lamas.
70. Mullin, *Mystical Verses...*, pp. 66-7. Also, Mullin, *Selected Works... II*, pp. 23, 206. Manjushri is a meditational deity that embodies discriminating awareness.
71. Mullin, *Mystical Verses...*, pp. 67-72.

one he received his *bhikshu* (full) ordination as a monk.[72] He then spent the next several years in retreat, meditation, and teaching in response to many invitations, throughout central and southern Tibet. Many miraculous events were recorded during these tours which suggested Gendun Gyatso's spiritual greatness. It was during this period that he met and received further teachings from the reclusive, eccentric *yogi* Khedrup Noryang Gyatso, another direct disciple of the First Dalai Lama. Noryang Gyatso was like a father to the young lama and it is said he was instrumental in bringing about the Second Dalai Lama's enlightenment.[73] His real father passed away in 1503, shortly after Gendun Gyatso had made a teaching pilgrimage to Tsang. Fortunately, his father was able to spend some time with Gendun Gyatso in meditation and review of the lineages taught by him.[74] For another decade following this event, Gendun Gyatso would spend his winters in Lhasa and the rest of his time on pilgrimage, in meditation retreat and teaching in response to the many invitations that came his way. Often he taught and meditated before audiences of several thousands.[75]

Next occurred the events for which the Second Dalai Lama is most remembered. According to prophecies — some attributed to the writings of Padmasambhava and Atisha — an emanation of Avalokiteshvara would build a monastery on the shores of Lhamoi Latso Lake (Lake of the Goddess) located about ninety miles south-east of Lhasa. This lake had long been a pilgrimage site. Gendun Gyatso, through a series of rituals, infused the lake with the power to be a source of visionary experience for all who visited it with a pure heart and meditated besides its waters, thus fulfilling the second part of the earlier prophecies. This all came about after Gendun Gyatso, in response to the entreaties of the local chieftains, decided to build a meditation hermitage and summer residence at Gyal Metoktang on

72. Mullin, *Selected Works . . . II*, pp. 206-7. Also, Mullin, *Mystical Verses . . .*, pp. 72-4.

73. Mullin, *Mystical Verses . . .*, pp. 75-9. Also, Mullin, *Selected Works . . . II*, pp. 207-8.

74. Mullin, *Mystical Verses . . .*, also mentions here that the father passed away at age seventy-two, fulfilling a prophecy made by his son at age three. Kunga Gyaltsen displayed his high state of mystical accomplishment by sitting in tukdam for fifteen days, pp. 79-80.

75. *Ibid.*, p. 80.

the lake, naming it Chokhor Gyal Monastery. Many miraculous occurrences were said to happen during construction, which was subsidized by the local kings and chieftains (as were all his teaching and pilgrimage tours). A year later, in 1511, the empowerment ceremonies took place. Since that time Lhamoi Latso Lake has been a pilgrimage site for hundreds of thousands of central Asians, all hoping to see a vision within its waters, which might reveal the mysteries of their lives. The lake has also been consulted to help discover reincarnated lamas, including the Dalai Lamas. In recent times, Regent Reting Rinpoche saw visions within the lake, which were instrumental in locating the present Dalai Lama.[76]

In 1511, during the construction of the Chokhor Gyal Monastery, Gendun Gyatso received a request from his former *guru*, Panchen Yeshey Tsemo of Tashi Lhunpo, to return and assume the abbotship. After nearly twenty years of exclusion he returned, was enthroned, took up his former residence (that of the First Dalai Lama) and proceeded to give many teachings. Before long the monastery more than doubled its enrollment of monks and its prestige, due to his fame, presence, and efforts. He also resumed studies with his former *guru*, until the pressures to finish the construction of Chokhor Gyal Monastery took him away.[77]

From the time he was twenty-one, and had completed his studies at Drepung, Gendun Gyatso hardly spent more than a month or two per year at Drepung due to his involvement with pilgrimage and teaching tours.[78] This changed in 1517 when he accepted the abbotship (Holder of the Fearless Lion Throne) of Drepung, the largest and most prestigious monastery in the Gelugpa fold. It had links to all of central Asia, and the best students and scholars from monasteries all over Tibet came there to study.[79]

---

76. *Ibid.*, pp. 80-7. Also, Mullin, *Selected Works. . . II*, pp. 17, 208. Also, Shakabpa, *Tibet A Political History*, pp. 91-2. See also, Norbu & Turnbull, *Tibet*, p. 229.

77. Mullin, *Mystical Verses. . .* , pp. 87-90. See also, Das, *Tibetan Studies*, who says he was abbot for only five years, p. 249.

78. Mullin, *Mystical Verses. . .* , pp. 87-90. Also, Snellgrove & Richardson, *A Cultural History. . .* , speculate that much of the reason for these extensive travels lay in the fact the Gelugpa were suffering the hostilities, especially in the Lhasa area, of the Karmapa and their patrons, p. 182.

79. Mullin, *Mystical Verses . . .* , p. 94. Mullin also notes that during Tibet's classical period (eleventh to seventeenth centuries) "it was quite common →

One of his first acts as abbot of Drepung was to confer with the *gongma* (king) of Lhasa and gain control over the *Monlam Chenmo*, or Great Prayer Festival. The festival was restored to the Gelugpa who, following the creative inspiration of Tsongkhapa, had first inaugurated it. The Karmapa had refused them attendance to the festival for the previous nineteen years. The restoration of these rights was considered one of the greatest accomplishments of the Second Dalai Lama's life.[80]

The Great Prayer Festival was a highlight of the Tibetan New Year, taking place in Lhasa over two to three weeks. For Tibetans the festival "represents the active presence of the enlightenment tradition in the world and the meritorious energy created by the festival is said to be a major factor in sustaining world peace and prosperity".[81] The Tibetans, much like the Hopi of New Mexico, regard themselves as contributors to universal well-being and as peacekeepers for the world community. Thus, tampering with the festival for sectarian and political purposes was considered a serious transgression.[82]

The *Rinpung* hierarchy was at the time the primary political force in Tibet and their patronage went to the Karmapa. The conflicts over the festival seem to have come about due to the intrigues of the Fourth Sharmapa Tulku, Chokyi Drakpa, who fomented much sectarian rivalry in order to further his own position within the Tibetan aristocracy. Apparently his schemes almost split the Karma Kargyu, his own sect, into two camps. His chief rival was the Eighth Karmapa Tulku, Mikyu Dorjee, with whom the Gelugpa had amiable relations.[83]

→ for a young monk scholar to study in numerous monasteries and to gain experience within a wide variety of lineages (or sects)", pp. 253-4. See also, Mullin, *Selected Works. . . II*, p. 209. Here too Mullin makes note of the freedom of monks to study where and with whom they wished, p. 19.

80. Mullin, *Mystical Verses. . .* , pp. 94-5.
81. *Ibid.*, p. 95.
82. *Ibid.*
83. Mullin, *Mystical Verses. . .* , goes on to say that the career of the Sharmapa Tulku suffered as a result of his actions as it did later during the time of the Eighth Dalai Lama when the then Sharmapa Tulku conspired to take over the Shigatse region which led to the Tibet-Nepal war, pp. 95-6, 274. The current Sharmapa Tulku is heavily involved with the intrigues surrounding the escape from Chinese-occupied Tibet of the Seventeenth Karmapa Tulku, promoting his own candidate as the real Karmapa.

From 1518 until he died twenty-four years later, Gendun Gyatso was the head lama in charge of the Monlam Festival. The Lhasa King was impressed by the Second Dalai Lama's conduct in these matters and either gave him or had constructed for him the *Ganden Phodrang*, a suite of buildings in Drepung Monastery. This became his principal residence in Lhasa and that of the subsequent Dalai Lama's to the middle of the Fifth's reign.[84] By the time of the Fifth Dalai Lama, the name, Ganden Phodrang, had become that of the Tibetan government.[85]

Like his predecessor, the Second Dalai Lama commissioned many images to be constructed, principally for Chokhor Gyal Monastery. As with the First, the Second Dalai Lama had gold collected from all over Tibet and crafted into a life-size image of Buddha Maitreya. These were not merely temple decorations. Because they were made from contributions from many disciples they created spiritual unity amongst those disciples. Tibetans regard such sacred images as vessels of power, able to transform the *karma* and energy of living beings and acting as generators of merit for the entire planet.[86] It would appear the Dalai Lamas were to play a considerable role in propagating such activities within Tibetan culture.

In 1525 Gendun Gyatso assumed the abbotship of Sera, his stewardship there increasing the numbers of monks as well as its general prosperity. He was now the spiritual head of four monasteries and engaged in a ceaseless round of teaching and meditation practices.[87] He was, however, also engaged in a great deal of writing activity. The Fourteenth Dalai Lama referring to Gendun Gyatso as a prolific writer — his collected works containing in four volumes several hundred items such as poems, essays, prayers, and meditation guides — also says "the Second Dalai Lama was the greatest of all the early Dalai Lamas", partially because of his scholarship.[88] These writings

---

84. Mullin, *Mystical Verses. . .* , pp. 97-8, 264. Also, Mullin, *Selected Works . . . II*, p. 209.

85. Hoffmann, *The Religions of Tibet*, p. 171. See also, Shakabpa, *Tibet: A Political History*, p. 91.

86. Mullin, *Mystical Verses. . .* , pp. 99-101.

87. *Ibid.*, pp. 101-3.

88. *Ibid.*, pp. xiii-xiv. See also, Mullin, *Selected Works. . . II*, pp. 21, 210. Mullin further notes that the breadth and scope of the Second Dalai Lama's writings were matched only by the Fifth and, perhaps, the Seventh Dalai Lamas, p. 17.

differed from those of his predecessor in that the First's were long, detailed treatises focussed primarily on the mainstream Vajrayana tantric traditions, the five principal themes of Sutrayana, and the doctrines of the Kadampa (based on doctrines introduced by Atisha) and New Kadampa (based on Tsongkhapa's reforms) traditions. The Second Dalai Lama, undoubtedly aware of his predecessor's work, chose to write short essays and monographs focussing on the lineages and practices of the lesser-known sects. "He seemed to want to cover the corners of Tibetan Buddhism, the aspects upon which his predecessor had not found time to write", says Mullin.[89] Yet another feature of the Second's writings were his spontaneously composed verses of poetry, mystical verse works, or *Nyam gur*, which arose out of his spiritual experience or knowledge. He would typically sign his works with names such as Nankhai Naljorpa, or "The Yogi of Space", Yangchen Sheypai Dorje, or "Melodious Laughing Vajra", and Tranguyon Gendun Gyatso, or "The Mad Beggar Gendun Gyatso", the latter referring to his detachment rather than a lack of possessions.[90] Also much of his writing came in the form of poems, essays or treatises pertinent to the spiritual life of those devotees who had requested he write them. Apparently this is a customary request made of spiritual masters in Tibet.[91]

The Second Dalai Lama's non-sectarian approach to Buddhism is also reflected in his teachings as well as his writings. He was known as the yellow hat master with no sectarian bias. His personal meditation practices were taken from many of the schools of Buddhism in Tibet as were his studies and doctrinal interests.[92] He studied with more than ten *gurus* including his father, a Nyingmapa master and later, his principle *guru*, Khedrup Norzang Gyatso, who led him, according to his own admission, to achieve *shunyata*, or emptiness, the ultimate level of reality.[93]

89. Mullin, *Selected Works. . . II*, p. 20.

90. Mullin, *Mystical Verses. . .* , pp. xiii-xiv.

91. Mullin, *Selected Works. . . II*, pp. 20-1.

92. Mullin, *Mystical Verses. . .* , p. xv. See also, Mullin, *Selected Works. . . II*, p. 210.

93. Mullin, *Selected Works. . . II*, p. 210. See also, Mullin, *Mystical Verses . . .* , p. xiii. Mullin suggests all the Dalai Lamas up to the Seventh combined Nyingmapa and Gelugpa traditions. The Eighth, according to his Tibetan biography, also started to follow this combined tradition just before he died, p. 254.

This self-assured assessment was in keeping with his assertive and outgoing personality, "confident of who he was, and fully at ease with the centre-stage role expected of him", according to the present Dalai Lama who also uses words such as outspoken, haughty, and loquacious to describe his former incarnation.[94] That he would reincarnate was certain in the mind of Gendun Gyatso. For sometime before he died he prepared his disciples for that eventuality, first by hinting of his approaching death and then giving signs as to where he would reincarnate. He also stated, several times before he died, that he would soon have to go to the north where he had work to do.[95] As he was dying he expressed the wish to return so that his life's work could be further forwarded.[96] In 1542, at the age of 68, Gendun Gyatso passed away seated in meditation and at a time of his choosing. According to his biography, after cremation his heart was found crystallized into the shape of a Buddha in the form of a tantric deity.[97]

The Second Dalai Lama continued the work of the First Dalai Lama in spreading the Buddha *dharma*. As the pre-eminent lama of his day his prestige carried the fortunes of the Gelugpa and that of the office of the, as yet to be named, Dalai Lama lineage further into central and southern Tibet. By the time he died there were few important lamas in Tibet who had not studied with him or received tantric initiations from him or one of his disciples.[98] Through his efforts, control of the Great Prayer Festival had been restored to the Gelugpa. Even though Gelugpa persecutions persisted — they, as yet, wielded but little political power — their overall growth was such that a *depa*, a special official to oversee its internal administration, had to be

---

94. Mullin, *Mystical Verses. . .*, pp. xv, 149.

95. Mullin, *Selected Works. . . II*, p. 211. Also, Mullin, *Mystical Verses . . .*, pp. 105-9. Mullin describes how the Second Dalai Lama, even though quite ill, travelled to the Tolung area and left strong signs he would be reborn there, pp. 109-10. Further along Mullin mentions that the Third Dalai Lama travelled to Mongolia, in the north and "tamed the violent Mongolian peoples . . . ushering in an era of peace and harmony", p. 115. In the foreword the present Dalai Lama states that Gendun Gyatso prophesized, towards the end of his life, that the Dalai Lama lineage would remain stable up to the Fifth Incarnation, p. xvi.

96. Norbu & Turnbull, *Tibet*, p. 217.

97. Mullin, *Mystical Verses. . .*, pp. 113-14.

98. *Ibid.*, p. 11.

appointed.[99] This growth was soon to take an exponential leap with the reappearance of the Dalai Lama incarnation.

Dalai Lama III

The third Dalai Lama was born in 1543 in the village of Khangsar, in the Tolung valley not too far from Lhasa.[100] His father, Depa Namgyal and his mother Paldzom Butri were of a distinguished family well connected to the Phagmotru family and to Sakya Monastery.[101] As with the first two Dalai Lamas, miraculous signs accompanied his birth. It is said, according to his Tibetan biography, that at birth he started to recite Tibet's great *mantra*, "*om mani padme hum*". After learning to talk he would speak often about his predecessor with some accuracy, even declaring he was Gendun Gyatso. These signs brought him to the attention of the delegation seeking the Second Dalai Lama's reincarnation.[102]

The search committee consulted the *Nechung oracle*, who was the channel for one of Tibet's principal protector deities, and with whom the Second Dalai Lama had established a special relationship, as he would with all subsequent Dalai Lama reincarnations. Upon being advised by the oracle that the Second Dalai Lama had reincarnated in a hundred bodies, Sungrab Gyatso, the head of the Drepung search committee and Gendun Gyatso's principal secretary, also searched for signs in the mystic Lahmoi Latso Lake. It was then that the Tolung candidate was singled out for consideration. After a formal recognition process the boy, now aged four, was quickly confirmed as the reincarnation. Sungrab Gyatso made arrangements for his enthronement and education.[103]

Placed in Drepung, he proved to be a precocious and brilliant scholar under the tutelage of Panchen Sonam Drakpa from whom he also took his *upaseka*, novice and final vows. He was given the

---

99. Norbu & Turnbull, *Tibet*, p. 217.
100. Glenn Mullin, *Essence of Refined Gold*, 1985, p. 221. See also, Shakabpa, *Tibet: A Political History*, p. 92.
101. Mullin, *Essence. . .* , p. 221. Also, Snellgrove & Richardson, *A Cultural History. . .* , p. 183. See also, Bell, *The Religion of Tibet*, p. 110.
102. Mullin, *Essence. . .* , pp. 221-2. See also, Norbu & Turnbull, *Tibet*, p. 217.
103. Mullin, *Mystical Verses. . .* , pp. xvi, 174.

monastic name Sonam Gyatso, which touched off a 'national scandal', according to Mullin, as it was expected he would be named Gendun Drakpa.[104] At the age of ten he was placed on the throne of Drepung, and four years later on that of Sera, all the while continuing his studies under various teachers.[105] In addition he presided over the Great Prayer Festival, instituting the practice, on the last day of each festival, of the monks repairing and maintaining the dikes of the Kyichu River. It had flooded Lhasa in 1562.[106]

Sonam Gyatso, while still quite young, made a pilgrimage to Chokhor Gyal Monastery. This was a trip all Dalai Lamas would be expected to make during their lifetime for the purpose of performing tantric meditation. Thousands lined his route to receive blessings, and he visited the various monasteries on the way. From that time he divided his time between Gyal and Drepung and his numerous teaching tours.[107] Responding to many invitations his travels took him amongst the nomads of northern Tibet, to southern Tibet where he declined the abbotship of Tashi Lhunpo but left a representative, and through central Tibet, giving teachings to the various monasteries he visited. Throughout, he maintained an extensive and rigorous daily meditation schedule as well as periodically going on retreat. He also became well known for the many miracles which occurred in his presence, developing, according to Norbu & Turnbull, "extraordinary powers".[108] Because of these extensive travels and teaching duties he found little time for writing; nevertheless, forty titles, modest by Tibetan standards, issued from his pen.[109] In this way, working with missionary zeal, he successfully reinforced and spread the teachings of Tsongkhapa throughout Tibet.[110]

---

104. Mullin, *Essence. . .*, pp. 19, 250.
105. Das, *Tibetan Studies*, pp. 249-50. See also, Mullin, *Essence. . .*, p. 224, and Shakabpa, *Tibet: A Political History*, p. 92.
106. Shakabpa, *Tibet: A Political History*, p. 92.
107. Mullin, *Essence. . .*, pp. 222-4. See also, Mullin, *Mystical Verses. . .*, p. 24.
108. Mullin, *Essence. . .*, pp. 226-9. See, Shakabpa, *Tibet: A Political History*, p. 93.
109. Mullin, *Essence. . .*, p. 14.
110. W.W. Rockhill, *The Dalai Lamas of Lhasa and their Relations with the Manchu Emperors of China 1644-1908*, 1910, p. 4.

The Third Dalai Lama had been appointed personal teacher to the Nedong king, one of the more powerful rulers of the Phagmotru family, who died in 1564. With his death the Phagmotru-supported Gelug fortunes suffered due to pressures from the supporters of the Karma Kagyud. Sonam Gyatso often acted as a mediator in these conflicts with some success.[111] In 1573 he founded *Namgyal*, which would be the personal monastery of all the Dalai Lamas, on the Potala hill just outside Lhasa, but it was taken over by the Tsang-backed Kagyud forces who were led by the Sharmapa Tulku. In 1574 Tsang invaded U and assumed political control.[112] It was in the midst of these circumstances that Altan Khan, prince of the powerful Tumed Mongols, who had been successfully raiding the Chinese borderlands for many years, invited Sonam Gyatso to Mongolia.[113]

The Mongols, having previously accepted the Buddhist faith in the time of Kublai Khan and Sakya Phagpa, had reverted back to their old shamanistic ways after the fall of the Yuan dynasty.[114] There is some evidence that Karmapa lamas had maintained links with Mongolia but these were not effective in preserving Buddhism.[115] However, some lamas brought to Mongolia from north-eastern Tibet had some success, just prior to this time, in reintroducing Buddhism into the country.[116] Because of these tenuous contacts and perhaps, as Bell speculates, because Altan Khan knew the power of the

---

111. Shakabpa, *Tibet: A Political History*, pp. 92-3.
112. Das, *Tibetan Studies*, p. 250. U and Tsang are districts within central Tibet, which is generally known as the province of U-Tsang.
113. Snellgrove & Richardson, *A Cultural History. . .*, p. 183. Also, Rockhill, *The Dalai Lamas of Lhasa. . .*, p. 4. See also, Bell, *The Religion of Tibet*, p. 111.
114. Bell, *The Religion of Tibet*, p. 112. See also, Hoffmann, *The Religions of Tibet*, p. 171. See also, Mullin, *Essence. . .*, who says Kublai's successor, Timor Khan rejected Buddhism due to its pacifying influence on the Mongolians, pp. 233-4.
115. R.A. Stein, *Tibetan Civilization*, 1972, p. 81. Also, Snellgrove & Richardson, *A Cultural History. . .*, pp. 183-4.
116. Rockhill, *The Dalai Lamas of Lhasa. . .*, says these contacts resulted in Altan Khan and his peoples being converted to Buddhism, pp. 4-5. Also, Hoffmann, *The Religions of Tibet*, p. 171. See also, Snellgrove & Richardson, *A Cultural History. . .*, who suggest the Buddhist presence in Mongolia at the time invalidates the Gelugpa claim of their reestablishing contact between Tibet and Mongolia, p. 183.

priesthood in Asia and was probably remembering the glory of the Kublai-Sakya alliance, the famed lama Sonam Gyatso was invited to Mongolia.[117] This was a move that, while meeting with initial resistance, was soon welcomed by the Chinese. Having been very much embarrassed by Mongolian raiding forces over the years, they could see the advantage of supporting the proselytizing efforts of the Tibetan lamas, in that it dampened the Mongolian martial spirit, effectively weakening their military intimidation.[118]

Wary of Mongolian intentions, Sonam Gyatso refused Altan Khan's invitation and sent a representative instead. A second invitation accompanied by a large delegation from the Khan as well as the now perceived opportunity to spread the Buddha Dharma throughout Mongolia persuaded Sonam Gyatso to take up the challenge.[119] Thus, it was in 1576, at age 34, that Sonam Gyatso began to fulfil the prophecy he had made towards the end of his previous incarnation that he would go to work amongst the peoples of the north. This work would affect much of the known world since aggressive Mongolian militarism had devastated much of Asia and even parts of Europe.[120]

Because of his reputation Sonam Gyatso was seen off by the leading secular and ecclesiastical figures of his day. A huge procession accompanied him many miles out of Lhasa before they tearfully, reluctantly, and with much apprehension sent him off.[121] The size of his retinue dictated a slow pace, the journey taking well over a year. This was primarily due to invitations from the many monasteries and noble families along his route to stop and impart his blessings and teachings.[122] Along the way, it is said, he tamed rushing torrents so

---

117. Bell, *The Religion of Tibet*, p. 111. Also, Norbu & Turnbull, *Tibet*, p. 218. See also, Malik, *Dalai Lamas of Tibet*, p. 16.
118. Snellgrove & Richardson, *A Cultural History . . .* , p. 184.
119. Hoffmann, *The Religions of Tibet*, pp. 171-2. Also, Norbu & Turnbull, *Tibet*, p. 218. See, Das, *Tibetan Studies*, p. 250. See also, Rockhill, *The Dalai Lamas of Lhasa . . .* , who mentions only one invitation, stating that Sonam Gyatso responded promptly, arriving in Mongolia in 1576 (other authorities place his arrival as 1578), p. 5.
120. Mullin, *Mystical Verses . . .* , p. 115. Mullin goes on to speculate that, had there been a Nobel Peace Prize in Sonam Gyatso's time, he certainly would have deserved it, p. 115.
121. Mullin, *Essence . . .* , pp. 230-1.
122. *Ibid.*, pp. 231-2.

his party could cross over, made a waterfall reverse its flow, and pulled a right winding conch-shell (a rare and auspicious manifestation in itself) from within a large rock. Because of these signs his fame preceded him and also demonstrated that "he, and his religion, were powers to be reckoned with".[123] In time a large advance party bearing rich gifts from Altan Khan greeted and then accompanied Sonam Gyatso's party to the camp of the Khan.

Sonam Gyatso, in his first address to the Mongols and the borderland Chinese, proclaimed the new laws of the land. In short, the precepts of the Buddha were to be followed. Blood sacrifices of all kinds were outlawed; those of humans, such as the immolation of widows, were punishable by death; any retaliation against the monkhood, to these injunctions, meant confiscation of one's property. The Mongolian deity *Ongghon* was no longer to be propitiated, his worship replaced with that of the Wisdom Protector Mahakala, an emanation of Chenrezig. The Mongols were also to cease their pillaging ways and their raids into China and Tibet. In general, the people were encouraged to integrate the Buddha's teachings into their way of life and emulate the gentler mannerisms of central Tibetans.[124] Altan Khan then proclaimed these precepts as law much to the relief of Tibet and China.[125]

After this, Altan Khan conferred upon Sonam Gyatso the title Tale (Dalai), which means "Ocean", the same as his Tibetan name Gyatso. The implied meaning was "Ocean of Wisdom". (This title was posthumously applied to the Third Dalai Lama's predecessors and all subsequent reincarnations.) For his part, Sonam Gyatso gave Altan Khan the title "King of Religion, Majestic Purity". It is said the Third Dalai Lama revealed that Altan Khan was the reincarnation of Kublai Khan and that he (Sonam Gyatso) was that of Phagpa, the Grand Lama of Sakya, thereby reinstating the priest-patron relationship.[126]

---

123. Norbu & Turnbull, *Tibet*, p. 218. Also, Bell, *The Religion of Tibet*, pp. 112-13. See also, Mullin, *Essence...*, pp. 231-2.

124. Mullin, *Essence...*, pp. 234-6. See also, Bell, *The Religion of Tibet*, p. 114, and Norbu & Turnbull, *Tibet*, p. 219.

125. Norbu & Turnbull, *Tibet*, p. 219.

126. Snellgrove & Richardson, *A Cultural History...*, also note that Altan Khan was "in no position to bestow his "priest" authority over any part of Tibet", p. 184. See also, Hoffmann, *The Religions of Tibet*, p. 172, and Mullin, *Essence...*, p. 14. Also, Malik, *Dalai Lamas of Tibet*, p. 17.

To solidify these proceedings Sonam Gyatso established the Tekchen Chokhor Monastery, following which many more monasteries were built.[127] He also left Lama Yonten Gyatso (not to be confused with the Fourth Dalai Lama), whose line was to continue as one of the most prominent within the Buddhism of Mongolia, as his representative. Sometime later Yonten Gyatso is credited with bringing the dying Altan Khan back to health, thereby solidifying the general faith of the Mongols in Buddhism.[128] Altan Khan had arranged for Sonam Gyatso to visit the imperial court, which he may or may not have done en route to eastern Tibet. In any event, an official was appointed to further relations between China and Tibet.[129] Sonam Gyatso did, however, teach in western China and was provided with translators by the governor.[130]

For the next few years the Third Dalai Lama travelled through the eastern Tibetan provinces of Amdo and Kham, teaching and establishing monasteries as he went. In particular he won the support of the king of Litang (also written as Lithang), formerly a patron of the Karmapa, establishing a monastery there. He also built the monastery of Kumbum on the site of Tsongkhapa's birthplace. Kumbum grew to be the foremost Gelugpa institution in eastern Tibet. These travels significantly enhanced the prestige of the Dalai Lama himself while furthering the Gelugpa cause in these regions, which were areas of Nyingmapa and Bonpo influence.[131]

In 1585 at the invitation of Dhuring Khan, Altan Khan's successor, Sonam Gyatso returned to Mongolia. During his time there he was asked to mediate a border dispute between Mongolia and China, perhaps the first time the Dalai Lama exercised purely political

---

127. Mullin, *Essence...*, p. 243. See also, Das, *Tibetan Studies*, p. 251.

128. Bell, *The Religion of Tibet*, pp. 116-17.

129. Bell, *The Religion of Tibet*, pp. 115-16, and Norbu & Turnbull, *Tibet*, p. 220, claim Sonam Gyatso did visit the imperial court. Other authors contend that while Sonam Gyatso did receive an invitation to the Chinese court he never made the trip. See, Snellgrove & Richardson, *A Cultural History...*, p. 184. See, Shakabpa, *Tibet: A Political History*, who also mentions that an official was appointed to further relations between Mongolia and Tibet, p. 96.

130. Shakabpa, *Tibet: A Political History*, p. 96.

131. Norbu & Turnbull, *Tibet*, p. 220. Also, Mullin, *Essence...*, p. 237, and Mullin, *Mystical Verses...*, p. 12.

authority.[132] He once again received an invitation to the Chinese court but declined, promising to come at a later date. Returning to north-eastern Tibet in 1588 he fell ill, and, sensing his life was ending, gave instructions to his disciples, telling them he would soon return in another body. As with his predecessors, he sat in meditation and ceased breathing. His ashes were returned to Lhasa and preserved in Drepung.[133]

The Third Dalai Lama was a man of prodigious spiritual energy. He established himself as a brilliant scholar and teacher as well as an able administrator very early in his career. Combining the Nyingmapa and Gelugpa traditions, he took care to maintain his meditation and retreat practices as an example to his disciples. His work in Mongolia and eastern Tibet greatly furthered the Buddha Dharma in general and the Gelugpa in particular. Because these activities involved Tibet with China, China soon involved itself with Tibet,[134] which was to prove consequential in time. Nevertheless, his greatest legacy is the conversion of Mongolia to Buddhism. Mongolia has remained a spiritually devoted nation ever since.[135]

Dalai Lama IV

As he was dying Sonam Gyatso's Mongolian converts implored him to remain longer since his religious leadership was sorely needed. He acceded to their requests in the form of a promise to be reborn in Mongolia.[136] Shortly thereafter, a child born in 1589 into the family of Altan Khan (his great-grandson) showed signs, such as visions of various gods and recognition of the Third's personal effects, indicating he was the reincarnation of the Third Dalai Lama.[137] The search committee sent out from Tibet to investigate confirmed these signs. A large delegation from central Tibet, including high lay officials, representatives of the three leading Gelugpa monasteries, and the

---

132. Norbu & Turnbull, *Tibet*, p. 220. See also, Bell, *The Religion of Tibet*, p. 117.
133. Mullin, *Essence. . .* , pp. 239-40. See also, Shakabpa, *Tibet: A Political History*, p. 96.
134. Richardson, *Tibet and Its History*, pp. 40-1.
135. Bell, *The Religion of Tibet*, p. 118.
136. Norbu & Turnbull, *Tibet*, pp. 220-1.
137. Gunther Schulemann, *Geschichte Der Dalai-Lamas*, 1958, p. 215.

Third Dalai Lama's treasurer, failed to convince the parents to let the child return with them. He subsequently received his early religious training in Mongolia with Tibetan monks sent to tutor him[138] and was enthroned there in 1591.[139] The Fourth Dalai Lama was named Yonten Gyatso (Ocean of Good Quality), later becoming known as Tutob Yonten Gyatso, or "Yonten Gyatso the Adept", since he exhibited great spiritual power in his youth.[140] His appearance in Mongolia, which was not doubted at all during the confirmation process, brought the Mongols closer to the Tibetan religious hierarchy without making them feel dependent.[141] This resulted in a closer spiritual relationship between Mongolia and Tibet. As well, the Gelugpa became the dominant sect in Mongolia surpassing whatever influence was left of the earlier Sakya hierarchy.[142]

In 1601 Yonten Gyatso, accompanied by a large Tibetan delegation and Mongolian escort, left to assume his duties in central Tibet. They travelled along the great wall of China to the Kokonor region where he gave teachings. They also stopped at Tongkhor, the diplomatic post established by Sonam Gyatso.[143] Upon arrival in Lhasa he was again enthroned and was given many gala receptions. He soon settled into Drepung, was ordained as a monk, and later became the student of the scholarly Tashi Lhunpo abbot, Lama Lobsang Chokyi Gyaltsen, who, in 1604, had been summoned to Lhasa. This eminent

---

138. Shakabpa, *Tibet: A Political History*, pp. 96-7. See also, K. Dhondup, *The Water-Horse and Other Years*, 1984, who makes the point that the Mongolian child was favoured over another popular candidate born in Tibet, p. 9.

139. Schulemann, *Geschichte* . . . , p. 215.

140. Das, *Tibetan Studies*, p. 251. See also, Mullin, *Mystical Verses* . . . , p. 12.

141. Schulemann, *Geschichite*. . . , p. 215. See also, Snellgrove & Richardson, *A Cultural History*. . . , who somewhat cynically note "this piece of diplomacy. . . gained conclusively the interested support of the Mongol ruling family", pp. 184-93.

142. Shakabpa, *Tibet: A Political History*, p. 97. See also, Mullin, *Mystical Verses*, p. 12.

143. Shakabpa, *Tibet: A Political History*, p. 97. Also, Snellgrove & Richardson, *A Cultural History*. . . , p. 193. See also, Schulemann, *Geschichte* . . . , p. 216.

lama instructed the young Dalai Lama in the *sutras* and tantras[144] and later officiated at his full ordination, which took place in 1614, at the age of twenty-five, somewhat later than would be expected.

Yonten Gyatso proved to be of a scholarly disposition, dedicating his time to study, practice, and teaching, although we are told he produced no writings of significance.[145] He seemed to mature slowly, appearing at times to be complacent and lacking in energy. Schulemann speculates that this was due to the relatively peaceful situation at the time of his arrival in Tibet. Nevertheless, he saw to his duties, which amongst others included receiving and giving blessings to high-ranking officials from Mongolia and Tibet, responding to various invitations to teach, and presiding over the annual Great Prayer Festival.[146] He was also, in 1615, invited to visit China by the emperor, for the purposes of blessing a temple in Nanking, but the Dalai Lama declined due to pressing responsibilities.[147]

The Mongols were very saddened to see their home-grown Dalai Lama leave, but were somewhat mollified by his sending, as his representative, a reincarnated high lama who was considered an embodiment of the future Buddha Maitreya. He was accorded the title Maidari Hutuhtu. This new hierarch of the Gelugpa in Mongolia took up residence in Urga under the patronage of the Khalkha Mongols.[148] A dispute arose as to the spiritual rank of this hierarch in

---

144. Shakabpa, *Tibet: A Political History*, p. 97. Also, Schulemann, *Geschichte. . .* , p. 216. See also, Doboom Tulku, "the lineage of the panchen lamas", *lungta*, no. 10, Winter 1996, p. 7. (These events were the beginnings of what would become a dynamic spiritual relationship between the Dalai and Panchen Lamas, the first of whom, would be Lobsang Chokyi Gyaltsen.)

145. Schulemann, *Geschichte. . .* , p. 217. See also, Mullin, *Essence . . .* , p. 244.

146. Schulemann, *Geschichte. . .* , pp. 216-17.

147. Mullin, *Essence. . .*, p. 244. See also, Shakabpa, *Tibet: A Political History*, p. 99.

148. Hoffmann, *The Religions of Tibet*, also mentions that the Chinese attempted to impose the condition that the Maidari Hutuhtu should be reincarnated only in Tibet, p. 174. Also, Rockhill, *The Dalai Lamas of Lhasa. . .* , p. 6. See also, Schulemann, *Geschichte. . .* , who points out this patriarch had been born in Mongolia in 1592, left for Tibet with the Fourth Dalai Lama, returning in 1604 to ascend the vacant throne of the Third Dalai Lama and holding office until 1635. His successor did much →

relation to the high lama of the Mongolian monastery of Gahdan, bringing their tribal patrons to the brink of war. The chief of the Celeuth (Qoshat) Mongols, the other contending party, was able to effect a reconciliation, for which service he was given the Buddhist title, Ta Kausri, by the Chinese emperor. Later, known as Gushri Khan,[149] he would play a prominent role in Tibetan affairs.

In Tibet the Red Hat Karmapa sect, whose patron was the Tsang king Karma Tensung Wangpo, resented the show of Gelugpa strength resulting from the Fourth Dalai Lama's arrival and enthronement. They sent messages and poems to the Dalai Lama that were considered, partially due to a lack of understanding, patronizing and insulting by the Dalai Lama's attendants who replied in kind.[150] The Dalai Lama's Mongolian cavalry raided the stables and houses of the Red Hat Karmapas. In retaliation Karma Tensung Wangpo invaded Lhasa in 1605, expelling the Mongolian guards, and in the ensuing struggle for political power several districts in the province of U were captured.[151]

In 1607 the Dalai Lama visited southern Tibet and in the following year, Tsang, at the invitation of Tashi Lhunpo where he was asked to assume the abbotship. Being already abbot of Drepung he accepted an honorary title, then proceeded to tour and teach at the other Gelugpa monasteries in the district. The Tsang king, Karma Tensung Wangpo, neither supported nor obstructed these activities. On his return to U the Fourth Dalai Lama stayed at Gongkhor monastery. Messages between him and the Red Hat Karmapa Lama who resided nearby may have led to a meeting with the possibility of a truce between the sects, but it seemed the attendants of both lamas did not wish it to be so. The Dalai Lama was hustled off to Drepung, quashing any hope of reconciliation.[152]

→ to entrench and spread Buddhism throughout Mongolia. Although the Dzungar Mongols of the western regions were not so accepting of the Gelugpa reforms Mongolian expansion led to an alliance with Peter the Great of Russia, which resulted in Buddhism spreading via "tent monasteries" as far as the Volga. To this day the Dalai Lamas are linked to this branch of Tibetan Buddhism, pp. 219-23.

149. Das, *Tibetan Studies*, pp. 251-2.

150. Snellgrove & Richardson, *A Cultural History . . .*, p. 193.

151. Shakabpa, *Tibet: A Political History*, pp. 97-8.

152. Shakabpa, *Tibet: A Political History*, p. 98. See also, Dhondup, *The Water-Horse. . .*, p. 11.

In 1610 the Phagmotru supporters of the Gelugpa, emboldened by a revival of their fortunes due to Gelugpa successes associated with the presence of the Dalai Lama, raided the Tsang-controlled Lhasa valley. The Tsang king later retaliated, gaining complete control of U and thereby, virtual political control of Tibet. Nevertheless, the new king, Karma Phutsok Namgyal, still allowed the Gelugpa to act as his representatives in Lhasa. Asking for an audience with the Dalai Lama, he was refused by Yonten Gyatso's attendants on the grounds that he was an enemy of the Gelugpa. This deeply offended the king. Shakabpa says public sympathies were with the king for he could have been won over peacefully; instead, he returned to Shigatse disappointed.[153]

In 1616 The Fourth Dalai Lama, apparently suffering from rheumatism, took treatments in some hot springs. In early 1617 he died at Drepung, aged twenty-eight. There is some speculation he was poisoned. His cremation was presided over by Lobsang Chokyi Gyaltsen and the ashes shared between Drepung, his father, and one of his Mongolian patrons.[154]

During his short life he remained primarily interested in spiritual matters, for which he showed a real aptitude. Political affairs were handled by his attendants with little success; rather, they contributed to the tense internal pressures within Tibet. The strong connection to Mongolia initiated by the Third Dalai Lama and reinforced by Yonten Gyatso reincarnating there, was making itself felt in Tibet through Mongolian interest in their spiritual source. China, occupied by its own internal strife, showed only peripheral interest in Tibet at this juncture.[155] The stage was now set for the arrival of one of the most dynamic political and spiritual figures ever to appear in Asia.

---

153. Shakabpa, *Tibet: A Political History*, pp. 98-9. See also, Dhondup, *The Water-Horse. . .*, p. 12.

154. Schulemann, *Geschichte . . .*, p. 217. Also, Shakabpa, *Tibet: A Political History*, p. 99. Various authors differ as to the date of Yonten Gyatso's death with Mullin, *Essence. . .* , concurring with Shakabpa, p. 244. Schulemann puts the year as 1616, as do Snellgrove & Richardson, *A Cultural History*, p. 193, Hoffmann, *The Religions of Tibet*, p. 173, and Rockhill, *The Dalai Lamas of Lhasa. . .* , who also says it could be 1615, as does Das, *Tibetan Studies*, p. 252.

155. Richardson, *Tibet and Its History*, p. 43.

Dalai Lama V

The Fifth Dalai Lama was born into a Tibet rife with internal struggles. As a result of being insulted by the attendants of the Fourth Dalai Lama, Karma Phuntsok Namgyal attacked Lhasa in 1618. His forces killed thousands, including monks at Sera and Drepung, the survivors finding refugee in Karmapa monasteries north of the city. Phuntsok Namgyal had some smaller Gelugpa monasteries forcibly changed to Karmapa institutions. Armed Tsang military camps were established to watch and restrict Gelugpa movements. Upon returning to Shigatse the Tsang king built a rival monastery to Tashi Lhunpo, to which considerable damage had been inflicted due to attacks by the Karmapa forces. Perhaps the cruelest blow was the decree that it was unlawful to search for the reincarnation of the Fourth Dalai Lama.[156]

The Fifth Dalai Lama was born in 1617 at Chingwoi Taktse in the Chongyas district on the eastern border of Tsang.[157] His father, an aristocrat and a highly placed Tibetan officer, was a Nyingmapa adherent with connections to Sakya and the Phagmotru family.[158] The Fifth Dalai Lama was discovered in 1619 by a delegation sent out by Sonam Chospel, the Fourth Dalai Lama's chief attendant. During the usual testing procedures, Ngawang Lobsang Gyatso, as the child was soon to be named, unerringly recognized his predecessor's personal articles. Further confirmation was provided, somewhat later,

---

156. Shakabpa, *Tibet: A Political History*, p. 100. Also, Das, *Tibetan Studies*, p. 252. See also, Dhondup, *The Water-Horse. . .* , who adds that the intervention of the Kargyupa Lama of Taklung Monastery, where the Sera and Drepung monks took refuge, resulted in their return to their own monasteries, pp. 12-14.

157. Shakabpa, *Tibet: A Political History*, p. 100. Also, Mullin, *Essence. . .* , p. 241. See also, Petech, "The Dalai Lamas and Regents of Tibet: A Chronological Study", *T'oung Pao*, no. 47, p. 372. Also, G. Tucci, *Tibet Land of Snows*, 1967, p. 38.

158. Rockhill, *The Dalai Lamas of Lhasa. . .* , p. 6. Also, Snellgrove & Richardson, *A Cultural History. . .* , p. 194. See also, Tucci, *Tibet Land. . .* , p. 38. Also, Michael, *Rule by Incarnation. . .* , who notes all Dalai Lamas were born into commoner families, except the Fourth and Fifth, helping to keep the institution "free of politically powerful connections", p. 48. This statement lends interest to a comment by Sir Charles Bell, *Tibet: Past and Present*, who recalls the Thirteenth Dalai Lama telling him that the Fifth Dalai Lama was the "son of a poor man", p. 35. In another work, Sir Charles Bell, *Portrait of the Dalai Lama*, 1946, says the Fifth was the son of a peasant at Chung-gye, p. 43.

by the Tashi Lhunpo abbot, Lobsang Chokyi Gyaltsen. Because of the political situation, Ngawang Gyatso's discovery and whereabouts were kept secret until 1622. In the meantime he was taken to Nakartse, near Lhasa, rather than Drepung.[159]

In 1620 the Mongol soldiers who had been expelled by the Tsang King in 1605, returned in the guise of pilgrims. They attacked the Tsang military camps outside Lhasa, killing most of the Tsang troops. Lobsang Chokyi of Tashi Lhunpo and the Ganden Tripa (head of the Gelugpa order) mediated between the two armies resulting in the Mongols agreeing to leave, the Tsang forces decommissioning their camps, and the converted monasteries being restored to the Gelugpa.[160] A year later Phuntsok Namgyal died, further easing military tensions between the provinces of U and Tsang. In 1622 the discovery and identity of the Fifth Dalai Lama were revealed and he was installed at Drepung. Unsettled conditions, however, dictated his further seclusion until 1625 when his teacher, Lobsang Chokyi, the future Panchen Lama, initiated the young Dalai Lama into the monastic order at Drepung.[161]

Ngawang Gyatso received the usual careful education expected of a Dalai Lama. Included were the Buddhist canonical texts and medicine. He also studied the *sutras* and tantras with his principle guru Lobsang Chokyi Gyaltsen.[162] His tantric studies included those of the Nyingmapa, whose meditation practices became a well-known feature of his life.[163] According to Hoffmann, a considerable number of the Fifth Dalai Lama's writings on theology and mysticism dealt with the Nyingmapa tradition.[164] He developed into an outstanding scholar whose prolific writings equaled those of all the previous Dalai Lamas combined. These writings included biographies of eminent personalities of his era, histories of Tibet, commentaries on classical

159. Shakabpa, *Tibet: A Political History*, p. 101. Also, Doboom Tulku, "the lineage of the panchen lamas", p. 7.

160. Shakabpa, *Tibet: A Political History*, p. 101. Also, Snellgrove & Richardson, *A Cultural History. . .*, p. 194. See also, Dhondup, *The Water Horse. . .*, p. 264.

161. Shakabpa, *Tibet: A Political History*, p. 101.

162. Doboom Tulku, "the lineage of the panchen lamas", p. 7. See also, Hoffmann, *The Religions of Tibet*, p. 173.

163. Snellgrove & Richardson, *A Cultural History. . .*, p. 196.

164. Hoffmann, *The Religions of Tibet*, p. 174.

Indian poetry, grammar and astrology, and a great deal of prose and poetry.[165]

In gratitude to his *guru*, for the many services rendered to himself and his predecessor, the Fifth Dalai Lama conferred the title Panchen (great scholar) on Lobsang Chokyi Gyaltsen (1570-1662), also declaring him to be an incarnation of Amitabha.[166] These announcements were made on the basis of an "old and miraculously discovered text", or *terma* (treasure), which had been hidden, according to the Nyingmapa tradition, since the time of Padmasambhava. On the same basis the Fifth Dalai Lama declared he was the reincarnation of Avalokiteshvara, Tibet's patron deity.[167] Both lineages were thus accorded divine status with that of the Panchen Lama being second only to that of the Dalai Lama in the religious hierarchy of Tibet. (From time to time supporters of the Panchen Lamas would argue that the reverse was true, at least spiritually, since Amitabha in the Buddhist pantheon is the spiritual father or guide of Avalokiteshvara.[168]) At any rate, all previous incarnations in the Dalai Lama line were accorded the same divine status, as were the known incarnations in Lobsang Chokyi Gyaltsen's line. While he is generally considered the First Panchen Lama, being already an incarnate lama, his previous three incarnations were accorded the same status by some Tibetans, making him the fourth in the line.[169]

---

165. Mullin, *Essence. . .* , p. 244. Also, Hoffmann, *The Religions of Tibet*, p. 173. See also, Glenn Mullin, *Path of the Bodhisattva Warrior*, 1988, p. 17. See also, Wylie, "Dalai Lama", *The Encyclopedia of Religion*, vol. 4, p. 201.

166. Stein, *Tibetan Civilization*, p. 84. See also, Doboom Tulku, "the lineage of the panchen lamas", p. 7.

167. Hoffmann, *The Religions of Tibet*, pp. 175-6. See also my text above, p. 39.

168. Stein, *Tibetan Civilization*, p. 84. Also, Bell, *Tibet: Past and Present*, pp. 35-6. See also, Richardson, *Tibet and Its History*, who observes that Amitabha is a *dhyani* Buddha (one of five "idea" Buddhas projected "into the plane of spiritual meditation", each of which are further projected into the material sphere as *bodhisattvas*). The Panchen Lama then is arguably more spiritual than the Dalai Lama but only "if he remains in spiritual contemplation and abstains from all contact with the temporal world". The Dalai Lama as the material projection (son) of Amitabha "is true to his nature when he influences the physical world", pp. 54-5.

169. Tucci, *The Religions of Tibet*, p. 42. Also, Stein, *Tibetan Civilization*, p. 84. See also, Doboom Tulku, "the lineage of the panchen lamas", →

The relationship between these two incarnations was to prove significant in the years to come.

As the Dalai Lama was developing through his studies and writings he was pulled again and again into the temporal sphere by the swirl of political events. Karma Phuntsok Namgyal was succeeded by his son Karma Tenkyang who became known as the Desi Tsangpa (Regent of Tsang).[170] He engaged in a number of activities to hinder Gelugpa influence and growth. When the Christian missionaries, the Jesuits Cacella and Cabral, arrived at Shigatse in 1627 via Bhutan, the Tsang ruler, who was perhaps hoping, as Bell speculates, for some help from the white strangers, warmly received them. His Karmapa allies were less tolerant of outside religious influence, however, so very little came of these contacts.[171] Karma Tenkyang apparently tried to have the young Dalai Lama assassinated. The attempt failed but not before the Dalai Lama's mother had been killed by throwing her from the upper story of her house.[172] Karma Tenkyang also conspired to restrict Gelugpa influence in the Kokonor region and eastern Tibet by encouraging his ally, the king of Beri, a Bonpo supporter, to persecute the monks of Litang Monastery.[173]

Gelugpa representatives along with Sonam Chospel, who was now the Fifth Dalai Lama's influential aid, approached the Oriat, Dzungar, and Choskar Mongol tribes who were all Gelugpa supporters. Chief amongst them was Gushri Khan of the Qoshot tribe, part of the Oriat confederacy. He had managed to take advantage of dissension amongst the Mongol tribes of the Kokonor region to establish an

---

→ *lungta*, who notes that previous Tibetan governments referred to Lobsang Chokyi Gyaltsen as the First Panchen Lama but in recent years the present Dalai Lama's government in exile refers to him as the fourth in the line, p. 6. See also, Richardson, *Tibet and Its History*, who noted that it was the Chinese writers who habitually placed Lobsang Chokyi Gyaltsen as fourth in the line of Panchen Lamas while the mass of Tibetans would regard him as the first, p. 55.

170. Shakabpa, *Tibet: A Political History*, p. 102.

171. Bell, *The Religion of Tibet*, p. 124. Also, Stein, *Tibetan Civilization*, p. 83. See also, Shakabpa, *Tibet: A Political History*, p. 102.

172. Bell, *The Religion of Tibet*, p. 124. See also, Malik, *Dalai Lamas of Tibet*, p. 23.

173. Shakabpa, *Tibet: A Political History*, p. 103.

orderly government.[174] Under his lead an alliance of Mongol tribes agreed to enter into a religious war in support of the Dalai Lama.

In the meantime the Desi Tsangpa had appealed to the Chogthu Mongols with whom Tsang rulers had long been allied. Ten thousand troops under Arsalang were sent to wipe out the Gelugpa sect but they were intercepted by Gushri Khan. As a result of Gushri Khan's persuasion, Arsalang changed his plans and upon arriving at Lhasa prostrated himself before the Dalai Lama. After receiving religious instruction from the Dalai Lama, Arsalang vowed not to harm the Gelugpa. For his troubles Arsalang was ordered killed by his father, the Chogthu chief. Realising the instability of the situation, Gushri Khan led his army against the Chogthu, wiping out the entire tribe, and thereby eliminating the threat to the Gelugpa. For these services the Dalai Lama awarded Gushri Khan the titles "Religious King" and "Holder of the Buddhist Faith" at a 1638 ceremony in Lhasa, to which the Khan had made a pilgrimage in order to receive spiritual instruction from the Dalai Lama.[175]

The Gelugpa learned of a plot between the king of Beri, who had already overrun much of eastern Tibet, and the Tsang king to wipe out the Gelugpa. This prompted an immediate response from Gushri Khan who planned to march against both. According to Shakabpa, the Dalai Lama approved of the move against Beri but opposed further aggression against the Tsang as relations with them had somewhat normalised. He also pointed out that the origins of much of the trouble lay with the Gelugpa for having snubbed the Tsang ruler during the time of the Fourth Dalai Lama. His chief attendant Sonam Chospel argued for all out war and apparently changed the orders of the Dalai Lama to indicate that the Tsang should be attacked as well. After a year Gushri Khan had defeated Beri, executed their king, and then marched on Tsang. The Dalai Lama objected when he heard of this, but Sonam Chospel again defied his master and left with troops to support the war.[176]

---

174. Snellgrove & Richardson, *A Cultural History*, p. 194. Also, Shakabpa, *Tibet: A Political History*, p. 103.

175. Shakabpa, *Tibet: A Political History*, pp. 103-5. Also, Dhondup, *The Water Horse...*, pp. 17-20.

176. Shakabpa, *Tibet: A Political History*, reports that the Dalai Lama objected to extensive hostilities on religious grounds, stating that he was supposed to be a lama, to study religion, meditate, and preach. Creating →

In the midst of these events the Dalai and Panchen Lamas and Gushri Khan from their side, and the Desi Tsangpa and Karmapa Lama from the other, had all sent envoys seeking support from the Manchu Emperor who was the rising power in the east and *de facto* ruler of China. His replies, which came much after the fact, favoured no side or sects "regardless of the colour of their robes", but did serve to open relations between China and Tibet.[177]

Even though the Tsang king had been weakened earlier by an invasion of Tibet by Ladakh and an increased absence of support from the Karmapa hierarchies, he put up a spirited defense.[178] Finally, with the help of the monks from Sera and Drepung, Sonam Chospel on one front and Gushri Khan on another defeated the Tsang king, who was then taken to U and made prisoner.[179]

The Dalai Lama was summoned to Shigatse where he was received with great respect. In 1642 he was placed on the throne of the Tsang ruler with Gushri Khan occupying another, though slightly lower, throne. Gushri Khan then conferred supreme authority over all of Tibet upon the Dalai Lama. Sonam Chospel, who was given the title of Desi, equivalent to prime minister, would be responsible for the political administration of the country, referring matters of importance to the Dalai Lama when deemed necessary. The Dalai Lama was now the temporal and spiritual ruler of Tibet, his realm stretching from west of Mt. Kailas to Kham in the east. He later declared that Lhasa would be the capital of Tibet and the government would be known as Ganden Phodrang, which was also the name of his residence at Drepung. He also drew up laws of public conduct

---

→ further disturbances was unnecessary he said, and would only cause more suffering. The Dalai Lama then added that what the Gelugpa already had was "more than sufficient", pp. 105-9. See also, Dhondup, *The Water-Horse. . .* , pp. 20-3.

177. Rockhill, *The Dalai Lamas of Lhasa. . .* , pp. 9-13. Richardson, *Tibet and Its History*, also notes the Manchus took full control of China in 1644, p. 43. See also, Snellgrove & Richardson, *A Cultural History. . .* , p. 197.

178. Snellgrove & Richardson, *A Cultural History. . .* , point out the Tenth Black Hat Karmapa disapproved of militarism and the Red Hat Karmapa had recently died, p. 195.

179. Shakabpa, *Tibet: A Political History*, pp. 109-10.

and appointed the government ministers and district governors.[180] Gushri Khan reserved for himself the title King of Tibet, becoming in effect the patron and protector of the Dalai Lama. A new priest-patron relationship had been formally established.[181]

Karmapa resistance still flared up but was ruthlessly suppressed by Gushri Khan and Sonam Chospel. Karma Tenkyang was executed and all resistance collapsed.[182] In the ensuing years many Karmapa and Kagyupa monasteries were forcibly converted to the Gelugpa, resulting in a self-imposed exile to other Himalayan countries by many of the Red Hats in order to escape the power of the Dalai Lama. One Red Hat Karmapa faction, the *Brugpa*, was able to establish a theocratic state in Bhutan.[183] On the whole, however, it was thought the Dalai Lama acted with tolerance in these matters, even allowing some Karmapa monasteries to re-establish themselves. He also allowed the Nyingmapa to establish Mindroling, an important monastic teaching centre in central Tibet. The Bonpo and the Nyingmapa operating primarily in eastern Tibet were allowed to function without hindrance as were the Sakya. On the other hand, the *Jonang*, which was a minor sect, all but ceased to exist with the conversion of their monasteries.[184] The primary purpose of all these moves was to take the secular power out of the hands of all sects except the Gelugpa while still retaining religious freedom. However, Gelugpa influences and standards soon affected how the other sects organized and conducted themselves since the Gelugpa were the better organized, most zealous, and freshest of all the sects.[185]

---

180. Shakabpa, *Tibet: A Political History*, pp. 110-11. Also, Snellgrove & Richardson, *A Cultural History. . .*, p. 195. See also, Dhondup, *The Water-Horse. . .*, pp. 25-6.

181. Snellgrove & Richardson, *A Cultural History. . .*, p. 195. See also, Richardson, *Tibet and Its History*, pp. 41-2.

182. Shakabpa, *Tibet: A Political History. . .*, pp. 111-12.

183. Hoffmann, *The Religions of Tibet*, p. 175. Also, Snellgrove & Richardson, *A Cultural History. . .*, pp. 195-6. See also, Shakabpa, *Tibet: A Political History*, p. 113.

184. Snellgrove & Richardson, *A Cultural History. . .* pp. 196-7. Bell, *The Religion of Tibet*, says, on the other hand, there was no tolerance at the time, p. 126.

185. Snellgrove & Richardson, *A Cultural History. . .*, p. 197. See also, Norbu & Turnbull, *Tibet*, p. 249.

The Fifth Dalai Lama's organizational skills set the country on a firm footing towards becoming a theocracy. Nevertheless, he is still regarded mostly for his spiritual greatness by Tibetans and for his firmly establishing the rule of religion. While keeping his steady hand on the helm he put most of the secular authority in the hands of the *desi* (regent), preferring to devote the bulk of his time to religious pursuits.[186] This would somewhat explain his prodigious writing output and his renown as a practitioner of the tantric arts. In the practical realm, he was successful in ordering a census of western Tibet, Tsang, and the eastern districts for taxation purposes, assigning a portion of the taxes to support the monasteries.[187] Under his guidance a centralised form of government was established which endured virtually unchanged to present times. The government was divided equally between monks and laymen, the final authority being with the Dalai Lama.[188] Perhaps the only real mistake during the Fifth Dalai Lama's administration was that of allowing a war with Bhutan to take place, in which the ill-prepared Tibetans and their Mongol allies were soundly defeated.[189]

A more successful foreign relations venture was the Dalai Lama's trip to China, made after receiving several invitations to Beijing from the Manchu emperor of China. The emperor was hoping the Dalai Lama's religious influence would keep the Mongols from invading

---

186. Norbu & Turnbull, *Tibet*, pp. 247-9. Also, Petech, "The Dalai Lamas and Regents. . . ," who notes that after the desi Sonam Chospel died in 1658, the Fifth Dalai Lama personally took charge of the administration until a new regent was appointed. The Dalai Lama did the same for one and a half years after the next regent died, pp. 378-9. See also, Robert Thurman, "Tibetan Buddhist Monastic and Intellectual Culture", *White Lotus: An Introduction to Tibetan Culture*, 1990, who notes that the Fifth Dalai Lama ushered in a form of monastic government when, at the same time, the secularisation process engendered by the Protestant Reformation was destroying the power of European monasteries, p. 40.

187. Shakabpa, *Tibet: A Political History*, pp. 112-13. See also, Stein, *Tibetan Civilization*, p. 84.

188. Norbu & Turnbull, *Tibet*, p. 249. Also, Malik, *Dalai Lamas of Tibet*, who notes no other Dalai Lama save for the Thirteenth was able to wield the temporal and spiritual authority of the Fifth, pp. 24-5.

189. Shakabpa, *Tibet: A Political History*, pp. 112-13. Also, Bell, *The Religion of Tibet*, pp. 125-6.

Chinese territory.[190] After the traditional visit to the Chokhor Gyal Monastery by the Lhamo Latso Lake, the Dalai Lama, with a large retinue, left for China. En route he was very well received by Tibetans and Mongols. The Dalai Lama, wishing to show his independent status, requested the first meeting with the emperor take place outside the Chinese frontier. A compromise was worked out and the emperor, against the wishes of his Chinese advisors, met the Dalai Lama at the walled city of Khothor, somewhat distant from Beijing. While official Chinese records indicate the emperor met the Dalai Lama while on a hunting expedition, the extensive preparations indicate the Manchu emperor had deliberately made the journey for the sole purpose of meeting the Dalai Lama.[191] Travelling on to Beijing the Dalai Lama stayed in the Yellow Palace especially built for his visit. The leaders exchanged gifts and banquets, the Dalai Lama being accorded the deference due a head of state. The Dalai Lama was also requested to give instructions to the Chinese and Mongols regarding the regulation of their monasteries. It was a successful visit; "clearly a meeting between equals".[192] This diplomatic contact was to bear fruit for the Chinese as the Dalai Lama's intervention in 1662, and on other occasions, curtailed Mongolian raiding into Chinese frontier towns.[193]

---

190. Dhondup, *The Water-Horse. . .* , p. 28. See also, Shakabpa, *Tibet: A Political History*, who points out that this visit occurred because of the Third Dalai Lama's prophecy that the descendants of Altan Khan would become the rulers of Mongolia and China. Mongolians and Manchus are closely related racially, seeming to lend credence to this prophecy, p. 114.

191. Shakabpa, *Tibet: A Political History*, pp. 114-16.

192. Snellgrove & Richardson, *A Cultural History. . .* , point out that this contravened Chinese political theory which "excluded entirely the possibility of equal diplomatic relations with any country whatsoever", p. 198. Also, Rockhill, *The Dalai Lamas of Lhasa. . .* , notes the Dalai Lama was treated as an "independent sovereign, and nothing can be found in Chinese works to indicate that he was looked upon in any other light", p. 18. See also, Norbu & Turnbull, *Tibet*, p. 250. See also, Bell, *Tibet: Past and Present*, p. 36.

193. Shakabpa, *Tibet: A Political History*, p. 119. Also, Snellgrove & Richardson, *A Cultural History. . .* , p. 199. See also, Bell, *Tibet: Past and Present*, p. 37.

Gushri Khan died in 1655 leaving the kingdom of Tibet to his two sons who divided the responsibilities. They had little interest in ruling Tibet nor did their successors so that gradually all power devolved into the hands of the Dalai Lama, including the power to appoint a regent.[194] This proved to be auspicious as the Dalai Lama's choice for regent in 1679 was the twenty-seven-year-old Sangye Gyatso (1653-1705) (see footnote 206), a nephew of the second regent Trinley Gyatso. Sangye Gyatso had been asked to assume the post in 1675 when the third regent, because of a scandal involving a mistress, was asked to resign. The brilliant young Sangye Gyatso, who became a well-known scholar and author of books on history, medicine, and astrology, had declined at that time, citing his youth.[195] Many scholars claim Sangye Gyatso was the natural son of the Dalai Lama perhaps, as Shakabpa speculates, out of conjecture arising from the young regent's age. However, nothing in Tibetan records corroborates these stories.[196] Sangye Gyatso quickly proved himself an able administrator and the Dalai Lama fully entrusted the affairs of state to him. Later Sangye Gaytso was to assume full secular authority over Tibet during the minority of the Sixth Dalai Lama.

The Panchen Lama had died in 1662 at the age of ninety-one. The monks of Tashi Lhunpo asked the Dalai Lama in 1665 to confirm his reincarnation, who was named Lobsang Yeshe. Later Lobsang

---

194. Snellgrove & Richardson, *A Cultural History. . .* , p. 198. See also, Richardson, *Tibet and Its History*, p. 45.

195. Shakabpa, *Tibet: A Political History*, pp. 121-2, 125. See also, Petech, "The Dalai Lamas and Regents. . . ," pp. 379-80.

196. Shakabpa, *Tibet: A Political History*, p. 125. See, Hoffmann, *The Religions of Tibet*, who strongly asserts that Ngawang Lobsang Gyatso broke his vows of celibacy, p. 175. Also, Rockhill, *The Dalai Lamas of Lhasa. . .* , who states Sangye Gyatso "is generally believed in Tibet, (to be) a natural son of the Dalai Lama", p. 19. See also, Norbu & Turnbull, *Tibet*, who mention the controversy in light of the Fifth Dalai Lama's Nyingmapa connections but draw no conclusions, p. 249. For his part Malik, *Dalai Lamas of Tibet*, refers to the desi as Ngawang Gyatso's "spiritual disciple", p. 25, while Tucci, *Tibet Land of Snows*, uses the tern "spiritual son", p. 41. Of special interest is Luciano Petech, *China and Tibet in the Early 18th Century*, 1950, who claims that Sangye Gyatso is the natural son of the Fifth Dalai Lama, p. 9. In his later work, Petech, "The Dalai Lamas And Regents of Tibet: A Chronological Study", refers to Sangye Gyatso as the nephew of the second regent, p. 380.

Yeshe would receive his novice ordination and much of his training at the hands of the Dalai Lama. At the time of Lobsang Yeshe's ordination, and after much deliberation, the Panchen Lama's throne was placed second in height to the Dalai Lama's.[197]

The Dalai Lama continued to strengthen ties with neighbouring countries with many of their princes and kings making visits to Lhasa. Trade and commerce developed as did scholarly contacts, which resulted in translations of Indian and Pali scriptures by visiting Indian scholars.[198] A war with Ladakh in 1684 resulted in established borders between the two countries.[199] Further military incursions into Bhutan proved more successful than the first, but relations remained strained.[200] When called upon by China to intervene in that country's internal revolt the Dalai Lama showed his independence by declining to give aid to either side.[201]

One of the most prominent achievements of the Fifth Dalai Lama was the building of the Potala, a fortress "of a size to dwarf the palaces of western monarchs".[202] Built on the Red Hill, just outside Lhasa, on the site of the palace built by Tibet's greatest king of the golden age, Songtsen Gampo, the Potala became symbolic of the spiritual greatness of the Fifth Dalai Lama. Its very name refers back to the mythical abode of Avalokiteshvara, a mountain called Potala.[203] The Potala would remain home to the Dalai Lamas and the Tibetan government for 300 years. The personal monastery of the Dalai Lama, Namgyal, was already on the site having been built by the

---

197. Shakabpa, *Tibet: A Political History*, p. 119. See also, Doboom Tulku, "the lineage of the panchen lamas", *Iungta*, vol. 10, Winter 1996, p. 7.
198. Malik, *Dalai Lamas of Tibet*, p. 25. See also, Snellgrove & Richardson, *A Cultural History. . .*, pp. 198-9.
199. Shakabpa, *Tibet: A Political History*, pp. 122-3. See also, Snellgrove & Richardson, *A Cultural History. . .*, p. 199.
200. Shakabpa, *Tibet: A Political History*, pp. 118-19. See also, Dhondup, *The Water-Horse. . .*, pp. 30-1.
201. Shakabpa, *Tibet: A Political History*, pp. 120-1.
202. Bell, *The Religion of Tibet*, p. 130.
203. Norbu & Turnbull, *Tibet*, pp. 250-1. See, Turrell Wylie, "Dalai Lama", *The Encyclopedia of Religion*, vol. 4, p. 200. See also, Hoffmann, *The Religions of Tibet*, p. 176. See also, Snellgrove & Richardson, *A Cultural History. . .*, p. 200.

Third Dalai Lama, Sonam Gyatso.[204] Begun in 1645, the completion of the Potala took 50 years. It became to Tibetans one of their most important places of spiritual pilgrimage and exemplified the genius of Tibetan national culture.[205]

Ngawang Lobsang Gyatso never lived to see the completion of the Potala, dying in 1682 at the age of 65, during a three-year retreat.[206] He became known as the Great Fifth for the enduring legacy he left. Tibet had become a unified country somewhat independent of foreign interference under his leadership. He created the forms of governance Tibetans were to live by, in the process enacting strict penal laws, a system of revenue collection, a national system of medical care, and a programme of national education.[207] He also reorganised the Great Prayer Festival into its current form.[208] An astute diplomat, he strengthened Tibet's relations with her neighbours. Also a deep thinker and scholar, he left a corpus of writings few would equal. Above all, Tibetans remember him as a spiritual adept who showed tolerance for religious traditions other than his own, while setting his on a firm footing. A strong figure like his was difficult to follow and this was to be proven all too true by his successor, though in many respects, the Sixth Dalai Lama had a more dramatic life than that of the Fifth.

Dalai Lama VI

Sangye Gyatso concealed the death of the Fifth and the discovery of

---

204. Wylie, "Dalai Lama", p. 200. See, Hoffmann, *The Religions of Tibet*, p. 176. See also, Norbu & Turnbull, *Tibet*, p. 250.

205. Snellgrove & Richardson, *A Cultural History. . .* , p. 200. See also, Norbu & Turnbull, *Tibet*, p. 251.

206. Mullin, *Essence. . .* , p. 244. Interestingly both Dhondup, *The Water-Horse. . .* , p. 33, and Shakabpa, p. 123, claim the Fifth Dalai Lama (1617-82) was sixty-eight when he died. Simple arithmetic proves otherwise unless using the Tibetan system of reckoning age, which counts the year of birth and the current year, which would make the Fifth Dalai Lama 67 when he died. See also, Sir Charles Bell, *Portrait of the Dalai Lama*, 1946, p. 53.

207. Malik, *Dalai Lamas of Tibet*, pp. 24-5. See also, Mullin, *Essence. . .* , p. 244.

208. Norbu & Turnbull, *Tibet*, p. 250. See also, Bell, *Tibet: Past and Present*, p. 37.

the Sixth Dalai Lama for close to fifteen years. It was announced that the Fifth Dalai Lama had undertaken a meditation retreat for an indefinite period of time, which was apparently accepted at face value by the populace and government officials.[209] Sangye Gyatso went to extraordinary lengths to keep this secret.[210] Only the Dalai Lama's personal attendants, a monk who impersonated the late Dalai Lama and the regent knew. The imposter monk had to be bribed, beaten or cajoled over the years to keep up the deception, which was required when, unavoidably, Mongol princes or others of like stature would request a personal audience with the Dalai Lama. Wearing a ceremonial robe, a hat and eyeshades the imposter was apparently able to deceive these dignitaries who had likely never seen the Dalai Lama before.[211] It is reported that the Fifth Dalai Lama himself ordered this deception so that the Potala could be finished without hindrance and to prevent the Manchus from sowing seeds of dissension amongst the Mongols of the Kokonor region.[212] Some scholars feel that Sangye Gyatso either made the decision for reasons of state security or because of the desire to retain personal control over Tibetan affairs.[213] Some scholars even maintain that the secret was in fact widely known amongst the Tibetan people.[214]

---

209. K. Dhondup, *Songs of the Sixth Dalai Lama*, 1981, p. 5. Also, Shakabpa, *Tibet: A Political History*, who notes Sangye Gyatso himself put the number at fifteen years in his book, the *Bai-durya-ser-po*, pp. 125-6. See, Wylie, "Dalai Lama", p. 201. Other authorities differ on the number of years this deception was carried out. See, Bell, *The Religion of Tibet*, who says it was 16 or 9 years, pp. 134-5. Malik, *Dalai Lamas of Tibet*, says it was 13 or 9 years, p. 25. Also, Norbu & Turnbull, *Tibet*, put the number at 9 years, pp. 282-3.

210. Dhondup, *Songs. . .* , states that it was said the regent, Sangye Gyatso, had the Nechung oracle and the oracle's mother murdered after secretly consulting the oracle regarding the rebirth of the Fifth Dalai Lama. When the Nechung oracle came out of his trance it was learned he still knew of the Fifth Dalai Lama's death, pp. 6-7. See also, Norbu & Turnbull, *Tibet*, p. 283.

211. Shakabpa, *Tibet: A Political History*, pp. 125-7. Also, Dhondup, *Songs . . .* , pp. 5-6.

212. Dhondup, *Songs . . .* , p. 5. Also, Mullin, *Essence. . .* , p. 224.

213. Snellgrove & Richardson, *A Cultural History. . .* , p. 204. See also, Rockhill, *The Dalai Lamas of Lhasa. . .* , p. 21.

214. Rockhill, *The Dalai Lamas of Lhasa. . .* , pp. 21-2. Also, Petech, *China and Tibet. . .* , p. 9. See also, Snellgrove & Richardson, *A Cultural History. . .* , pp. 204-5.

Nevertheless, it was quite apparent that Sangye Gyatso carried out the general administration of the country in an admirable fashion.[215] Malik goes so far as to say "Sangye Gyatso saved his country from possible foreign intervention and, by not taking his own people into his confidence, from internal instability and national confusion".[216] In 1695 the Potala was completed and only then, in 1696, was it announced that the Fifth Dalai Lama had died and his reincarnation had long before been discovered; the same announcements were formally presented, a year later, to the Chinese court.[217]

In the meantime, in 1683, a boy was born in the Monyul district of southern Tibet (these days known as Tawang district in the state of Arunachal Pradesh, India).[218] His father, Ridgzin Tashi, was a reputed Nyingmapa tantric lama; a *terton*, or treasure finder, in the line of Padmaglingpa according to Hoffmann; his mother, Tsewang Lhamo, was considered a devout Buddhist.[219] According to local legends, several miracles are attributed to the young Tsanyang Gyatso (Precious Ocean of Pure Melody), as he would later be named. These included leaving his footprints, skullmark (the imprint made by his head while lying down), and mystic finger writing in solid rock, all of which can still be seen today. Another incident considered miraculous has to do with three sandalwood trees Tsanyang Gyatso is said to have planted before leaving Tawang. He said the three trees would grow to equal height and when they did he would return. It was noticed the trees were of equal height, size, and shape in 1959. Shortly thereafter the Fourteenth Dalai Lama passed through Tawang on his way to exile in

---

215. Shakabpa, *Tibet: A Political History*, p. 127. See, Dhondup, *Songs. . .* , p. 5. Also, Rockhill, *The Dalai Lamas of Lhasa . . .* , p. 22.

216. Malik, *Dalai Lamas of Tibet*, p. 26.

217. Shakabpa, *Tibet: A Political History*, p. 128. See, Petech, *China and Tibet. . .* , p. 9. Also, Bell, *The Religion of Tibet*, who says the emperor complained of being deliberately misinformed for sixteen years, p. 135.

218. Dhondup, *Songs. . .* , p. 7. Also, Claude Apri, "In the footsteps of the 6th Dalai Lama", *Tibetan Review*, August 1996, who notes that the Fifth Dalai Lama had been invited to the Monyul district to consecrate a monastery built in 1645 by Mera Lama. Unable to go, the Dalai Lama promised to come in the future. The local people of Monyul believe it is in fulfilment of this promise that the Fifth Dalai Lama's reincarnation appeared amongst them, p. 16.

219. Apri, "In the footsteps. . . ," p. 16. See, Hoffmann, *The Religions of Tibet*, p. 178. Also, Dhondup, *Songs. . .* , p. 10.

India.[220] They also caught fire at a time of great unrest due to the Chinese occupation of Tibet.

The regent, Sangye Gyatso, had a secret search conducted for the Fifth Dalai Lama's reincarnation. Guided by divinations, the search committee, in 1685, reported the birth of an extraordinary child. He was confirmed as the Dalai Lama after two subsequent visits by trusted aids and further consultations with the oracles.[221] It seems that, at the age of six, the young Dalai Lama and his mother were taken to the nearby Tsona Monastery and kept there under tight security until 1697.[222] At that point he was taken to Nakartse near Lhasa, where his *guru*, the Second Panchen Lama Lobsang Yeshe, gave him religious instruction and the monastic name of Tsanyang Gyatso along with his novice ordination.[223] Following this, the Sixth Dalai Lama was taken to Lhasa. There, before a large assembly of monks, including the abbots of Drepung, Sera, and Ganden, as well as high state officials, Sangye Gyatso gave a detailed report of his deception as per the Fifth Dalai Lama's instructions.[224] Tsanyang Gyatso was then installed in the Potala and enthroned as the Sixth Dalai Lama before a gathering of high lay and ecclesiastical figures and foreign dignitaries.[225]

The young Dalai Lama received his spiritual training under the supervision of Sangye Gyatso and the Second Panchen Lama. However, Tsanyang Gyatso preferred to spend his time practising archery and enjoying the outdoors with his friends, much to the

---

220. Dhondup, *Songs...*, pp. 34-5. See also, Apri, "In the footsteps...," who relates the story as having to do with three branches of the same tree, which he saw at the time of this writing, pp. 16-17.

221. Shakabpa, *Tibet, A Political History*, p. 128. See, Dhondup, *Songs ...*, p. 7. Also, Apri, "In the footsteps...," p. 17. See also, Norbu & Turnbull, *Tibet*, who state the search for the new Dalai Lama was not begun for nine years and he was at least twelve by the time he was confirmed, p. 283.

222. Apri, "In the footsteps ...," p. 17. See, Dhondup, *Songs...*, pp. 7-8.

223. Doboom Tulku, "the lineage of the panchen lamas", pp. 7-8. See, Dhondup, *Songs...*, pp. 8-9. Also, Apri, "In the footsteps...," p. 17. See also, Shakabpa, *Tibet: A Political History*, who says the Dalai Lama was taken to Nakartse in 1688 and instructed by teachers selected by Sangye Gyatso and the Second Panchen Lama, p. 128.

224. Dhondup, *Songs...*, pp. 8-9.

225. Dhondup, *Songs...*, p. 9. Also, Shakabpa, *Tibet: A Political History*, p. 128.

consternation of the regent.[226] A simple and austere personality, the Sixth Dalai Lama disdained ceremony and servants, preparing his own tea, and sharing it willingly with anyone who had come for his audience and blessings. He was carefree as regards his monastic training but is known to have had a keen intellect and to have composed a number of learned treatises. He was also a skilled architect, beautifying the Potala Palace and building the Lu Khang palace (the Serpent Home) below the Potala. As a dancer Tsanyang Gyatso contributed to the development of *cham*, the Tibetan monastic opera.[227]

At age twenty, the Sixth Dalai Lama went to Tashi Lhunpo, supposedly to take his final vows from his *guru*, the Panchen Lama. However, Tsanyang Gyatso long delayed doing so despite entreaties by the leading lay officials, such as Thanyang Khan, who was the brother of the Qosot ruler (in name only) of Tibet, the Panchen Lama, and the abbots of Drepung, Sera, and Ganden. Tsanyang Gyatso renounced his novice vows instead and returned to the status of a layman. He could no longer be the religious leader of Tibet but still was able to keep his temporal position as Dalai Lama.[228]

From that time Tsanyang Gyatso preferred to distance himself from Sangye Gyatso. Further, to the regent's horror and that of all the leading figures of the country, the Dalai Lama engaged in behaviour considered unbecoming of a monk. Dressing as a layman in blue silks and brocades and letting his hair grow long he would take to the taverns of Lhasa and Shol, the town at the foot of the Potala. He would also spend time with his many lovers in a special tent in the park or his private palace, the Serpent Home. To this day the wine houses where he spent his time are painted yellow in his

---

226. Shakabpa, *Tibet: A Political History*, pp. 128-9. Also, Dhondup, *Songs* . . . , pp. 10-11.

227. Dhondup, *Songs*. . . , who says The Sixth improved upon the Norbu Lingka palaces (which had yet to be built), pp. 10-11. See, Norbu & Turnbull, *Tibet*, pp. 281-4. Also, Bell, *The Religion of Tibet*, p. 137. See also, Malik, *Dalai Lamas of Tibet*, p. 30.

228. Dhondup, *Songs*. . . , pp. 11-15. Also, Shakabpa, *Tibet: A Political History*, p. 129. See also, Rockhill, *The Dalai Lamas of Lhasa*. . . , who suggests Tsanyang Gyatso renounced his vows because he was informed by the emperor of China and the Mongol prince Lazang Khan that he could not be regarded as the reincarnation of his predecessor, p. 32.

honour. He also spent much time composing lyrical poetry and love songs, singing these during his revels with his friends.[229]

The regent, Sangye Gyatso, outraged by the behaviour of the Dalai Lama, was increasingly concerned about the effect it was having on the Mongol supporters of his ably administered regime. These supporters and much of the clergy were beginning to waver in their faith. While instructing his officials to avoid outward criticism of the incarnation of Avalokiteshvara, Sangye Gyatso plotted to kill Thargyanas, a close companion of Tsanyang Gyatso, whom the regent believed was arranging rendezvous with women for the Dalai Lama. The plot failed and the conspirators were harshly dealt with. Knowing the regent's hand was behind the plot the Dalai Lama avoided Sangye Gyatso even further.[230]

While the Sixth Dalai Lama's behaviour was viewed with great consternation in official circles, both secular and religious, he was revered by the common people and remains so to this day in most of Tibet. Malik points out it was "inconceivable for any Tibetan for even a moment to believe that their saviour was not the best and the highest amongst human beings".[231] Bell adds to this, referring to the deeply religious loyalty and faith of the Tibetans, in stating, "his subjects could not question his acts. The ministers of a Dalai Lama are freely blamed if things turn out badly, but the God-King is above human criticism".[232]

---

229. Shakabpa, *Tibet: A Political History*, p. 129. See, Dhondup, *Songs. . .* , p. 15. Also, Norbu & Turnbull, *Tibet*, p. 284. See also, Snellgrove & Richardson, *A Cultural History. . .* , p. 205.

230. Shakabpa, *Tibet: A Political History*, pp. 129-30. Also, Dhondup, *Songs. . .* , pp. 16-17. Dhondup later points out that Tsanyang Gyatso likely resented the regent's hypocrisy, for Sangye Gyatso was known for his loose ways, a fact Dhondup suggests was partially responsible for the young Dalai Lama's behaviour.

231. Malik, *Dalai Lamas of Tibet*, pp. 31-2.

232. See, Bell, *The Religion of Tibet*, p. 141. See also, Glenn Mullin, *Songs of Spiritual Change*, 1981, who observes another reason the Dalai Lama had such a wide popular appeal was that he was not exclusively associated with any one sect. The *Ganden Tripa*, not the Dalai Lama, was head of the Gelug order. The Dalai Lama studied with lamas of all sects and was a member of the Gelugpa, which was an amalgam of the other major sects, p. 17.

The Sixth Dalai Lama is especially loved for his poetry, perhaps as Norbu and Turnbull say, "apart from Milarepa . . . the most lyrical . . . in Tibet".[233] While many of his poems contained a sharp satire dealing with social injustices and the hypocrisy of many monks, most were clearly love poems. These however, also showed a profound religious emotion according to Norbu and Turnbull.[234] These poems are also considered by Tibetan scholars to be the work of a tantric master, containing hidden meanings lost to ordinary readers, an opinion supported by the Sixth Dalai Lama's tantric treatises.[235] It is thought that Tsanyang Gyatso was acting in the capacity of a tantric master, an adept who taught "that life itself, in whatever form it appears to us, is one of our greatest teachers".[236]

Dhondup suggests that Thubten Jigme Norbu, the current Dalai Lama's older brother, is able to convey some of the hidden meaning in Tsanyang Gyatso's poetry. For instance, the concept of the 'Compassionate One' is brought forth in the following:

> My compassionate One, be like the holy
> mountain, Rirab Lhunpo.
> Stay still, and let the sun and moon encircle you.
> Day and Night,
> Faithful, like the sun and moon,
> Shall I be to you.[237]

---

233. Norbu & Turnbull, *Tibet*, pp. 284-6. Also, Malik, *Dalai Lamas of Tibet*, p. 30. Dhondup, *Songs. . .*, quoting H.E. Richardson says that Tsanyang Gyatso was "the only writer of lyrical verse that Tibet has produced", and Luciano Petech, saying Tsanyang Gyatso was "one of the finest poets of Tibet, nay the only erotic poet of the country". Dhondup adds that the Sixth Dalai Lama was a poet of the people, pp. 36-7.

234. Norbu & Turnbull, *Tibet*, pp. 284-5. See also, Dhondup, *Songs . . .*, p. 39. (Both these works deal at length with the poetry of Tsanyang Gyatso.)

235. Dhondup, *Songs . . .*, pp. 38-9.

236. Norbu & Turnbull, *Tibet*, p. 293. The authors go on to discuss the significance of Tsanyang Gyatso's tantric teachings. One interesting facet of his relationship with women is that the Sixth Dalai Lama claimed to have never allowed a drop of semen to emit in all his relations with women. This would be considered a highly advanced tantric practice leading to a higher spiritual awareness. See, Norbu & Turnbull, *Tibet*, pp. 284-93. Also, Malik, *Dalai Lamas of Tibet*, pp. 34-5. See also, Alexandra David-Neel, *Initiates and Initiations in Tibet*, 1975, p. 123.

237. Dhondup, *Songs. . .* (quoting from Norbu & Turnbull, *Tibet*), p. 42.

Another reason put forward by some authors for the behaviour of Tsanyang Gyatso is that he did not receive the strict religious training and upbringing that all other Dalai Lamas and other high incarnations would be subjected to from a very early age. Due to the circumstances surrounding the death of the Fifth Dalai Lama, the young incarnate Sixth was able to live in relative freedom for some years. He had time to develop a taste for the pleasures of the world, showing traits and preferences that could not readily be put aside. It is no wonder then, according to this line of thinking, that the young carefree Dalai Lama would have balked at the burden of his newly imposed responsibilities.[238]

Yet another theory, suggested by the present Dalai Lama, is that the Sixth Dalai Lama felt it would be better to discontinue his line of reincarnations in favour of a hereditary line of succession, as in the Sakya school. This would eliminate the power vacuum, which inevitably exists between the time a Dalai Lama dies and his successor reaches maturity, a problem solved by a mature and fully prepared son of the ruler stepping in to succeed the father.[239] As a Gelugpa monk this could only be possible by renouncing his vows and living as a layman. In one of many versions of the story, Tsanyang Gyatso is said to have had a special lover by whom he had a male child. Accordingly, the high Gelugpa officials, fearing the possibility of a hereditary succession, had the child and mother imprisoned and drove the young Dalai Lama into exile where he lived as a goatherd.[240]

Whatever the reasons for the behaviour of Tsanyang Gyatso it clearly was used as a pretext for his removal from office. The politics of the day were rife with intrigue. Sangye Gyatso had allied himself, during the reign of the Fifth Dalai Lama, with the Dzungar Mongols who, under their chief Galden, were hostile to China. The Qosot chief, Lhazang Khan, who assumed the titular kingship of Tibet by poisoning his brother, became allied with the Manchu emperor of China, K'ang Hsi. Lhazang Khan also wished to assume more control

---

238. Norbu & Turnbull, *Tibet*, pp. 282-3. See also, Malik, *Dalai Lamas of Tibet*, pp. 29-30. Malik goes on to speculate that the Sixth Dalai Lama chose this life to work out the accumulated *karmas* of some previous lives, p. 32.

239. From the foreword, Mullin, *Mystical Verses of a Mad Dalai Lama*, p. 13. Also, Malik, *Dalai Lamas of Tibet*, p. 33.

240. Norbu & Turnbull, *Tibet*, p. 290.

of Tibetan affairs than his immediate predecessors had held. Sangye Gyatso had also tried to unite the Qosot and Dzungar Mongols; asking them to restore to Tibet territories encroached upon by the Manchu dynasty. However, the K'ang Hsi emperor made use of the anger and betrayal, that everyone felt after Sangye Gyatso concealed the death of the Fifth Dalai Lama, to split the Mongols into opposing factions. The emperor, looking for an opening into Tibetan affairs, was concerned with the religious influence of the Dalai Lama over the Mongols. He was worried they could unite and threaten the empire once again.[241]

Lhazang Khan still held the title, King of Tibet, first claimed by his grandfather, Gushri Khan. Lhazang Khan and Sangye Gyatso grew increasingly antagonistic towards one another. In 1703, Sangye Gyatso was forced to resign, due to the discontent of the Mongols with him. Before doing so he had a golden mausoleum built in the Potala to house the preserved body of the Fifth Dalai Lama. Upon resigning he appointed his eldest son Ngawang Rinchin as the regent, but he still effectively maintained political control from behind the scenes. Quarrels over religious practice and the failure of Sangye Gyatso to rectify the conduct of the Dalai Lama further exacerbated tensions with Lhazang Khan. Finally Sangye Gyatso tried to have Lhazang Khan and one of his ministers poisoned, but Jamyang Shepa of Drepung Monastery saved them.[242]

There was an attempt to mediate this conflict by the abbots of the three principal Gelugpa monasteries, a representative of the Panchen Lama, the Sixth Dalai Lama, and the *Lamo* oracle. As a result Lhazang Khan was ordered by the Lamo oracle to leave for the Kokonor region, an order he could not refuse.[243] Travelling a

---

241. Tucci, *Tibet Land of Snows*, pp. 41-2. See, Dhondup, *Songs. . .*, pp. 17-19. Also, Shakabpa, *Tibet: A Political History*, pp. 127-31. See also, Richardson, *Tibet and Its History*, pp. 46-7. Also, Snellgrove & Richardson, *A Cultural History. . .*, mention that Galden, the leader of the Dzungar Mongols since 1676, had once been a monk in Lhasa and was closely associated with the Fifth Dalai Lama and the regent, Sangye Gyatso, pp. 205, 207-8.

242. Dhondup, *Songs. . .*, pp. 19-20. Also, Shakabpa, *Tibet: A Political History*, p. 131. See also, Rockhill, *The Dalai Lamas of Lhasa. . .*, who says Sangye Gyatso twice attempted to poison Lhazang Khan and his minister, p. 33.

243. Shakabpa, *Tibet: A Political History*, p. 131. Also, Dhondup, *Songs. . .*, pp. 20-1.

short distance, the wily Lhazang Khan regrouped and marched on Lhasa with his army. Interventions by the Panchan Lama and the abbots of the three monasteries did not, according to Dhondup, and did, according to Shakabpa, produce a cease-fire.[244] Dhondup reports that Sangye Gyatso and his Tibetan forces were quickly defeated. Following this the ex-regent left for Gongkar in retirement but on the orders of Lhazang Khan's wife, was intercepted and, in 1706, executed. This action was much disapproved of by Tibetans, since Sangye Gyatso, for all his faults, was regarded as a champion of Tibetan interests. Lhazang Khan was now in complete control of Tibetan political affairs.[245]

Lhazang Khan then agitated for the removal of the Dalai Lama. He tried to win the support of the three principle monasteries and of the Panchen Lama through the presentation of rich gifts. He also sought the support of the K'ang Hsi emperor who complied by issuing an arrest warrant for the Dalai Lama to be brought to Beijing. Lhazang Khan tried to have the leading abbots depose the Dalai Lama on the grounds that he was unfit for the position. Although they did not go that far, they did issue a decision that indicated that, while Tsanyang Gyatso was the rightful Dalai Lama, the spirit of enlightenment no longer dwelt with him.[246] On this pretext Lhazang Khan ordered the Dalai Lama to be taken to the Mongol military camp at Lhalu, which was outside Lhasa, and for the Dalai Lama's personal belongings to be removed from the Potala. From Lhalu, Tsanyang Gyatso was able to send this prophetic note to a lady friend, which read:

White Crane!
Lend me your wings

---

244. Dhondup, *Songs. . .*, p. 21. Also, Shakabpa, *Tibet: A Political History*, p. 132.

245. Dhondup, *Songs. . .*, pp. 22-3. Also, Shakabpa, *Tibet: A Political History*, who places the year as being 1705, p. 132.

246. Dhondup, *Songs. . .*, p. 24. Also, Petech, *China and Tibet in the Early 18th Century*, pp. 11-12. See, Rockhill, *The Dalai Lamas of Lhasa. . .*, pp. 33-4. See also, Snellgrove & Richardson, *A Cultural History. . .*, who point out that Lhazang Khan already had the emperor's support when he invaded Lhasa. In return for the emperor's formal recognition of his rule, Lhazang Khan sent tribute to China, indicating Tibet was a vassal of China, p. 208.

I will not fly far
From Lithang, I shall return.[247]

On June 27, 1706, it was announced that the Dalai Lama had been deposed and would be taken into exile. As his escort approached Drepung the large unarmed crowd following attacked, attempting to save the Dalai Lama. The crowd was beaten off but monks from Drepung, supported by monks from Sera and Ganden and led by the Tri Rinpoche (head of the Gelugpa order), joined the crowds and attacked once again. They carried the Dalai Lama off to Drepung. The following day the Nechung oracle was consulted and he declared Tsanyang Gyatso to be the true incarnation of the Fifth Dalai Lama. Meanwhile Lhazang Khan brought in troops and artillery, threatening to destroy the monastery. Seeing a massacre about to occur the Dalai Lama insisted on leaving though his friends were all killed in the attempt to protect him from the Mongol troops. Lhazang Khan, in his anger, none the less, attacked and sacked the monastery before leaving for China with the deposed Dalai Lama.[248] In November of 1706, at a small lake named Gunganor, just south of Kokonor, Tsanyang Gyatso, the Sixth Dalai Lama, disappeared. According to official Chinese and Tibetan records he died of an illness. His body was never recovered and it was widely speculated that he was murdered.[249]

There persists in popular legend and in some Tibetan chronicles, the story that the Sixth Dalai Lama, using his mystical powers, just disappeared from his captors. He proceeded first to eastern Tibet and, after much travel, came to Mongolia. There he lived a quiet life of meditation and acquired many disciples according to some

---

247. Shakabpa, *Tibet: A Political History*, pp. 132-3. Also, Dhondup, *Songs* . . . , pp. 1, 24-5.

248. Petech, *China and Tibet*. . . , pp. 12-13. See, Dhondup, *Songs*. . . , pp. 25-6. Also, Rockhill, *The Dalai Lamas of Lhasa*. . . , p. 34. See also, Shakabpa, *Tibet: A Political History*, p. 133. Also, Mullin, *Songs of Spiritual Change*, says that the people only allowed the Dalai Lama to leave Drepung after he promised that he would not leave Tibet and would return to them unharmed, p. 18.

249. Dhondup, *Songs*. . . , pp. 26-7. See, Shakabpa, *Tibet: A Political History*, p. 138. Also, Petech, *China and Tibet*. . . , p. 13. See also, Snellgrove & Richardson, who state that the K'ang Hsi emperor ordered that the Sixth Dalai Lama's "body should be dishonoured", p. 208.

Mongolian records. This *Secret Biography of the Sixth Dalai Lama* also says he built monasteries and finally died in 1746.[250] In a slightly different version, the Sixth Dalai Lama, after disappearing from his captors, wandered as a monk, appearing from time to time but vanishing as soon as he was recognised. He finally settled in Mongolia and worked as a goatherd.[251]

The Sixth Dalai Lama was a tragic figure in many respects, a victim of the power struggles which swirled around him. He rebelled against the high office he was born to, preferring instead a life of pleasurable pursuits, which many have interpreted in a tantric light, raising his activities "above the usual affairs of ordinary human beings".[252] He was a man of the people who expressed himself through his remarkable poetry. Though he was a source of exasperation to Tibetan officialdom, he was deeply loved and revered by the Tibetan populace. To them he was a god whose

> compassion was so great that he condescended to have feelings like a human being. He even acted like a human being while still remaining Avalokiteshvara incarnate, the bodhisattva of compassion, the Precious Protector of the Land of Snow.[253]

Dalai Lama VII

When the Sixth Dalai Lama was declared to have passed away Lhazang Khan decided to appoint his own choice as the new Dalai Lama. He

---

250. Mullin, *Songs of Spiritual Change*, says that before leaving Tibet, Tsanyang Gyatso "dressed in his tantric cloak, sat in meditation and mysteriously passed away", p. 19. See also, Apri, "In the footsteps. . . ," pp. 17-18. See, Malik, *Dalai Lamas of Tibet*, p. 34. Also, Dhondup, *Songs. . .* , pp. 29-30.

251. Norbu & Turnbull, *Tibet*, pp. 291, and p. 77 of the text above. For even more variations on this story see, Mullin, *Mystical Verses. . .* , p. 256.

252. Dhondup, *Songs. . .* , goes on to say that some Western and Tibetan scholars claim Tsanyang Gyatso was at the centre of a secret Nyingmapa tantric cult, p. 33. See also, Hoffmann, *The Religions of Tibet*, who, taking this idea further, suggests that the Sixth Dalai Lama and the regent Sangye Gyatso were supporting "heretical" Nyingmapa teachings, pp. 179-81.

253. Apri, "In the footsteps. . . ," p. 18.

did so in spite of Tibetan indignation and the anger of the Dzungar Mongols and Mongol tribes of the Kokonor region over his treatment of Tsanyang Gyatso. He announced that Tsanyang Gyatso had not been the true reincarnation of the Fifth Dalai Lama. He then put forth as the true reincarnation a twenty-five-year-old monk from the Chakpori Medical College of Lhasa, one Yeshe Gyatso, who was reputed to be the natural son of Lhazang Khan.[254] The Panchen Lama, apparently forced to do so by Lhazang Khan, officiated at the enthronement of this new Sixth Dalai Lama.[255] Yeshe Gyatso was neither accepted by the Tibetan people nor by much of the aristocracy, who referred to Lhazang's puppet as *kushab*, or "mister".[256] The emperor, realising that Lhazang had gone too far, delayed his approval of the new Dalai Lama, using this delay to gain leverage in Tibetan affairs. After investigations by the emperor's envoys, it was agreed that Lhazang Khan's regime would pay regular tribute to China and accept a Chinese representative in Lhasa in return for imperial recognition of the new Dalai Lama. This was granted in 1710.[257]

Tibetan hopes were raised when reports out of eastern Tibet indicated that a child born in Litang in 1708, and in accordance with the prophecy of Tsanyang Gyatso, showed all the signs of being the reincarnation of the recently deposed Sixth Dalai Lama. The child's father, Sonam Dargye, was a former monk of Drepung who had returned to the life of a layman. His mother was named Sonam Chotsu. It is reported wondrous signs accompanied the child's birth, and he was later named Kelsang Gyatso.[258] A delegation secretly sent out

---

254. Richardson, *Tibet and Its History*, p. 48. See, Shakabpa, *Tibet: A Political History*, p. 133. Also, Dhondup, *The Water-Horse and Other Years*, pp. 55-6. See also, Tucci, *Tibet Land of Snows*, p. 42. See also, Petech, *China and Tibet. . .*, who puts Yeshe Gyatso's age as twenty-one or twenty-two, p. 13.

255. Dhondup, *The Water-Horse. . .* , p. 56. Also, Petech, *China and Tibet. . .* , p. 13. See also, Rockhill, *The Dalai Lamas of Lhasa. . .* , who, in reference to this incident, calls the Panchen Lama an "easy going opportunist", p. 34.

256. Shakabpa, *Tibet: A Political History*, p. 134. Also, Dhondup, *The Water-Horse. . .* , p. 56.

257. Dhondup, *The Water-Horse. . .* , p. 56. See, Richardson, *Tibet and Its History*, p. 48. Also, Petech, *China and Tibet. . .* , pp. 14-15. See also, Rockhill, *The Dalai Lamas of Lhasa. . .* , pp. 36-7.

258. Mullin, *Songs of Spiritual Change*, p. 166. Also, Petech, *China and Tibet. . .* , pp. 16-17.

from Lhasa by Tibetan ecclesiastical officials found that the child bore the distinctive body markings looked for in the Dalai Lama. The boy was also able to correctly identify his predecessor's personal effects. Furthermore, the Nechung oracle later declared him the correct incarnation. Officers sent out by Lhazang Khan, however, declared the child to be a fraud.[259]

When the Mongol princes of the Kokonor region recognized and became protectors of the Litang child, the emperor of China took fresh notice. Lhazang Khan saw the Litang incarnation as a threat to his authority, a cornerstone of which was his control over the puppet Dalai Lama in whose name he ruled. A Tibetan general in the second investigating party sent out by Lhazang Khan, fearing for the child's safety, declared the Litang discovery to be irrelevant since his alleged former incarnation had been an impostor. Later, that same general secretly advised the family to leave for safety. In 1714, under the escort of Mongol and Derge troops, Kelsang Gyatso and his family arrived at the monastery of Derge.[260] From there he was brought to the Kokonor region. The Manchu emperor tried to have the child brought to Beijing but the Mongols balked at this suggestion. Finally, in 1716, the Litang incarnation was brought[261] to Kumbum Monastery where he stayed under the watchful eyes of Manchu and Qosot Mongol guards.

Throughout these events and from the age of six Kelsang Gyatso received his religious education, first under Losang Tempa, and later under Chuzang Nomonkan. He immediately showed great aptitude and was soon requested to give initiations and discourses during which his brilliance and depth became apparent. In 1716, when he was eight years old, he was placed on the throne of the Third Dalai Lama at Kumbum, from which he gave a discourse to several thousand

---

259. Mullin, *Songs of Spiritual Change*, p. 19. See, Dhondup, *The Water-Horse . . .*, p. 57. Also, Dhondup, *Songs of the Sixth Dalai Lama*, p. 28. See also, Petech, *China and Tibet*, pp. 16-17.
260. Dhondup, *The Water-Horse. . .*, pp. 58-9. Also, Petech, *China and Tibet. . .*, p. 17. See also, Shakabpa, *Tibet: A Political History*, p. 134.
261. Dhondup, *The Water-Horse. . .*, pp. 58-9. Also, Petech, *China and Tibet. . .*, pp. 18-19.

monks. He was later ordained by his two *gurus*, following which, he entered into intensive studies of fundamental logic and debate.[262]

The Litang incarnation was also sought after by the Dzungar Mongols, "the last of the rising nomad empires of Central Asia", according to Dhondup.[263] They saw in Kelsang Gyatso the key to control over all the Mongol tribes whose faith in the 'true' Dalai Lama was now total — a development not lost on the emperor. The Dzungar chief Tsewang Rabten was looking for a way to avenge himself on Lhazang Khan for the deaths of the Sixth Dalai Lama and Sangye Gyatso, with whom the Dzungars had been allied. He also wished to check Manchu influence in Tibet through the restoration of ecclesiastical rule. The pretext to act on these aims came in the form of an appeal from the three principal Gelugpa monasteries at Lhasa to overthrow Lhazang Khan and restore the rightful Dalai Lama to his throne. The Dzungars knew they would need to gain hold of the Litang incarnation, who was under Manchu protection at Kumbum, in order to succeed and gain the approval of the Tibetan people.[264]

The Dzungar army was able to penetrate deeply into Tibet, catching Lhazang's forces unprepared. The governor of Tsang, Pholanas, was a keen supporter of Lhazang Khan, and he was able to mount a Tibetan army and offer a spirited resistance, in spite of the half-hearted efforts of his troops, whose true loyalties were to the Litang incarnation. The Dzungars had secretly announced they were coming to avenge the Sixth Dalai Lama and were escorting his reincarnation to Lhasa. In 1717, despite the efforts of Pholanas, Lhazang Khan was defeated and killed, ending Qosot rule in Tibet.[265]

---

262. Mullin, *Songs of Spiritual Change*, says that Kelsang Gyatso was invited to travel to the monasteries of Kham and Amdo provinces and eventually to Kumbum, pp. 167-8. (It is interesting to note how the Tibetan biography of Kelsang Gyatso, as translated by Mullin, makes no reference to the swirl of political intrigue around him, focussing instead on the religious events only.)

263. Dhondup, *The Water-Horse. . .* , p. 58.

264. Dhondup, *The Water-Horse. . .* , pp. 58-9. See, Shakabpa, *Tibet: A Political History*, p. 135. Also, Dhondup, *Songs. . .* , pp. 27-8. See also, Petech, *China and Tibet. . .* , pp. 25-6.

265. Shakabpa, *Tibet: A Political History*, pp. 134-7. See, Dhondup, *The Water-Horse. . .* , pp. 60-9. Also, Snellgrove & Richardson, *A Cultural History. . .* , pp. 227. See also, Petech, *China and Tibet. . .* , pp. 26-41.

The Dzungars were welcomed as liberators but as soon as their commander Tsering Dhondup took control of Lhasa, his soldiers began a savage campaign of looting, rape, and arson. It was also learned that the force the Dzungars had sent to Kumbum to secure the Litang incarnation had failed, in spite of Dzungar claims to the contrary. The Dzungars also started to repress the Nyingmapa and other sects, destroying monasteries and killing the monks. These actions destroyed any Dzungar support from the Gelugpa hierarchy and the Tibetan nobility, in spite of the deposition of the false Dalai Lama, Yeshe Gyatso, and the subsequent recognition of Kelsang Gyatso, who was still in Chinese hands, as the true Dalai Lama.[266]

The Dzungars installed a Tibetan noble, Lhagyal Rabten Tagtsepa, as their puppet prime minister. They also carried their repression into Tsang where their siege of Shigatse was repulsed by the efforts of the Panchen Lama. At this juncture two of Lhazang's firmest supporters amongst the Tibetan nobility, Khangchennas, the governor of western Tibet and Pholanas, the governor of Tsang, organised the Tibetan resistance. They soon secured the whole country except the Dzungar-controlled province of U and Lhasa.[267]

Meanwhile the emperor of China had responded to the overthrow of Lhazang Khan by sending an expeditionary force to Tibet, which was wiped out by the Dzungars in 1718. In 1720 he ordered a larger army, under the command of his son, to escort the Litang incarnation to Lhasa. The emperor had by now recognised Kelsang Gyatso as the true Dalai Lama.[268] Hearing of the Chinese advance, Pholanas

266. Shakabpa, *Tibet: A Political History*, p. 137. See, Dhondup, *The Water-Horse. . .*, pp. 67-71. Also, Snellgrove & Richardson, ,, pp. 217-18. See also, Petech, *China and Tibet. . .*, pp. 43-5.

267. Dhondup, *The Water-Horse. . .*, pp. 70-1. Also, Shakabpa, *Tibet: A Political History*, pp. 137-9. See also, Rockhill, *The Dalai Lamas of Lhasa. . .*, who says that the Panchen Lama's efforts managed to save Tashi Lhunpo and its treasures, but the town of Shigatse was largely destroyed, p. 39.

268. Shakabpa, *Tibet A Political History*, pp. 137-9. See, Snellgrove & Richardson, *A Cultural History. . .*, p. 218. Also, Petech, *China and Tibet. . .*, who suggests that the recognition of Kelsang Gyatso by the emperor was a pragmatic decision since there was now only one Dalai Lama, pp. 57-60. See also, Rockhill, *The Dalai Lamas of Lhasa*, who says the emperor saw an opportunity to put in place a 'Pontiff of his own choice' while proclaiming himself as the champion who was returning the rightful Dalai Lama to his throne, pp. 40-1.

and Khangchennas led their troops against Dzungar-occupied Lhasa. The Dzungars took flight, allowing the Manchu army to escort the Dalai Lama into Lhasa to a rapturous welcome.

According to the Chinese edict of recognition, Kelsang Gyatso was enthroned as the Sixth Dalai Lama, implying that the previous two Sixth Dalai Lamas had not been true incarnations.[269] The Manchus eventually had to concede to Tibetan opinion, however, which recognised Tsanyang Gyatso as the true Sixth Dalai Lama, making Kelsang Gyatso the Seventh.[270] Prior to his enthronement, Kelsang Gyatso gave a discourse, before the great temple of Lhasa, to thousands of people. The Panchen Lama officiated at his enthronement and novice ordination, giving him the monastic name of Lobsang Kelsang Gyatso (Ocean of Good Fortune). The Panchen Lama then gave religious instructions to the Dalai Lama. They also officiated together at the Monlam Prayer Festival of 1721.[271]

The Chinese set about restoring order. The false Dalai Lama, Yeshe Gyatso, was deported to China and the Tibetans who had collaborated with the Dzungars and the Dzungar lamas were tried and executed. Among those executed was the puppet prime minister, Rabten Tagtsepa, who was not spared despite the entreaties of Pholanas and the Seventh Dalai Lama. The office of *desi* was abolished and replaced by a counsel of Tibetan ministers. Its chairman, Khangchennas, was an unofficial member, who was appointed in 1723; he worked in consultation with Pholanas. Another unofficial member was Sonam Dargye, the father of the Dalai Lama, who was a politically ambitious man. A Chinese garrison was also established which, after a few years, was removed, leaving only a Chinese representative. At any rate, Tibet had come under Chinese protection, a relationship that would endure in some form until 1911.[272]

---

269. Shakabpa, *Tibet: A Political History*, p. 138.

270. Richardson, *Tibet and Its History*, p. 49.

271. Bell, *The Religion of Tibet*, p. 143. Also, Mullin, *Songs of Spiritual Change*, p. 168.

272. Shakabpa, *Tibet: A Political History*, pp. 140-1. See, Richardson, *Tibet and Its History*, pp. 50-1. Also, Petech, *China and Tibet . . .*, pp. 63-9. See also, Rockhill, *The Dalai Lamas of Lhasa . . .*, who mentions that in 1720 the Dalai Lama was given temporal sovereignty over Tibet by the emperor. He also adds that the garrison left by the Chinese was comprised of Mongol troops, pp. 41-2.

The position of the Dalai Lama in this new arrangement was of a figurehead who had no real temporal power. The Chinese treated him with great deference, however, because of his immense spiritual influence.[273] This situation was likely preferable to the Dalai Lama as he showed very little interest in politics whatsoever.[274] In other respects he proved to be the opposite of the Sixth Dalai Lama. He took to his studies conscientiously, first with the Panchen Lama and later with the Ganden throne holder, Lozang Dargye. After more studies, often at Drepung during the summer months, he was given his full ordination by the Panchen Lama in the presence of thirty-one of the most prominent lamas in Tibet.[275]

The pursuit of religion marked Kelsang Gyatso's life. He was the perfect monk, a simple unassuming man who rarely slept more than three hours a night, passing his time in study, meditation, teaching, and writing. His writings were "straightforward, earthy, and alive with a natural disarming imagery", according to Mullin.[276] He was renowned for his compositions of informal spiritual poetry and a large number of prayers and hymns. The corpus of tantric literature he left is still widely studied. In all, his hundreds of titles are collected into eight volumes.[277] He led an austere life and travelled widely, often on foot and simply dressed so as to move incognito amongst the people, to whom he would give teachings, frequently by means of everyday life situations. His religious discourses were often given in a park in Lhasa and were well attended. As time went on he retired more and more into solitary religious contemplation and a life of renunciation, seeking

---

273. Petech, *China and Tibet . . .*, p. 69.

274. Mullin, *Songs of Spiritual Change*, p. 19. See, Norbu & Turnbull, *Tibet*, who say Kelsang Gyatso "showed a disinclination to make use of the power that had come to him" leaving "most secular matters to others, particularly to the Panchen Rinpoche", p. 297.

275. Mullin, Songs of Spiritual Change, p. 169. Also, Petech, *China and Tibet . . .*, p. 70.

276. Mullin, *Songs of Spiritual Change*, p. 19.

277. Mullin, *Songs of Spiritual Change*, p. 20. Also, Mullin, *Essence of Refined Gold*, p. 245. In another book Mullin, *Mystical Verses . . .*, notes that the Seventh Dalai Lama was the first to not incorporate Nyingmapa lineages into his spiritual life. Mullin speculates this was due to years of Nyingmapa persecutions by the Dzungar Mongols and also the tragic example of the Sixth Dalai Lama, "a Nyingmapa by birth and inclination", p. 254.

to restore authority through religious devotion rather than political manoeuvering.[278]

Of the latter, there was a great deal in Tibetan political affairs. The death, in 1722, of the K'ang Hsi emperor had brought about a retrenchment policy in Chinese foreign affairs. The Yung Chen emperor withdrew the garrison at Lhasa leaving an *amban*, or representative.[279] The *Kashag*, or governing council, made up of district governors, was divided along regional and sectarian lines. The majority of the council, including the Dalai Lama's father, who was always seeking greater powers for the son he influenced, secretly worked for a lessening of Manchu interference. Pholanas and Khangchennas were inclined to rapprochement with the Manchus.[280] In this regard Pholanas was instrumental in helping the Manchus suppress a Qosot uprising in the Kokonor region, as was the Dalai Lama whose religious influence kept the other Mongol tribes out of the conflict. The Dalai Lama was later able to convince the emperor to restore the rights of the Kokonor monasteries that had supported the uprising.[281]

When an edict from the Yung Chen emperor arrived, ordering a suppression of the Nyingmapa, it was rejected by the Kashag and most vociferously by Pholanas, who was a Nyingmapa supporter at heart. At a suggestion by the Dalai Lama's father, more authority was concentrated in one person's hands. Khangchennas was made prime minister, but, after carrying out the Nyingmapa persecution, he estranged himself from Pholanas and even further from the Kashag. Finding his position untenable, Pholanas submitted his resignation to the Dalai Lama, but the request was denied. At that point Pholanas returned to Tsang to attend to a serious illness of his wife.[282]

---

278. Norbu & Turnbull, *Tibet*, pp. 298-9. Also, Mullin, *Songs of Spiritual Change*, p. 19.
279. Shakabpa, *Tibet: A Political History*, p. 141. Also, Petech, *China and Tibet . . .*, pp. 78-81.
280. Dhondup *The Water-Horse . . .*, pp. 82-3. Also, Shakabpa, *Tibet: A Political History*, p. 141.
281. Petech, *China and Tibet . . .*, pp. 82-8.
282. Dhondup, *The Water-Horse . . .*, pp. 86-9. Also, Shakabpa, *Tibet: A Political History*, pp. 141-2. See also, Petech, *China and Tibet . . .*, pp. 92-8.

During Pholanas' absence Prime Minister Khangchennas, his family, and many of his supporters were murdered by three members of the Kashag, who then sent troops to kill Pholanas. Forewarned, Pholanas saw to the safety of his family and fled, gathering supporters and an army as he went. The ensuing civil war lasted from 1727 to 1728 despite the interventions of the Panchen Lama and the Dalai Lama. The latter was still quite young and influenced by his father, who was found to be a party to the conspiracy to form a new government.[283] Finally in 1728, spurred on by the efforts of the Panchen Lama and the Sakya abbot and at the urging of the Dalai Lama and his father, who was now seeking a peaceful solution, both sides agreed to stop fighting. They exchanged prisoners, agreed to disband their armies, and awaited a decision from the emperor to whom both sides had sent reports.[284] Pholanas kept his forces intact and, when he saw the opportunity, attacked. He was able to reach Lhasa with little opposition and became the *de facto* power in Tibet.[285]

The rebel ministers had taken refuge in the Potala. Fearing for the safety of the Dalai Lama, the abbots of the three monasteries assured Pholanas that the Dalai Lama and his father were innocent of Khangchennas' murder. In the end, at the suggestion of the Dalai Lama and much against the wishes of his commanders, Pholanas allowed the ministers to live under house arrest.[286] Upon the arrival of the Chinese force sent to quell the rebellion, the ministers and their supporters were put on trial, found guilty, and executed. Pholanas managed to have many of the lesser conspirators shown clemency.

---

283. Dhondup, *The Water-Horse . . .* , pp. 89-93. See, Shakabpa, *Tibet: A Political History*, pp. 141-3. Also, Petech, *China and Tibet . . . .* mentions that the father of the Dalai Lama became allied to the minister Lumpanas when the latter gave him his two daughters in marriage, pp. 99-116. See also, Rockhill *The Dalai Lamas of Lhasa . . .* , who comments that it was said the outbreak was incited by the Dalai Lama and his father, p. 42.

284. Petech, *China and Tibet . . .* , pp. 117-19. See, Dhondup, *the Water-Horse . . .* , p. 93. Also, Shakabpa, *Tibet: A Political History*, p. 143.

285. Dhondup, *The Water-Horse. . .* , pp. 93-5. See, Shakabpa, *Tibet: A Political History*, p. 143. See also, Petech, *China and Tibet. . .* , pp. 119-23.

286. Shakabpa, *Tibet: A Political History*, p. 143. Also, Dhondup, *The Water-Horse . . .* , p. 95. See, Petech, *China and Tibet . . .* , pp. 126-9.

He also refused to punish many of those that fought against him, later including some of them in his administration upon formation of a new government.[287]

Over the protests of the Panchen Lama, Pholanas, and the people, and in order to limit his power, the emperor sent the Dalai Lama and his father to Garthar, which was near Litang, where they were to remain for seven years.[288] The Chinese also tried to set-up the position of the Panchen Lama in opposition to that of the Dalai Lama. The Panchen Lama was offered the temporal and administrative sovereignty over Tsang and western Tibet, which he wisely refused. He did, however, accept authority over the three sub-districts in the vicinity of Tashi Lhunpo Monastery. While this action had no immediate effect on his relations with the Dalai Lama it was to prove a recurring point of contention between the officials of the subsequent Dalai and Panchen Lamas as time went on.[289]

Pholanas became head of the government, appointing ministers to the Kashag himself. He was immediately able to acquire the support of the Panchen Lama and the monasteries knowing these were essential towards maintaining a stable government. He slowly consolidated his power and proceeded to oversee a just and peaceful administration for eighteen years. During his rule many improvements were made to systems of taxation, justice, postal service, and trade. He also had new editions of the Tibetan canonical literature produced and oversaw the cessation of religious persecution. He had the confidence of the Manchu administration of China such that the Tibetan garrison was kept to a minimum and the two ambans never had a real hand in Tibetan affairs. In foreign affairs Tibet secured suzerainty

---

287. Dhondup, *The Water-Horse . . .* , pp. 95-6. Also, Shakabpa, *Tibet: A Political History*, pp. 143-4. See also, Petech, *China and Tibet . . .* , who states there is no evidence to show the conflict was any more than an internal Tibetan affair and that it was not directed against Chinese suzerainty, pp. 131-5.

288. Dhondup, *The Water-Horse . . .* , pp. 96-7. See, Shakabpa, *Tibet: A Political History*, p. 144. Also, Petech, *China and Tibet . . .* , pp. 136-8.

289. Snellgrove & Richardson, *A Cultural History . . .* , pp. 219-20. Also, Richardson, *Tibet and Its History*, p. 53. See also, Petech, *China and Tibet . . .* , who says that the Panchen Lama refused the most valuable part of the Chinese offer and that he had to give up pretensions to control over eastern Tsang, pp. 138-9.

over Bhutan and maintained good relations with Ladhak. Pholanas also raised and trained a small standing army. He reigned as a king, and his power was close enough to being absolute that he was able to ignore the demands of the monasteries and the people to return the Dalai Lama to Lhasa.[290]

The Seventh Dalai Lama and his father had been taken to Litang in 1728 and to the Chinese garrison town of Garthar in 1730, where a monastery had been built for the Dalai Lama by the Chinese. During this period his father was taken to Beijing, where, chained to his two wives, he was brought before the emperor. But because he was no longer deemed a threat, he was punished no further and returned to his son. The Chinese then announced that the official reason for the Dalai Lama's removal was his (and his father's) intrigue with the Dzungar Mongols before and during the civil war.[291]

During his exile the Dalai Lama received many visitors, mostly religious figures and the occasional Mongol prince seeking blessings. A son of the Manchu emperor was especially taken by the Dalai Lama whilst on an official visit. Kelsang Gyatso primarily attended to his studies, having taken his tutor, the Ganden throne holder, Palden Drakpa with him. Later, the Dalai Lama's guru Ngawang Chokden was sent to tutor him.[292]

In 1735, with the situation in Tibet normalized and firmly under Pholanas' control, the Dalai Lama was permitted to return to Lhasa. He travelled with a large retinue, feted all the way by local dignitaries and lamas. En route the Dalai Lama gave many discourses and blessings to all that sought them. His arrival in Lhasa was triumphal and a great relief to all, for he had been missed. What was not said, however, was that his return was conditional on his attending only to his spiritual duties. As for his father, he was made to reside a three

---

290. Dhondup, *The Water-Horse . . .* , pp. 97-8. See, Shakabpa, *Tibet: A Political History*, pp. 144-5. Also, Richardson, *Tibet and Its History*, pp. 52-3. See also, Petech, *China and Tibet . . .* , pp. 140-55.

291. Petech, *China and Tibet . . .* , pp. 155-7. Also, Bell, *The Religions of Tibet*, pp. 145-6.

292. Mullin, *Songs of Spiritual Change*, p. 170. Also, Petech, *China and Tibet . . .* , p. 157.

days' journey outside of Lhasa, being allowed to visit but once a year. He was also ordered to refrain from politics.[293]

The Seventh Dalai Lama travelled to Tashi Lhunpo shortly after his return, and there he received further teachings from the Second Panchen Lama, and from his *guru* Ngawang Chokden, who gave him the complete Kalachakra Tantra, which had been in danger of extinction. Kelsang Gyatso later made the traditional pilgrimage to Chokhor Gyal Monastery. Over the course of his life he fulfilled his religious calling, giving many teachings, initiations, and monastic ordinations to thousands of aspirants. He was also constantly engaged in writing. According to Mullin, the Seventh Dalai Lama "greatly restored the essence of Buddhism in general and, in particular, the essential doctrine of Lama Tsongkhapa".[294]

In 1738, the Seventh Dalai Lama recognised Palden Yeshe, the Third Panchen Lama, as the reincarnation of Lobsang Yeshe, who had died the year before. Subsequently, Palden Yeshe received his novice ordination and extensive spiritual instruction from Kelsang Gyatso, including a 'panoramic transmission of Dharma', which lasted everyday for over half a year.[295] When his own *guru*, Ngawang Chokden, passed away, the Dalai Lama showed the greatest respect and all the correct attitudes, as he had during his training, thus leaving an inspiring example for others to follow. During his lifetime, Kelsang Gyatso was recognised throughout Tibet as the foremost amongst lamas in learning and realisation.[296]

---

293. Petech, *China and Tibet . . .* , pp. 157-8. Also, Dhondup, *The Water-Horse . . .* , p. 98. See also, Mullin, *Songs of Spiritual Change*, p. 171.
294. Mullin, *Songs of Spiritual Change*, notes, in quoting the Tibetan biography of the Seventh Dalai Lama, that the Dalai Lama and Panchen Lama showed great affection for one another, pp. 171-4, 178. See also, Petech, *China and Tibet . . .* , who, quoting from "the official biography" of the Seventh Dalai Lama, says that the Panchen Lama did not meet with the Dalai Lama during this visit, giving his infirm condition as a reason. Petech goes on to speculate the Dalai Lama's real purpose for making this visit was to affirm his "suzerainty over the whole of Tibet, including the *Tashi Lama's* new possessions", pp. 2, 159-60.
295. Doboom Tulku, "the lineage of the panchen lamas", p. 8. Also, Mullin, *Songs of Spiritual Change*, pp. 174-7. See also, Petech, *China and Tibet . . .* , p. 164.
296. Mullin, *Songs of Spiritual Change*, p. 176.

After some years a rift developed between Pholanas and the Dalai Lama, the origin of which likely stemmed from the fact that Pholanas did everything in his power to keep the Dalai Lama under his thumb.[297] Apparently, the Dalai Lama, so long denied any real voice in temporal affairs, had sent a complaint to the emperor, who sent a representative to smooth over the quarrel. Pholanas died before that could happen and in 1747 was succeeded by his son Gyurmed Namgyal who acted towards the Dalai Lama with the same coldness as his father. Contrary to his father, however, Gyurmed Namgyal strongly disliked the Manchu presence in Tibet.[298]

Gyurmed Namgyal plotted to expel the Manchus from Tibet. It was later learned he did so in collusion with the Dzungar Mongols who were still a threat to the Manchu empire.[299] In order to facilitate his plans, Gyurmed Namgyal asked that the Manchu garrison in Lhasa be reduced. He later requested that it be replaced with Tibetan soldiers. The Chinese became increasingly suspicious of his intentions and were worried when Gyurmed Namgyal had his brother, the governor of western Tibet murdered, despite the efforts of the Dalai Lama to mediate their differences. When some pro-Manchu Tibetans disclosed Gyurmed Namgyal's true intentions, the ambans took matters into their own hands and lured the Tibetan ruler into a trap where they killed him. This prompted a violent reaction from a Tibetan mob, which, despite the efforts of the Dalai Lama to stop them, put to death the ambans and well over 100 Chinese soldiers and citizens. Another 200 or so survived in the refuge of the Potala, under the protection of the Dalai Lama.[300]

Once the mob had settled down the Dalai Lama took control of the situation. He appointed a minister, Duke Pandita, as chief administrator, forbade any help to the mob leaders and had them

---

297. Shakabpa, *Tibet: A Political History*, p. 147.

298. Petech, *China and Tibet . . .*, pp. 175-6. See, Dhondup, *The Water-Horse . . .*, p. 101. See also, Shakabpa, *Tibet: A Political History*, p. 147.

299. Petech, *China and Tibet . . .*, p. 210. See, Shakabpa, *Tibet: A Political History*, p. 148. Also, Richardson, *Tibet and Its History*, p. 56.

300. Shakabpa, *Tibet: A Political History*, pp. 147-9. See, Dhondup, *The Water-Horse . . .*, pp. 101-10. Also, Richardson, *Tibet and Its History*, pp. 56-7. See also, Rockhill, *The Dalai Lamas of Lhasa . . .*, pp. 44-5. See also, Petech, *China and Tibet . . .*, pp. 198-201.

taken into custody. He then sent reports to the emperor, who recalled a retaliatory force and sent a smaller one with investigative powers instead. The Chinese commissioner who arrived first, acting unilaterally, had the accused executed in spite of pleas from the Dalai Lama for clemency. In the subsequent administrative reorganisation in 1751 responsibility was invested in the Kashag but the overall power, both secular and spiritual, was vested in the Dalai Lama.[301]

The restoration of the Dalai Lama to power marked the end of lay supremacy in Tibet.[302] The council of four ministers, one a monk in charge of ecclesiastical concerns, was to handle the affairs of the country. All important decisions were to be referred to the Dalai Lama for his approval.[303] The records show that the Dalai Lama was consulted by neighbouring countries to mediate disputes and to confer blessings at important state occasions.[304] In this way Kelsang Gyatso was able to attend principally to his spiritual duties of teaching, writing, and giving blessings, initiations, and ordinations. His popularity and fame drew disciples from all over central Asia, even so far to the east as the "great ocean". Finally, in 1757, deciding "his work for his disciples was complete", the Seventh Dalai Lama sat in meditation and passed away.[305]

The Seventh Dalai Lama was a pious and scholarly man who is respected, by many Tibetans, above all the other Dalai Lamas for his saintliness and his devotion to the practice, preservation, and

---

301. Dhondup, *The Water-Horse* . . . , pp. 110-13. Also, Shakabpa, *Tibet: A Political History*, pp. 149-50. See also, Petech, *China and Tibet* . . . , who goes on to say that the Chinese implicitly understood the sovereignty of the Dalai Lama and that they were restoring the regime, which had existed during the time of the Fifth Dalai Lama. In proclaiming the new government of Tibet the Chinese document stated "the Dalai Lama is the ruler of Tibet", pp. 201-13.
302. Snellgrove & Richardson, *A Cultural History* . . . , p. 225.
303. Petech, *China and Tibet* . . . , p. 220. Also, Shakabpa, *Tibet: A Political History*, p. 150.
304. Shakabpa, *Tibet: A Political History*, p. 151.
305. Mullin, *Songs of Spiritual Change*, pp. 179-80. Also, Shakabpa, *Tibet: A Political History*, who notes that the Dalai Lama had been in poor health for some time, pp. 151-2.

transmission of the Dharma.[306] In those turbulent times Lhazang Khan and then, Pholanas, whom Kelsang Gyatso regarded as a just and able administrator in spite of their difficulties, overshadowed him. During the short reign of Gyurmed Namgyal, the Dalai Lama, his character having matured, became more determined in political matters. When matters came to a crisis he proved he could rule effectively.[307] With his passing it would be almost 140 years before another Dalai Lama could rule with any degree of effect.

Dalai Lama VIII

There is very little in the histories on the lives of the next five Dalai Lamas: the Eighth, because he did not teach or write to any extent and only ruled for a brief time and, the Ninth to Twelfth, because they all died young.[308] During their lifetimes Tibet was ruled by a series of regents,[309] all Gelugpa lamas from one of six select monasteries near Lhasa, none of which were Drepung, Sera or Ganden. One of their head lamas would normally be selected for the post.[310] The first of these regents, appointed by the Tibetan government, was Jampal Delek, a high lama of Drepung, who was also head of Tengyeling monastery. While he and other earlier regents were conscientious, later regents acquired a taste for office and were to misuse their powers to further their own interests.[311]

The Eighth Dalai Lama was born at Thopgyal, in upper Tsang, in 1758. Miraculous occurrences were said to accompany his birth, including rainbows surrounding the house of his birth. Delegations

---

306. Norbu & Turnbull, *Tibet*, p. 311. See, Shakabpa, *Tibet: A Political History*, p. 152. Also, Mullin, *Songs of Spiritual Change*, p. 179.

307. Richardson, *Tibet and Its History*, p. 59.

308. Mullin, *Mystical Verses of a Mad Dalai Lama*, p. 14.

309. Petech, "The Dalai-Lamas and Regents of Tibet: A Chronological Study", defines "the regent as the caretaker of the spiritual and temporal rights of the Dalai Lamas", p. 377.

310. Bell, *The Religion of Tibet*, p. 184. Also, Bell, *Portrait of the Dalai Lama*, in mentioning the number of monasteries, states there are seven from which the regents are chosen, p. 53. See, Snellgrove & Richardson, *A Cultural History . . .*, who say that the office of regent became the special preserve of three of these monasteries, namely, Reting, Tengyeling, and Tshomoling, p. 228.

311. Shakabpa, *Tibet: A Political History*, p. 153.

from Lhasa, giving him the usual tests, confirmed he was the reincarnation of the Seventh Dalai Lama.[312] In 1761 he was formally declared the reincarnation of Kelsang Gyatso by the Panchen Lama and brought to Lhasa the following year, by the regent, where he was enthroned in the Potala.[313] The Panchen Lama named him Jampal Gyatso at his upaseka ordination. The Panchen Lama also officiated at his novice ordination in 1765 and his full ordination in 1777. The Panchen Lama educated Jampal Gyatso, giving him instructions in the *sutras* and tantras over the years.[314] His training, as with the Seventh, was in the Gelugpa tradition. Later in life, however, he followed the tradition of the early Dalai Lamas and combined the Gelugpa and Nyingmapa teachings in his practice.[315]

When asked to assume power in 1777, upon the death of the regent Jampal Delek, the Dalai Lama declined, as he had not completed his training. Ngawang Tsultrim of Tsernonling Monastery, who had achieved fame as a brilliant scholar and as imperial preceptor for fifteen years was appointed as regent. In the following year he was also elected as Tri Rinpoche (head of the Gelugpa order and third highest ecclesiastical rank in Tibet), a post he held for the full seven-year term.[316]

During the minority of the Eighth Dalai Lama the prestige of the Third Panchen Lama increased greatly. Richardson speculates this was because the Eighth Dalai Lama developed slowly and was undistinguished compared to Palden Yeshe. He also notes the Panchen Lama, "a man of remarkable character, learning and ability",[317] unlike the regent under Chinese watchfulness, was free to act without

---

312. Mullin, *Songs of Spiritual Change*, p. 180.

313. Petech, "The Dalai-Lamas And Regents . . . ," p. 373. Also, Shakabpa, *Tibet: A Political History*, p. 153. See also, Doboom Tulku, "the lineage of the panchen lamas", p. 8.

314. Doboom Tulku, "the lineage of the panchen lamas", p. 8. See also, Shakabpa, *Tibet: A Political History*, p. 153. See also, Mullin, *Essence . . .*, p. 246.

315. Mullin, *Mystical Verses . . .*, p. 255.

316. Shakabpa, *Tibet: A Political History*, p. 155. See also, Petech, "The Dalai-Lamas and Regents . . . ," who mentions that Ngawang Tsultrim was appointed imperial preceptor in 1762 by the Dalai Lama (who was four at the time), the regent, and the Panchen Lama, pp. 383-4.

317. Richardson, *Tibet and Its History*, p. 65.

interference. He was greatly respected by the emperor and was often consulted on spiritual and political matters. The British representative, George Bogle, who came to Tashi Lhunpo to discuss trade and potential diplomatic ties, much to the consternation of the Lhasa administration, regarded the Panchen Lama as the "real champion of the rights of Tibet and of the Dalai Lama".[318]

The Panchen Lama, at the invitation of the Ch'ien Lung emperor, and after much deliberation by the Kashag and regent, travelled to China in 1780. He resided there in the Yellow Palace built earlier for the Fifth Dalai Lama. He enjoyed great influence and respect and was appointed imperial preceptor. He was able to prevent Manchu interference in Tibetan affairs and enhance the authority of the Dalai Lama. Petech goes so far as to say he "was cherished and honoured by the emperor as no Tibetan churchman before him".[319] His stay was short-lived, however, as he died of smallpox in late 1780.

The death of the Panchen Lama spurred the Chinese into granting the Dalai Lama his long overdue full powers. He agreed to accept these responsibilities at imperial urging and the request of the regent and Kashag, taking power in July of 1781. However, the Dalai Lama requested the regent to assist him in this regard, which was the case until 1786, when Ngawang Tsultrim, at the emperor's request, returned to China. During this period, in 1783, the Dalai Lama ordered the construction of the Norbulingka Palace (Jewel Park), which would be the summer residence of the Dalai Lamas.[320] In the

---

318. Richardson, *Tibet and Its History*, pp. 65-6.

319. Petech, "The Dalai-Lamas and Regents . . . ," p. 384. See, Shakabpa, *Tibet: A Political History*, p. 155. Also, Doboom Tulku, "the lineage of the panchen lamas", p. 8. See also, Bell, *The Religion of Tibet*, p. 155. See also, Rockhill, *The Dalai Lamas of Lhasa . . .* , pp. 47-9.

320. Petech, "The Dalai-Lamas and Regents . . . ," p. 384. See, Mullin, *Essence of Refined Gold*, p. 246. Also, Shakabpa, *Tibet: A Political History*, p. 156. It is interesting to note that Malik, *Dalai Lamas of Tibet*, gives the Seventh Dalai Lama credit for building the Norbulingka, p. 38, as does R. Rahul, "The Institution of Dalai Lama", *International Studies*, vol. 10, no. 4, April 1969, p. 504. See also, The Fourteenth Dalai Lama, *My Land and My People*, 1962, who says the Norbulingka was started by the Seventh Dalai Lama, pp. 55-6. It is plausible to speculate that the Norbulingka was started by the Seventh Dalai Lama with much of the work being continued by the Eighth (Author's note).

same year the Dalai Lama recognised the reincarnation of the Panchen Lama and named him Tenpe Nyima at his *upaseka* ordination. The Dalai Lama would go on to give the Fourth Panchen Lama his novice ordination in 1789 and the full ordination in 1801 as well as to instruct the young Panchen Lama in the *sutras* and tantras.[321]

When the Third Panchen Lama died, his younger brother, who was his treasurer and an incarnate lama (*tulku*) himself, took possession of the Panchen Lama's considerable estate. He would share none of it, which displeased the people and the monasteries, but especially annoyed the youngest brother of the Panchen Lama, the Ninth Red Hat Karmapa, also known as the Ninth Sharmapa Tulku. He had retired some time before to Nepal, living amongst the Gurkhas with whom he now conspired to claim his share of his late brother's property. The Gurkhas, who were orthodox Hindus and generally contemptuous of Tibetans, had earlier overthrown the Newari kingdoms and consolidated their power in Nepal. They were annoyed with Tibet over border disputes and complaints by Tibet concerning monetary policies. The complaint of the Ninth Sharmapa Tulku became their pretext for invading Tibet.[322]

The Gurkhas invaded Tibet, capturing three frontier districts. A Chinese army was sent to deal with the situation but their generals, much against Tibetan wishes, concluded a treaty in which Tibet agreed to pay tribute annually to Nepal. The Chinese generals sent a false report to the emperor who later, upon hearing the truth, severely punished those responsible. The Tibetan accounts generally describe the Chinese as being a hindrance while Chinese accounts report the opposite.[323]

---

321. Doboom Tulku, "the lineage of the panchen lamas", p. 8. Also, Shakabpa, *Tibet: A Political History*, p. 156.

322. Richardson, *Tibet and Its History*, pp. 68-9. See, Shakabpa, *Tibet: A Political History*, pp. 156-7. Also, Rockhill, *The Dalai-Lamas of Lhasa . . .*, p. 49. See also my text above, which describes the intrigues of the Fourth Sharmapa Tulku during the time of the Second Dalai Lama, also mentioning the troubles this later incarnation would foment during the reign of the Eighth Dalai Lama, p. 44, footnote # 83.

323. Petech, "The Dalai-Lamas and Regents . . . ," reports that "the unworldly and weak Dalai Lama failed to rise to the occasion", prompting the emperor to appoint a new vice-regent, Tenpai Gonpo of Kundeling, whose position as prime minister and collaborator of the Dalai Lama meant "a practical suppression of the authority of the Dalai Lama", →

According to Petech, the new vice-regent, Tenpai Gonpo was soon recalled to Beijing because he supported certain administrative malpractices perpetrated by the Dalai Lama's younger brother. Shakabpa mentions that the Dalai Lama's two younger brothers, a finance secretary, the treasurer, and others (but not the vice-regent) were all sent into exile by the regent Ngawang Tsultrim who had been recalled from Beijing.[324] The regent upbraided the whole administration for allowing the treaty, and instead put Tibet on a war footing, while refusing to send any more tribute, one payment of which had been forwarded to Nepal. He died in 1791, however, forcing a recall of the vice-regent who was en route to Beijing.[325]

The Gurkhas again invaded Tibet, this time penetrating as far as Shigatse where they looted the treasures of Tashi Lhunpo. The Panchen Lama fled to Lhasa where he and the Dalai Lama were urged to flee to Kham by the ambans. The populace, starting to panic, was reassured by the Dalai Lama's refusal to leave Lhasa and further, by the abbots of the three great monasteries who promised to protect the Dalai Lama, the Potala, and the Jokang temple. Tibetan troops started driving the Gurkhas back, aided by an epidemic amongst the Nepalese troops. A Chinese army arrived and together with the Tibetans drove the Nepalese back, penetrating into Nepal almost to the capital. The Sharmapa Tulku poisoned himself and, in the war's aftermath, his goods and estates were confiscated by the Tibetan government. The concluding treaty had the Gurkhas paying tribute to the emperor and returning the looted treasures of Tashi Lhunpo.[326]

→ pp. 384-5. See, Shakabpa, *Tibet: A Political History*, who reports the Tibetan minister Tenzin Paljor Doring, sent to accompany the Chinese army, wrote that the Chinese commanders were reluctant to fight, pp. 158-62. See also, Rockhill, *The Dalai Lamas of Lhasa . . .* , pp. 50-1.

324. Petech, "The Dalai-Lamas and Regents . . . ," also adds, quoting Chinese sources, that the Dalai Lama "was very pious and well read in the sacred texts, but too credulous in front of others and without authority and wisdom", pp. 385-6. Also, Shakabpa, *Tibet: A Political History*, pp. 162-3.

325. Shakabpa, *Tibet: A Political History*, pp. 162-3. See, G. Tucci, *Tibet Land of Snows*, who says it was the Dalai Lama who refused to send the second installment of tribute to the Gurkhas, p. 47.

326. Shakabpa, *Tibet: A Political History*, pp. 164-9. See, Richardson, *Tibet and Its History*, p. 69. Also, Rockhill, *The Dalai Lamas of Lhasa . . .* , pp. 51-3.

The emperor, Ch'ien Lung, ordered a reform of the Tibetan administration as emperors had so often done in the past. The ambans were given more power and the Dalai and Panchen Lamas were to report to them rather than the emperor. Snellgrove and Richardson and Shakabpa point out that the Chinese were only holding up their end of the priest-patron relationship in sending troops to aid Tibet. They also note that Chinese overlordship was short-lived and that the changes of 1792-3 "existed mainly on paper".[327] A more lasting change was the closing of Tibet's borders to all foreigners, likely in response to a similar policy adopted by the Chinese. Shakabpa suggests that the Tibetans did so under pressure from the great monasteries of Lhasa who feared a threat to the Buddhist religion from foreign influences. Tibet would be a closed land throughout the nineteenth century.[328]

The most contentious change imposed on Tibet in 1793 was the introduction of a system to choose the reincarnation of high lamas by lottery. The Chinese felt the choosing of the great ecclesiastical figures in Tibet and Mongolia had been subject to abuse, citing the frequency of occurrences in which *tulkus* were chosen from aristocratic families.[329] A golden urn was sent from China, into which the names of the candidates for a reincarnate lama were to be placed and a winner drawn. However, the first time it was to be used to choose a Dalai Lama the system was ignored.[330]

Jampal Gyatso, the Eighth Dalai Lama, died in 1804. According to Mullin "he exhibited wonderful spiritual qualities mixed with a distaste for political intrigue".[331] His disciple, Tenpe Nyima, the Fourth Panchen Lama, had great respect for him.[332] Because he was concerned with

---

327. Snellgrove & Richardson, *A Cultural History . . .*, p. 226. See, Richardson, *Tibet and Its History*, p. 70. Also, Shakabpa, *Tibet: A Political History*, pp. 169-70. See also, Rockhill, *The Dalai Lamas of Lhasa . . .*, p. 53.
328. Snellgrove & Richardson, *A Cultural History . . .*, pp. 227-8. See, Richardson, *Tibet and Its History*, pp. 71-2. See also, Shakabpa, *Tibet: A Political History*, pp. 173-4.
329. Rockhill, *The Dalai Lamas of Lhasa . . .*, pp. 54-6.
330. Richardson, *Tibet and Its History*, p. 71. See, Shakabpa, *Tibet: A Political History*, p. 172. Also, Malik, *Dalai Lamas of Tibet*, p. 41. See also, Bell, *The Religion of Tibet*, p. 157.
331. Mullin, *Essence . . .*, p. 246.
332. Doboom Tulku, "the lineage of the panchen lamas", p. 8.

religious matters, he left the administration of Tibet to his regents. During his reign Tibet came under Chinese suzerainty once again due to the circumstances of the Tibet-Nepal war. The Eighth Dalai Lama is best remembered for having built the summer palaces of the Dalai Lamas, the Norbulingka, just outside of Lhasa.[333]

Dalai Lama IX

The Ninth Dalai Lama was born at Dan Chokhor in the province of Kham in 1806.[334] There were two candidates for Dalai Lama, the other from Amdo, but preliminary investigations favored the Kham child. When both were brought to Lhasa, the Kham child, who also possessed extreme intelligence, was able to recognize his predecessor's personal effects. The regent announced that the candidate from Kham was the Dalai Lama, bypassing the selection from the golden urn as proposed by the Chinese. In 1808 the envoys, sent by the emperor to examine the Tibetan choice, concurred with the decision on the basis of the child displaying all the requisite signs of a Dalai Lama. The Dalai Lama was subsequently enthroned in the Potala at an impressive ceremony attended by representatives from China, Mongolia, Bhutan, and Nepal. The Fourth Panchen Lama officiated and named him Lungtok Gyatso.[335] At the time Lungtok Gyatso received his *upaseka* ordination from the Panchen Lama as he would his novice ordination in 1812.[336]

In 1810 the regent, Tenpai Genpo Kundeling, died and was replaced by Demo Thubten Jigme who was, it is said, subject to occasional mental disorders. The country was administered quite well, however.[337] In spite of its closed border policy the disguised Englishman, Thomas Manning, was able to enter Tibet in 1811 and

333. Shakabpa, *Tibet: A Political History*, p. 170. Also, Mullin, *Essence . . .*, p. 246.

334. Shakabpa, ., puts the year as 1806, p. 172, as does Jetsun Pema, *Tibet, My Story*, 1997, p. 230. Malik, *Dalai Lamas of Tibet*, p. 179 and Mullin, *Essence . . .* , p. 246, put the year as 1805.

335. Shakabpa, *Tibet: A Political History*, p. 172. See, Gunther Schulemann, *Geschichte Der Dalai-Lamas*, 1958, p. 337. See also, Rockhill, *The Dalai Lamas of Lhasa . . .* , pp. 63-4.

336. Doboom Tulku, "the lineage of the panchen lamas", p. 8.

337. Shakabpa, *Tibet: A Political History*, p. 173.

to have an audience with the young Dalai Lama. Manning described him as having a simple, unaffected manner, a graceful smile, an exuberant yet friendly character, and a natural but reserved bearing.[338]

In 1815 the Dalai Lama, in order to ascertain his future, propitiated the goddess Palden Dorje, implying he had made the traditional journey to the Chokyor Gyal Monastery by the sacred Lama Latso Lake.[339] There was a prophesy that the Ninth Dalai Lama would have "obstacles to his life-span, but . . . should he live to old age would perform the greatest deeds of all the Dalai Lamas".[340] He passed away, however, in 1815, at the age of ten, after attending the Monlam festival and contracting a cold, which led to pneumonia.[341] It was as if, according to Schulemann, Avalokiteshvara had decided to remove the aura of great expectation around the child and not let anything continue. It also appears that death threats and rumors of certain people trying to get rid of the young Dalai Lama were circulating at the time.[342] In any event all Tibet mourned his loss.[343]

Dalai Lama X

The Tenth Dalai Lama was born in 1816 at Litang, in the province of Kham.[344] He was one of three candidates and was soon confirmed as the Dalai Lama by the Kashag and representatives of the three big monasteries. This decision, which was rejected by the imperial regime in 1818, was not made public at the time, and it was made despite the amban's insistence on the use of the golden urn. The parents of the two rival candidates dropped their claims, due to strong public opinion in favour of the Litang child. Also, the ambans accepted the choice already made but managed to convince the newly appointed regent, Lama Jampal Tsultrim of Tsemoling, to announce that the

---

338. Rockhill, *The Dalai Lamas of Lhasa. . .* , p. 64. Also, Schulemann, *Geschichte . . .* , pp. 347-8.
339. Schulemann, *Geschichte . . .* , p. 348.
340. Mullin, *Essence . . .* , p. 246.
341. Shakabpa, *Tibet: A Political History*, p. 174.
342. Schulemann, *Geschichte . . .* , pp. 348-9.
343. Mullin, *Essence . . .* , p. 246.
344. Malik, *Dalai Lamas of Tibet*, p. 179.

Litang candidate had been drawn by lot so as to not offend the emperor. (Shakabpa says this short-sighted action on the part of the regent was to be cited later as proof of so-called Chinese "sovereignty" over Tibet.[345])

The Tenth Dalai Lama was enthroned in 1822. The Fourth Panchen Lama, Tenpe Nyima, performed the hair cutting ceremony at the *upaseka* ordination and gave him the name Tsultrim Gyatso. He later gave him the novice ordination and in 1833 the full ordination. Tenpe Nyima also instructed the Tenth Dalai Lama in the *sutras* and tantras.[346] Lama Geshe Jampal (a *geshe* is one who has attained the Tibetan equivalent of a doctoral degree in religious studies), also instructed the young Dalai Lama.[347] Little is known from the sources consulted about Tsultrim Gyatso's writings except that he composed a Tibetan grammar.[348]

During his reign Tsultrim Gyatso preferred to mingle with the common people, and he was often found with his office clerks, sunning himself. He was in poor health throughout his life despite the ministrations of the best physicians the government could find. Prayer services were often held for the recovery of the Dalai Lama.[349] In 1837 he died, just as he was about to assume full control of the government. It was generally thought in Lhasa that the regent, hoping

---

345. Shakabpa, *Tibet: A Political History*, pp. 174-5. See, Rockhill, *The Dalai Lamas of Lhasa . . .* , who says that the amban Yu Lin was complicit in the attempt to have the Litang candidate recognised without resort to the golden urn. In their discussions, leading to their 1818 decree of rejecting the Tibetan recognition of the Tenth Dalai Lama, the Chinese said the decree should state that the Litang child's name was the first drawn from the vase, pp. 64-6. See also, Petech, "The Dalai-Lamas and Regents . . . ," pp. 387-8.

346. Doboom Tulku, "the lineage of the panchen lamas", p. 8. Also, Mullin, *Essence* . . . , p. 246. See also, Petech, "The Dalai-Lamas and Regents . . . ," pp. 374-5.

347. Schulemann, Geschichte . . . , p. 351.

348. Bell, *Portrait of the Dalai Lama*, who remembers the Thirteenth Dalai Lama pointing out a book he had authored. Bell noticed the author was the Tenth Dalai Lama, p. 109.

349. Shakabpa, *Tibet: A Political History*, p. 176. Also, Mullin, *Essence* . . . . p. 246.

to extend his authority during the minority of the next Dalai Lama, had hastened the death of the Tenth Dalai Lama.[350]

Dalai Lama XI

The Eleventh Dalai Lama was born of poor parents near Garthar, in the province of Kham, in 1838.[351] He was selected from two candidates brought to Lhasa in 1841 and subjected to the usual tests. Shakabpa casts some doubts as to whether this Dalai Lama was chosen according to the lottery, but some accounts, such as Petech's, claim that he was.[352] The Fourth Panchen Lama performed the Eleventh Dalai Lama's hair cutting ceremony, giving him the name Khedrup Gyatso (wise and insightful ocean). The Panchen Lama later instructed the Dalai Lama in the sutras and tantras and in 1846 gave Khedrup Gyatso his novice ordination.[353] The Eleventh Dalai Lama was enthroned in 1844 in the Potala.[354] The young Dalai Lama showed

---

350. Rockhill, *The Dalai Lamas of Lhasa . . .* , adds in a footnote, that documents addressed to the emperor in 1877 and published that year referred to a wound in the neck of the Tenth Dalai Lama and the strong suspicions of the Panchen Lama and the amban who were investigating the conduct of the regent at the time, pp. 66-8. See also, Schulemann, *Geschichte . . .* , who says the cause of death was the collapse of a ceiling on the sleeping Dalai Lama. He adds the regent did not seem overly sad at the news and said very little about it, p. 352. There is some inconsistency as to the date of Tsultrim Gyatso's death with Rockhill and Schulemann, above, putting it in 1838. See, Shakabpa, *Tibet: A Political History*, p. 176, Malik, *Dalai Lamas of Tibet*, p. 179, Mullin, *Essence . . .* , p. 246, and Petech, "The Dalai-Lamas And Regents . . . ," p. 375, who all state the year was 1837.
351. Malik, *Dalai Lamas of Tibet*, p. 179. See, Schulemann, *Geschichte . . .* , p. 353. See also, Mullin, *Essence . . .* , p. 246.
352. Shakabpa, *Tibet: A Political History*, states no details were given. No disputes arose over the selection between the Tibetans and the Chinese, p. 176. See, Petech, "The Dalai-Lamas and Regents . . . ," p. 375. See also, Mullin, *Essence . . .* , who states the Twelfth Dalai Lama was the only one selected from the golden urn, p. 246.
353. Doboom Tulku, "the lineage of the panchen lamas", p. 8. See also, Schulemann, *Geschichte . . .* , p. 353.
354. Schulemann, *Geschichte . . .* , p. 353. See, Rockhill, *The Dalai Lamas of Lhasa . . .* , p. 66. See also, Petech, "The Dalai-Lamas and Regents . . . ," who puts the year as 1842. p. 375.

great understanding and the people were very satisfied with him. His predecessor's *guru*, Lama Geshe Jampal, became his teacher.[355]

During the Eleventh Dalai Lama's reign there was an invasion into western Tibet, in 1841 by the Dogras, who had previously invaded Ladakh. Tibet won that war in 1842.[356] Closer to home, an investigation in 1844 of the regent's activities resulted in his being stripped of power. His estates were confiscated and he was sent into exile in Manchuria but not before some monks of Sera who supported the regent had killed a minister of the Kashag. The regent was accused of abusing his powers and enriching himself at the expense of the people, according to Chinese accounts. Shakabpa, noting that the Tibetan accounts do not give a reason for the investigation, speculates that the principal cause was bad blood between the regent and the Panchen Lama who instigated the investigation. The Panchen Lama later acted as interim administrator while a new regent, Yeshe Gyatso of Reting Monastery, was appointed.[357] The Panchen Lama passed away in 1854.[358] A year later Tibet was once again invaded by the Gurkhas of Nepal who, in the ensuing treaty of 1856, won tribute from Tibet.[359]

In 1855 the Eleventh Dalai Lama, who was still continuing his education, was asked to assume power, which he did in March of that year. His health broke down shortly thereafter, apparently because he was deeply affected by a brutal revolution in China and also unable to bear the rigours of his training and the many ceremonies over which he had to preside. He died of an illness in 1856.[360]

---

355. Schulemann, *Geschichte . . .*, p. 353.

356. Shakabpa, *Tibet: A Political History*, pp. 176-80.

357. Schulemann, *Geschichte . . .*, pp. 352-4. See, Rockhill, *The Dalai Lamas of Lhasa . . .*, pp. 66-7. Also, Shakabpa, *Tibet: A Political History*, p. 180.

358. Doboom Tulku, "the lineage of the panchen lamas", p. 8.

359. Shakabpa, *Tibet: A Political History*, pp. 181-2. See, Richardson, *Tibet and Its History*, p. 72.

360. Petech, "The Dalai-Lamas and Regents . . .," p. 375. See, Shakabpa, *Tibet: A Political History*, p. 181. Also, Schulemann, *Geschichte . . .*, who says the Dalai Lama died in 1855, p. 357. See also, Rockhill, *The Dalai Lamas of Lhasa . . .*, who says there were no grounds to confirm the Dalai Lama had been murdered. He also gives 1855 as the year of death, p. 69, while Mullin, *Essence . . .*, says it was 1856, p. 256.

Dalai Lama XII

The Twelfth Dalai Lama was born in 1856, at Olga, in the province of U.[361] One of three candidates, he was chosen by lot, a method much against the wishes of the people, but at the insistence of the regent. The lottery was held in 1858 during the Monlam festival. No troubles ensued, however, since "the name of the candidate already selected came up first", according to Shakabpa.[362] The Twelfth Dalai Lama was enthroned in the Potala in 1860 with the Reting regent presiding since the newly incarnated Panchen Lama was too young. The Dalai Lama was given the name Trinley Gyatso (renowned wise person of high expectation).[363]

In 1862, using the misuse of the regent's power and the regent's handling of the selection of the Twelfth Dalai Lama as a pretext, a Kashag minister, Wangchuck Gyalpo Shastra, with the backing of the monks of Ganden and Drepung, effected a coup. The regent was deposed and fled to China while Shastra declared himself *desi,* or prime minister. The attendants of the Dalai Lama, who effectively brought the populace into Desi Shastra's camp by having the Dalai Lama publicly confer blessings on the prime minister, had supported him in this. The prime minister put the Dalai Lama in nominal power even though Trinley Gyatso was only a child and still in training. At the request of the emperor the ex-regent had his confiscated property restored to him, but he died before he could return to Tibet.[364]

Desi Shastra died in 1864. Palden Dondup, the most influential minister in the Kashag, appointed the former Tri Rinpoche and teacher of the Dalai Lama, Khenrab Wangchuk, regent to the Dalai Lama. Palden Dhondup became Lord Chamberlain giving him much control over the Dalai Lama. When he threatened to remove the Dalai Lama from office in 1871, Khenrab Wangchuk successfully arranged Palden Dhondup's fall, during which the errant Lord Chamberlain committed

---

361. Malik, *Dalai Lamas of Tibet*, p. 179. See, Petech, "The Dalai-Lamas and Regents . . . ," pp. 375-6.

362. Shakabpa, *Tibet: A Political History*, p. 183.

363. Schulemann, *Geschichte* . . . , p. 357. See, Shakabpa, *Tibet: A Political History*, p. 183.

364. Shakabpa, *Tibet: A Political History*, pp. 183-7. Also see, Petech, "The Dalai-Lamas and Regents . . . ," pp. 390-1.

suicide.[365] His body was decapitated and the head displayed in public as a lesson to all. These events so shocked the young Dalai Lama that he eschewed all company and wandered about as though demented.[366]

When Khenrab Wangchuk died in 1872 the Dalai Lama was asked to assume his temporal responsibilities. He did so in 1873 but only ruled for two years before passing away in 1875. Two favourites of the Dalai Lama, who seemed to be able to influence him, were later imprisoned and exiled, having been accused of hastening the Dalai Lama's illness.[367] It seems that Trinley Gyatso, quite ill and sickly, made the journey to the sacred Lama Latso Lake. Shortly thereafter he died.[368]

Amongst Tibetans there is considerable speculation concerning the early deaths of Dalai Lamas nine through twelve. A natural inference is that at least one or two of them were killed by the regent of the day, not wishing to release his grip on power.[369] Another theory, according to Norbu and Turnbull, is that these Dalai Lamas were poisoned, either by "Tibetans for being Chinese-appointed imposters or by the Chinese for not being properly manageable".[370] It would seem the perfect opportunity was the visit of the Dalai Lama to the sacred Lhamoi Latso Lake, made to secure a vision of his future and to propitiate the goddess Mogsomora, the protector of all incarnations of Avalokiteshvara. Only the Dalai Lama could enter her shrine, a visit requiring proper preparation. Perhaps because of their age or because they were imposters, the theory goes, these four died shortly after the traditional visit to the lake. It is also possible they were poisoned by cooks in the Dalai Lama's retinue or by the regents when the Dalai Lama was given a specially prepared pill, meant to

---

365. Shakabpa, *Tibet: A Political History*, pp. 188-9. See, Petech, "The Dalai-Lamas and Regents . . . ", pp. 391-2. Also, Bell, *The Religion of Tibet*, p. 158.
366. Schulemann, *Geschichte . . .* , p. 358. Also, Bell, *The Religion of Tibet*, pp. 158-9.
367. Shakabpa, *Tibet: A Political History*, p. 190.
368. Petech, "The Dalai-Lamas and Regents . . . ", p. 376
369. Bell, *The Religion of Tibet*, p. 159.
370. Norbu & Turnbull, *Tibet*, p. 311.

increase his vitality.[371] Whatever the causes, the early deaths of these Dalai Lamas had a destabilising effect on Tibetan affairs.[372] Tibet was desperately in need of strong, reliable leadership. The Thirteenth Dalai Lama would fill that void.

Dalai Lama XIII

The Thirteenth Dalai Lama was born in mid-1876 at Thakpo Langdun in south-east Tibet. His father, Kungah Rinchin, and his mother, Lobsang Dolma, both of peasant stock were known for their deep faith, compassion, and wisdom.[373] According to the Tibetan biographies consulted by Mullin, many miraculous signs preceded and accompanied his birth.[374] Signs provided by the Twelfth Dalai Lama when he died initially guided the search committee under the new regent. The Twelfth Dalai Lama had passed away seated in meditation and facing south. But shortly thereafter his head had turned to the south-east as it did later, while he lay in his coffin. The Nechung oracle next described the landscape where the birth would take place and the names of the parents. A former abbot of Gyudto, one of the tantric colleges, received a vision through the frozen surface of the sacred Lhamoi Latso Lake. It was of the child incarnation with his parents and of their home in its distinctive surroundings and landscape. Guided by these signs, the child was discovered and found to bear the distinctive body markings of a Dalai Lama. A year later, as the boy was but ten months old when discovered, he was given the usual tests. The child was recognized from amongst two other candidates as the reincarnation of the Twelfth Dalai Lama.[375]

---

371. Norbu & Turnbull, *Tibet*, pp. 311-12. See, Bell, *Portrait of the Dalai Lama*, pp. 49-50. Also, Schulemann, *Geschichte . . .* , who says the ambans' involvement in the deaths were never fully explained, p. 359. See also, Rockhill, *The Dalai Lamas of Lhasa . . .* , who suggests these Dalai Lamas were not robust enough to withstand the rigours demanded of a Dalai Lama and were possibly, upon "reaching manhood . . . physical and mental wrecks" who died of natural causes, p. 70.
372. Mullin, *Essence . . .* , p. 256.
373. Shakabpa, *Tibet: A Political History*, p. 192. See, Mullin, *Path of the Bodhisattva Warrior*, 1988, p. 19. Also, Malik, *Dalai Lamas of Tibet*, p. 179.
374. Mullin, *Path . . .* , pp. 19-21.
375. Mullin, *Path . . .* , pp. 22-6. See, Bell, *Portrait . . .* , pp. 40-2. Also, Shakabpa, *Tibet: A Political History*, p. 192. See also, Norbu & Turnbull, *Tibet*, p. 312.

In 1878 the young incarnation was brought in procession to Lhasa. The Fifth Panchen Lama, Tenpe Wangchuk, performed the hair cutting ceremony and preliminary ordination of the Thirteenth Dalai Lama, naming him Thubten Gyatso. Thubten Gyatso spent the next year at Samteling Monastery just north of Lhasa undergoing the training and preparation necessary for his formal enthronement. His principal guru was Purchokpa Jampa Gyatso, though the regent, Tatsak Rinpoche, was named his senior tutor.[376] Another reason for the wait was the "blessing" and confirmation of Lhasa's choice by the emperor. The golden urn lottery had not been used. Because the choice had been so clear, Beijing did not contest it.[377] Subsequently, in 1879 the Thirteenth Dalai Lama was installed and enthroned in the Potala.[378]

The training and education of Thubten Gyatso began in earnest after he presided over the Monlam Prayer Festival for the first time, an event he was to dedicate much energy to; restoring it to a level of prestige enjoyed during the reigns of the early Dalai Lamas. Besides Purchokpa, the regent and the Panchen Lama, close to 100 respected teachers taught the Thirteenth Dalai Lama. These studies were primarily in the Gelugpa tradition but also drew strongly from the Nyingmapa tradition as well. In this regard the Thirteenth followed the example of the Fifth more closely than any other Dalai Lama. He was even considered a terton, or Nyingmapa treasure finder.[379]

Practice was considered of paramount importance. Thubten Gyatso would typically rise at four a.m. for a lengthy period of prayer and meditation before proceeding to his studies. He would also periodically enter into a prolonged meditation retreat in order to further his practice. The first of these, while still a young child, lasted

---

376. Mullin, *Path . . .* , who notes Purchokpa was much loved by Thubten Gyatso. Later Purchokpa's reincarnation would write the biography of the Thirteenth Dalai Lama, pp. 26-9. See also, Shakabpa, *Tibet: A Political History*, p. 193.

377. Mullin, *Path . . .* , pp. 32-3. See, Bell, *Portrait . . .* , p. 46. See, Shakabpa, *Tibet: A Political History*, p. 192. Also, Petech, "The Dalai-Lamas and Regents . . . ," pp. 376-7. See also, Rockhill, *The Dalai Lamas of Lhasa . . .* , who claims the lottery was resorted to in selecting the Thirteenth Dalai Lama, p. 71.

378. Mullin, *Path . . .* , pp. 33-4. See, Shakabpa, *Tibet: A Political History*, p. 193.

379. Mullin, *Path . . .* , pp. 34-40.

two months and twenty-five days.[380] He was a keen student and deeply interested in his religious studies. By the age of twelve he was able to successfully engage in debate with monks and scholars from the three principle monastic universities. As his *guru* Purchokpa later commented, "no one who was there had the slightest doubt that he was truly the incarnation of Avalokiteshvara, . . . all we could do was look on in awe".[381] In 1898, at the age of twenty-three, the Thirteenth Dalai Lama stood for his *geshe* exams, culminating an outstanding academic career by debating with the best scholars in the land over a period of six weeks and before audiences of up to 20,000 monks.[382]

Though he was to be thoroughly occupied with secular affairs throughout his life, the Thirteenth Dalai Lama strove to maintain his spiritual practices. He meditated four times daily and often did short meditation retreats. His first attempt at the traditional three-year retreat was broken after fourteen months due to the British invasion of 1903. He was, however, able to complete this retreat and its preliminaries from 1916 to 1920, in the process gaining "complete inner experience of the essence of the Vajra Vehicle" and upholding the legacy of the early Dalai Lamas.[383]

His writings not only reflected his devotion to spiritual practice but also his many activities in the religious and temporal spheres. These comprised several hundred titles arranged in seven volumes. Although he wrote no textbooks he did compose biographies, many sermons, liturgical works, tantric writings, letters of advice to individuals and monasteries, personal and official letters, guidebooks to the temples he had restored, as well as much prose and poetry. His scholarly output matched that of the First, Third, Fifth, and Seventh Dalai Lamas, in both quantity and quality.[384] In addition to his writings and like all Dalai Lamas, the Thirteenth had a myriad of religious duties to perform. Throughout his life he would be called upon to confirm or even locate the reincarnations of the important incarnate lamas of the land. He performed thousands of ordinations and

---

380. Mullin, *Path . . .*, p. 35. Also, Bell, *Portrait . . .*, p. 47.
381. *Ibid.*, p. 35. Also, Bell, *Portrait . . .*, p. 48. See also, Malik, *Dalai Lamas of Tibet*, p. 44.
382. Mullin *Path . . .*, pp. 41-2.
383. *Ibid.*, pp. 42-3. See also, Bell, *Portrait . . .*, p. 214.
384. Mullin, *Path . . .*, pp. 93-7.

initiations as well. He gave the Sixth Panchen Lama, Chokyi Nyima, his novice ordination in 1888 and the full ordination in 1902.[385] The Dalai Lama also had students and was "dedicated to raising the standard of scholarship in the monasteries", according to the Fourteenth Dalai Lama.[386]

The regent, Demo Trinley Rabgyas, of Tengyeling Monastery, who was reluctant to relinquish power, delayed the Dalai Lama's accession to temporal power for two years. After the Dalai Lama's empowerment ceremony in 1895, the now ex-regent and his brothers were found conspiring to bring about the death of the Dalai Lama by means of sorcery. Through the warnings and revelations of the Nechung oracle magical incantations had been discovered in a pair of boots destined as a gift for the Dalai Lama. The Dalai Lama, an opponent of capital punishment, forbade the death penalty, but the perpetrators were jailed for life. Later, the monks of Tengyeling, unable to let go of their resentment at the treatment of the ex-regent, circulated the prophecy that Thubten Gyatso would be the last Dalai Lama. They would also fight on the side of the Chinese during the 1910 invasion of Tibet, prompting the government to order the destruction of Tengyeling Monastery.[387]

It was noted earlier that Tibet had, at China's suggestions, adopted an isolationist policy. Their experience with proselytizing Christian missionaries, who showed little regard for Buddhism, if not outright disdain, instilled in Tibetans the fear that the British would attempt to destroy their religion. There were also fears of being colonized as Tibet watched the British steadily encroach upon the Himalayan frontier with their annexations of several regions within the Tibetan cultural sphere.[388] This was the era of the "Great Game", a struggle between the Russian and British Empires for control of central Asia.[389]

---

385. Doboom Tulku, "the lineage of the panchen lamas", p. 9. See, Mullin, *Path* . . . , pp. 14, 91.

386. The Fourteenth Dalai Lama, *Freedom In Exile*, 1990, p. 35. Also, Mullin, *Path* . . . , pp. 14, 38.

387. Mullin, *Path* . . . , pp. 43-9. See, Shakabpa, *Tibet: A Political History*, pp. 195-6. Also, Bell, *Portrait* . . . , pp. 53-6. See also, Malik, *Dalai Lamas of Tibet*, pp. 43-4.

388. Mullin, *Path* . . . , pp. 48-54. See, Richardson, *Tibet and Its History*, p. 71. See also, Bell, *Portrait* . . . , p. 60.

389. Peter Hopkirk, *Tresspassers on the Roof of the World*, 1995, p. 3.

The British, who were interested in expanding their trade into Tibet and also to use Tibet as a natural buffer to Russian southward expansion, negotiated treaties with China in 1876, 1890, and 1893. The British recognised Chinese control over Tibet as a means of checking Russia. The Chinese recognised Britain's annexation of Burma and gave permission for the British to enter Tibet. The Tibetans, who had not been consulted, repeatedly refused to negotiate with the British, and in 1887 established an armed garrison within Sikkim's borders which the British were forced to drive out. The British finally realized that Chinese control over Tibet was a fiction.[390]

Russia's expansion of her empire, having covered much of northern Asia, was pushing towards the Himalayas. Tibet had some natural links with Russia through the Kalmuks and Buriat Mongols, Buddhist adherents, who were now part of the Russian domain. A Buriat monk called Dorjieff, who had risen to be a trusted teacher of the Dalai Lama, made trips to Russia in 1898 and 1901, which resulted in the exchange of gifts and invitations between the Czar and the Dalai Lama. This set off alarm bells in British India, especially with the new viceroy, Lord Curzon, who was an expert on Russian affairs.[391]

Lord Curzon, realizing that only direct negotiations with Lhasa would secure relations with Tibet, ordered an armed trade mission into Tibet. The expeditionary force under Colonel Younghusband met Tibetan resistance, and several battles ensued en route to Lhasa, with the ill-equipped Tibetans suffering significant losses. In 1904, as the British force neared Lhasa, the Dalai Lama fled towards Mongolia leaving the Ganden Tri Rinpoche as regent. The treaty, which was forced on Tibet, called for that country to recognize the British protectorate over Sikkim, to accept the establishment of three trade marts within Tibetan borders, and to prevent other foreign nations from exercizing influence in Tibet. On their return to India the British left a representative at Gyantse who promptly established a rapport with the Panchen Lama. A month later the Panchen Lama travelled

---

390. Mullin, *Path . . .* , pp. 54-6. See, Shakabpa, *Tibet: A Political History*, who quotes the British political officer of Sikkim, Claude White, as saying the Chinese had "no authority whatever in Tibet" and "was suzerain over Tibet only in name", pp. 196-204. See also, Bell, *Portrait . . .* , pp. 60-1.

391. Richardson, *Tibet and Its History*, pp. 78-82. See, Mullin, *Path . . .* , pp. 57-9. See also, Bell, *Portrait . . .* , pp. 61-2.

to India where he met the Prince of Wales and Lord Minto. This created much discord between the Panchen Lama and Lhasa.[392]

The Dalai Lama travelled to Mongolia, stopping to give blessings and teachings to the hundreds of nomadic tribes who came to see him. In Urga (modern-day Ulan Bator) he was the guest of the Jetsun Dampa Lama, the head of Mongolian Buddhism. Pilgrims from surrounding regions came to seek his blessings and Russian diplomats visited him. He also sent Dorjieff to consult with the Czar. Some scholars report that the Mongolian hierarch became jealous of the Dalai Lama and resentful of the tribute and attention accorded to him, even though Thubten Gyatso had been Jetsun Dampa's *guru*. Mullin says there is no evidence to support this, and likely the story resulted from rumors started by the British who were frustrated at having let the Dalai Lama escape.[393]

In 1906 Thubten Gyatso travelled to eastern Tibet where he visited numerous monasteries, giving teachings and blessings. At Kumbum, an invitation to visit Beijing arrived as well as requests to return to Lhasa. The British and Russians, who were negotiating with each other, sent advice for him to refuse the request from China. The eventual Anglo-Russian treaty of 1907 saw Tibet established as a buffer state between British India and Russia, under nominal Chinese suzerainty. In the face of these uncertainties the Dalai Lama sent

392. Shakabpa, *Tibet: A Political History*, says the Tibetan government felt the Dalai Lama should leave in case he was forced to sign any long-term treaty harmful to Tibet. He also says that under the Anglo-Tibetan Convention of 1904 China was seen as a foreign power, pp. 205-20. See, Richardson, *Tibet and Its History*, pp. 82-90. Also, Bell, *Portrait . . .*, pp. 62-3. See also, Mullin, *Path . . .*, who points out that the Anglo-Tibetan dispute of 1904 was a "collision of two radically different cultures: the one intensely spiritual and the other both militant and secular". While the British were anxious to settle affairs with Tibet, the Tibetans were proceeding at their customary casual pace. The Dalai Lama must have felt there was no immediate danger, for he was in the middle of a three-year retreat when he was forced to leave Lhasa. Also of interest are the non-worldly reasons given, in one of his Tibetan biographies, for the Dalai Lama's departure. These included the needs of trainees in Mongolia and China for his attentions and the wish of the Dalai Lama to visit the holy places to the north and in China, pp. 65-7.

393. Mullin, *Path . . .*, pp. 68-70. See, Bell, *Portrait . . .*, pp. 65-8. Also, Shakabpa, *Tibet: A Political History*, pp. 220-1.

orders to Lhasa, including the appointment of a new prime minister. He accepted the emperor's invitation but determined, first of all, to attend to his spiritual responsibilities; he then made a pilgrimage to a sacred mountain in China.[394]

The Thirteenth Dalai Lama visited Beijing in 1908, being greeted with a grand reception, and staying at the Yellow Palace built for the Fifth Dalai Lama. He was in a much weaker position than the Fifth had been; none the less, he refused to meet the emperor when told he would be required to *kowtow* (bow low in the manner of a visiting vassal). Demanding equal treatment, he waited while arrangements were made for him to meet the emperor and empress dowager (the real power at the time). He had meetings with a number of foreign delegations and negotiated with the Chinese over their abuses in the province of Kham, where they were asserting their authority. When the empress died, preceded by the emperor by one day, the Dalai Lama was asked to officiate at the funeral. He later attended the enthronement of the new and last Manchu emperor of China. From the Chinese standpoint, it was hoped that the Dalai Lama would be subordinate to the emperor, and that more influence in Tibet could be arranged. From the Tibetan standpoint, the Dalai Lama later wrote that he went to discuss the duties of the emperor as patron within the priest-patron relationship earlier re-established by the Fifth Dalai Lama.[395]

The Dalai Lama's return to Lhasa was slowed by religious preoccupations, since he was required to visit monasteries on the

---

394. Mullin, *Path . . .* , who also notes that the British had attempted to set-up the Panchen Lama as a replacement to the Dalai Lama, but the Panchen Lama had refused, pp. 70-3. See, Shakabpa, *Tibet: A Political History*, p. 221. See also, Rockhill, *The Dalai Lamas of Lhasa. . .* , who met the Dalai Lama at the sacred mountain Wu-tai-shan. Rockhill says the Dalai Lama was induced to visit Beijing by an announcement that the Panchen Lama had requested an audience with the emperor, pp. 220-1.

395. Bell, *Portrait . . .* , notes that the Dalai Lama bent one knee to the ground while greeting the emperor, pp. 72-7. See, Mullin, *Path . . .* , pp. 73-4. Also, Shakabpa, *Tibet: A Political History*, pp. 221-3. See also, Rockhill, *The Dalai Lamas of Lhasa . . .* , pp. 77-8. (It is of interest to watch the opening scenes of Bernardo Bertolucci's 1987 film, "The Last Emperor". Prominent in the vast retinue assembled for the young emperor's enthronement are numbers of yellow-hatted Tibetan monks.)

way to teach and give blessings. He also paused for sometime to restore discipline at Kumbum, in spite of resistance from the monastery. It was a year before he reached Lhasa.[396] In the meantime, China, determined to check growing British influence in Tibet, had launched an invasion into eastern Tibet. The sacrilegious behaviour of the Chinese troops was resented fiercely by the Tibetans. In 1910, barely two months after his arrival in Lhasa, the Dalai Lama and his ministers were forced to flee the Chinese advance. Were it not for the heroic rearguard actions of a few Tibetan soldiers the Dalai Lama might have been captured by the Chinese who had put a price on his head.[397]

Seeking asylum in India, where Charles Bell was assigned to act as his British liaison, the Dalai Lama asked the British to intervene; London, however, had decided to remain neutral. Appeals to the Czar and Nepal for assistance only brought non-committal replies. Upon hearing that the Chinese had declared the Dalai Lama deposed, Thubten Gyatso decided never to have direct negotiations with the Chinese. The Chinese for their part soon discovered it was a mistake to depose the Dalai Lama since the populace responded by harassing the Chinese in every way possible. The Chinese requested the Dalai Lama to return, and take up office under Manchu administration, but the Dalai Lama refused. Tibetan resistance was organized and began to have some effect on the Chinese, who were suffering as a result of internal dissension. When revolution in China broke out, the Tibetans increased their efforts by openly declaring war in 1912. The Dalai Lama and his ministers had orchestrated all these efforts from India. In the meantime, the Dalai Lama had maintained his spiritual practices and religious responsibilities, receiving visitors for

---

396. Bell, *Portrait . . .*, p. 78. See, Shakabpa, *Tibet: A Political History*, p. 223. Also, Mullin, *Path . . .*, p. 74.

397. Shakabpa, *Tibet: A Political History*, gives considerable detail as to the murders of thousands of monks and the looting of their monasteries during the Chinese advance into Tibet, pp. 224-30. See, Mullin, *Path. . . .*, pp. 74-6. See also, Bell, *Portrait . . .*, pp. 82-9. See also, Richardson, *Tibet and Its History*, pp. 97-8. See also, Tucci, *Tibet Land of Snows*, who says the Chinese invasion of 1910 was sparked by a revolt in eastern Tibet, p. 51.

blessings, and making a retreat to the main Buddhist pilgrimage sites in India.[398]

The Tibetans were able to subdue the Chinese troops so that the Dalai Lama could enter Lhasa in early 1913. He ordered that all the Chinese be driven out of Tibet. Chinese prisoners were shown leniency and returned to China via India as per British requests. The Dalai Lama declared Tibet independent and in the process he outlined five principal policies for implementation. The first was the preservation of Tibetan cultural traditions. Mutual respect through the observation of religious traditions, with less involvement of religious institutions in politics and business, was another. Others included a fairer and more just administration, with the abolition of capital punishment, a national defense policy, and the reform and modernization of land distribution and taxation.[399] The Dalai Lama took measures to secure the country by raising and equipping an army. He later appointed a governor in Kham and sent troops to control the area which still had a Chinese military presence close to the eastern frontier.[400]

In the hope that Tibet's independence would be acknowledged by treaty, the Dalai Lama pressed for negotiations between Tibet, China, and Britain. The British, however, did not wish to antagonize the new Chinese regime led by Sun Yat Sen and, with strong persuasion, the Tibetans agreed to a nominal Chinese suzerainty over the provinces of Amdo and Kham, which were now referred to as Outer Tibet. The Chinese never did sign the 1914 Simla Convention. Later, the decision reached in Simla, namely, that Tibet was an autonomous region, proved to be an obstacle to Tibetan admission into the League of Nations and its successor the United Nations.[401]

Having secured Tibetan autonomy, the Dalai Lama set to work implementing the changes he had proposed in his declaration of

---

398. Shakabpa, *Tibet: A Political History*, pp. 230-42. See, Mullin, *Path . . .* , who notes that the visits of the Thirteenth Dalai Lama to re-consecrate the chief Buddhist pilgrimage sites rekindled lagging interest in them. This work has been carried on by the present Dalai Lama, pp. 76-80. Also, Bell, *Portrait . . .* , pp. 90-125. See also, Richardson, *Tibet and its History*, pp. 100-1.

399. Mullin, *Path . . .* , pp. 80-1. See, Shakabpa, *Tibet: A Political History*, pp. 242-8.

400. Shakabpa, *Tibet: A Political History*, pp. 250-1.

401. Mullin, *Path . . .* , pp. 80-3. See, Tucci, *Tibet Land of Snows*, p. 51.

independence. As mentioned, he tried to build an army, having realized foreign powers could not be relied on to defend Tibet. The military was to be run along Japanese lines since Japanese training methods were considered superior. After 1920 Tibet adopted a British orientation in military affairs. The Thirteenth Dalai Lama also ordered an overhaul of the monastic communities and their educational facilities as well as of medical colleges and hospitals. He encouraged the performing arts and fine arts. He ordered the political institutions to start reorganizing themselves. By 1916, feeling his reforms were in motion, the Dalai Lama entered into a three-year retreat.[402]

In order to meet the expenses of maintaining a standing army, the system of taxation was revised. Monasteries and families with large estates that formerly paid little tax now had to pay according to the size of their holdings. The Tashi Lhunpo authorities, when their taxes were raised significantly, felt they were being punished for their role in the Chinese invasion of 1910. At the time, the Panchen Lama, at the urging of his followers, seemed to curry favour with the Chinese. The Chinese had, of course, long tried to exploit the position of the Panchan Lama's office, setting it in opposition to the Dalai Lama's office. The Chinese offered to place the Panchen Lama at the head of the government in Tibet, as the British had tried to do during the Dalai Lama's flight in 1904. Once again the Panchen Lama declined, though he was apparently tempted. The Dalai Llama's centralization policies threatened Tashi Lhunpo's autonomy. That, combined with the Panchen Lama's apparent desire for a more expanded role, caused him and his court to leave suddenly, in 1923, on a purported teaching tour to China. The Panchen Lama never did return to Tibet, though his officials and Lhasa made several attempts to negotiate his return. It was a sad situation as the Dalai Lama and Panchen Lama were personally quite fond of each other, showing that fondness whenever they were together, with the Dalai Lama even restraining his officials from retaliating against Tashi Lhunpo. The Panchen Lama controversy would prove itself to be quite injurious to Tibet.[403]

---

402. Mullin, *Path . . .*, pp. 84-6.

403. Mullin, *Path . . .*, pp. 99-107. See, Shakabpa, *Tibet: A Political History*, pp. 237-8, 243, 263-4. Also, Bell, *Portrait . . .*, pp. 362-3. See also, Tucci, *Tibet Land of Snows*, pp. 51-2. See also, Richardson, *Tibet and Its History*, pp. 125-7.

Except for the period of his three-year retreat, the Dalai Lama worked very hard to reform Tibetan society. Aside from the general reforms that were mentioned earlier, he reformed those corrupt administrative practices at the Great Prayer Festival, which had led to the people staying away from it. He personally supervised the final exams for the *geshe* degree, which had also become subject to corruption and bribery. He restored Tibet's oldest temples and monasteries including their art works. He had new editions of the Tibetan scriptural collection, the *Kangyur*, printed. During the process he had the editor-in-chief removed when it was found that certain interpretations were slanted towards that editor's monastery of Drepung. The Dalai Lama finished the work himself. He punished monk officials who were found to be oppressing tenants on the monastic estates.[404] The Dalai Lama was able to tighten up monastic discipline and reduce the pervasive monastic influence on government. While this eventually came to be appreciated by the monasteries, as it allowed them to concentrate on spiritual matters,[405] there was so much resistance to the Dalai Lama's reforms that he was impelled to slow down the process of reformation. He was simply moving too fast for Tibetan opinion, according to Richardson.[406]

The Dalai Lama had tried to use the opportunity presented by contact with the modern world to modernize Tibet. Under constant pressure from the monastic institutions, which saw little benefit from British influence including British failure to contain China, the Dalai Lama allowed those innovations, which mostly acted as deterrents to monastic rule. The Dalai Lama's efforts at modernization were designed to bring Tibet to a point where it could hold its own against others while maintaining a state of balance between its powerful neighbours.[407]

Malik says the Dalai Lama took a pragmatic approach to the political necessities facing Tibet.[408] He was a man of action who was often impulsive and quick-tempered, though cheerful and kindly in

---

404. Mullin, *Path . . .*, pp. 86-9. Norbu & Turnbull, *Tibet*, pp. 316-17.
405. Norbu & Turnbull, *Tibet*, p. 319.
406. Richardson, *Tibet and Its History*, p. 131.
407. Snellgrove & Richardson, *A Cultural History . . .*, p. 244. See, Malik, *Dalai Lamas of Tibet*, p. 55.
408. Malik, *Dalai Lamas of Tibet*, p. 55.

disposition. The former traits he tended to display with his officials, the latter, with his people at large. It was said he possessed miraculous powers and psychic abilities, which he apparently displayed on one occasion when, observing some monks improperly performing their rites during the Great Prayer Festival, he stamped his foot to redirect their attentions. An imprint of the Dalai Lama's foot was left in the stone verandah of the Jokang temple.[409]

The Dalai Lama devoted the last decade of his life to the essential duties of a lama: teaching, philosophical discussion, and composing spiritual treatises.[410] He continued his tireless revival, promotion, and promulgation of Tibetan culture. He was able to hold the Chinese at bay, even as he hoped for a change in British attitudes. The general populace loved him for his unyielding stance on corruption, exemplified by his harsh attitude towards his officials. For this he came to be called the Great Thirteenth. He had improved the lot of the people so far as systems of education, medicine, justice, and government were concerned, taking an active role in these reforms. Thus it was that he was asked for his advice as to what could further be done, when, in 1932, the Nechung oracle warned him of dangers to his life.[411]

In his final testament, the Thirteenth Dalai Lama reviewed his life and his work. He warned the Tibetan people that the communists, who were actively seeking power in China, posed a great danger to them with their antipathy towards religion. He prophesized the destruction of Tibet and its culture if steps were not immediately taken to build a strong, modern army. He then hinted it would not be long before he passed away. His words proved to be prophetic, for much of what he predicted in this testament came to pass, including his own death, of an illness, one year later in 1933.[412]

Bell conjectures that the Thirteenth Dalai Lama died due to overwork.[413] One Tibetan theory states that he chose to die when he

---

409. Malik, *Dalai Lamas of Tibet*, p. 48. See, Bell, *Portrait . . .* , pp. 169, 296-7. Also, Mullin, *Path . . .* , p. 91.

410. Mullin, *Path . . .* , p. 107.

411. *Ibid.*, pp. 107-8.

412. *Ibid.*, pp. 109-14. See, Shakabpa, *Tibet: A Political History*, pp. 270-1. Also, Malik, *Dalai Lamas of Tibet*, pp. 49-54.

413. Bell, *Portrait . . .* , p. 388.

did so that his reincarnation would be in the vigour of youth when the communist blow fell on Tibet.[414] Whatever the case, he would be remembered as a tireless worker for Tibetan welfare and the Buddhist religion.[415] The present Dalai Lama, in recalling the achievements of the Great Thirteenth, mentions how his predecessor improved living standards, reorganised the army, sent students abroad to study, established industry and electrical service, introduced postal and telegraph services, made changes in the Gelugpa monastic curriculum, and concluded a number of international agreements.[416] The Fourteenth Dalai Lama also tells of the time when the Great Thirteenth, on his way back from China, paused in the village of Taktser, and remarked on the beauty of the house where the present Dalai Lama was born. After some meditation the Dalai Lama said he would like to return to the area. Leaving behind a pair of boots at a nearby monastery, the Great Thirteenth rode off to Lhasa.[417]

Dalai Lama XIV

After the death of the Thirteenth Dalai Lama it was some two years before the birth, in 1935, of the Fourteenth Dalai Lama. A mood of despondency was prevalent within the nation, and political conditions were marked by instability. The Chinese Nationalist government, refusing to recognize Tibetan independence, was pushing further into the eastern districts. China had established an unofficial representation at Lhasa when the condolence mission, sent to pay respects to the Great Thirteenth, simply stayed on. A former commander-in-chief of the army and advisor to the Dalai Lama, Lungshar, tried to overthrow the government of Tibet and establish a republic; as a result of this attempt, he was blinded and imprisoned for life. The regent, Reting Rinpoche, who had been a favorite of the Thirteenth Dalai Lama, was barely out of his teens. He was somewhat frivolous and had allowed himself to be influenced by Lungshar. Furthermore, the

414. Mullin, *Path . . .*, pp. 114-15.
415. Malik, *Dalai Lamas of Tibet*, pp. 54-5.
416. The Fourteenth Dalai Lama, *My Land and My People*, 1962, p. 73.
417. *Ibid.*, p. 24. See, Mullin, *Path . . .*, pp. 11-12.

Panchen Lama, a highly revered figure, was still in exile, his return being negotiated.[418]

When Thubten Gyatso's embalmed body sat in state in a southward-facing direction his head turned to the east on two occasions. A large star-shaped fungus was found on the north-east pillar of the chapel containing the body. These and other signs prompted the regent to seek a vision in the sacred Lhamoi Latso Lake. After receiving one, the regent consulted the Nechung oracle who directed search parties to the east. The party sent to Amdo found that a temple at Kumbum Monastery and the house where a likely candidate was found conformed to the regent's vision. This house, in the village of Taktser, was the same one that the Thirteenth Dalai Lama had remarked upon while in the area in 1909. The young boy, now two years of age, was one of three candidates suggested by the Panchen Lama, whom the search party had sought out at Jyekundo in Chinese-controlled eastern Tibet. The boy, whose favourite game was pretending to go to Lhasa, recognised members of the search party and, upon testing, was able to unerringly select his predecessor's belongings from amongst clever imitations. Furthermore, Lhamo Dondup, for that was his name, bore all the distinctive body markings of a Dalai Lama. All of this was a surprise to his father, Chokyong Tsering, and his mother, Sonam Tsomo, both humble farmers. They had already produced a high-ranking *tulku* in Thubten Jigme Norbu, the Taktser Rinpoche, who was at Kumbum.[419]

---

418. Michael Goodman, *The Last Dalai Lama*, 1986, p. 8. See, Richardson, *Tibet and Its History*, pp. 139-43. Also, Shakabpa, *Tibet: A Political History*, pp. 274-7. See also, John Powers, *Introduction to Tibetan Buddhism*, 1995, who says Reting Rinpoche proved to be corrupt and heavy-handed, that he was known to have sexual relations with women, was rumoured to be homosexual as well, and that popular resentment grew against him, p. 161.

419. Goodman, *The Last . . .*, pp. 7-15. See, Claude Levenson, *The Dalai Lama*, 1988, pp. 47-53. Also, Shakabpa, *Tibet: A Political History*, who accompanied the regent to Lhamoi Latso Lake, reports the regent was contemplating his resignation after receiving the vision. Shakabpa goes on to detail how the Tibetan government, though wishing the Panchen Lama to return quickly to Tibet, in accordance with the terms negotiated by the Thirteenth Dalai Lama, balked when the Chinese insisted on an armed escort of 500 soldiers to accompany the Panchen Lama. Chokyi Nyima passed away in Jyekundo in 1937 and his body was returned to

→

Lhamo Dondup was kept at Kumbum for two years, under the care of a paternal uncle and in companionship with his two brothers who were monks there. The long delay in taking Lhamo Dondup to Lhasa resulted from the demands of the local Chinese warlord for a huge ransom before allowing the boy's departure.[420] The party, including the parents, finally left in 1939, arriving to find a huge reception at Lhasa. Those who witnessed these proceedings remarked on the composure of the four-year old Dalai Lama. In October of 1939 the regent performed the hair cutting ceremony and *getsul* (novice) ordination of the Dalai Lama, naming him Tenzin Gyatso.[421] In February of 1940 he was enthroned in the Potala before a large assembly of monks and abbots with representatives from neighbouring countries in attendance. His senior tutor, Reting Rinpoche, and junior tutor, Taktra Rinpoche, presided. The British representative, Sir Basil Gould, later remarked on how the young incarnation's "attention never wavered" and on his "infallible skill in doing the right thing to the right person at the right time".[422]

Tenzin Gyatso settled into the Potala accompanied by his older brother, Lobsang Samten, who had been a novice monk at Kumbum. His family, who now only saw him from time to time, called the Dalai Lama, Kundun (the Presence). His life was taken over by adult monks.

→ Tashi Lhunpo, pp. 278-83. See also, Doboom Tulku, "the lineage of panchen lamas", p. 9. See also, Powers, *Introduction* . . . , pp. 164-7. See also, Bell, *Portrait* . . . , pp. 397-8.

420. Powers, *Introduction* . . . , p. 168. See, Goodman, *The Last* . . . , pp. 15-18. Also, Levenson, *The Dalai Lama*, pp. 53-4. See also, Bell, *Portrait* . . . , who adds that the governor and the abbots of Kumbum were reluctant to let the young child be taken to Lhasa unless he was declared to be the Dalai Lama, a fact Lhasa wished to keep secret, pp. 398-9.

421. Shakabpa, *Tibet: A Political History*, p. 285. See, Tenzin Gyatso, The Fourteenth Dalai Lama, *Freedom In Exile*, 1990, who says that at the time of his getsul ordination there were rumours the Reting Regent, having broken his vows of celibacy, was not fit to perform the ceremony, pp. 17-18.

422. Goodman, *The Last* . . . , pp. 65-9. See, Shakabpa, *Tibet: A Political History*, who notes that the Chinese claimed their representative Wu Chung-hsin had been sent to officiate at the enthronement, pp. 285-6. Also, Richardson, *Tibet and Its History*, who also mentions the claims of Wu, calling them "ritual fictions" and a "fanciful account", p. 154. See also, Bell, *Portrait* . . . , who says the Chinese claims were false, pp. 399-400.

Kenrap Tenzin, a member of the search party, became the Master of Robes and later the Dalai Lama's chief of staff. Kenrap Tenzin and Ketswang Rinpoche, who was appointed third tutor, gave the Dalai Lama his early education, which started in earnest a year after his enthronement. The young Dalai Lama proved a bright and capable student. He also showed a phenomenal memory, never forgetting a story once it was told to him. In 1946 after a fight, during which the high-spirited and often aggressive Tenzin Gyatso injured Lobsang Samten, the latter was sent to live with his parents.[423]

In late 1940 the Reting regent resigned due to his unpopularity.[424] The elderly and conservative Taktra Rinpoche was appointed regent and senior tutor to the Dalai Lama. Ling Rinpoche, a brilliant scholar and abbot of Gyudto, the new junior tutor, and Trijang Rinpoche, another noted scholar, would supervise the education of the Dalai Lama from the age of eight. His studies became increasingly complex, but after some initial resistance Tenzin Gyatso showed himself equal to his teachers in aptitude. His interest turned quickly to advanced treatises, well beyond what was required. When it came to dialectics Tenzin Gyatso, like his predecessor, excelled at an early age. By the age of thirteen he was debating in front of hundreds of monks at Sera and Drepung, to which he was admitted as a monk at the same age.[425] These studies, along with hours of daily meditation and the initiations that consecrated his mind and body towards an ever deepening spiritual development, would continue until Tenzin Gyatso was able to successfully earn his geshe degree at the age of twenty-five.[426]

The Dalai Lama was intensely interested in the outside world and gleaned what he could from the one newspaper in Tibet, which

---

423. Goodman, *The Last . . .*, pp. 90-101. See, the Fourteenth Dalai Lama, *Freedom . . .*, who says his memorisation of Buddhist scripture was so boring he often forgot passages as soon as he had learned them, pp. 15-21.

424. Richardson, *Tibet and Its History*, pp. 157-8. See, Shakabpa, *Tibet: A Political History*, who says the regents' life was predicted to be cut short, by the state astrologer and the soothsayer, if he did not devote his life to prayer and meditation, p. 286. Also, Powers, *Introduction . . .*, p. 169

425. Goodman, *The Last . . .*, pp. 105-8. See, the Fourteenth Dalai Lama, *My Land . . .*, pp. 44-8. Also, Levenson, *The Dalai Lama*, pp. 58-60.

426. The Fourteenth Dalai Lama, *My Land . . .*, pp. 48-50.

was printed in India, from newspapers sent by the British mission in Lhasa, and from books and papers given to the Thirteenth Dalai Lama by Sir Charles Bell. He wished to learn English, beginning with books that had been used briefly in an English language school established in Lhasa in 1945. The school soon closed under pressure from the monasteries, who feared it would be harmful to their religion. The Dalai Lama was also interested in all sorts of mechanical devices and machinery, and he would often tinker with the cars of the previous Dalai Lama. His interest in a film projector presented to the Thirteenth Dalai Lama was the pretext for inviting Heinrich Harrer to the Norbulingka to oversee the building of a movie theatre. The Austrian, who had escaped from a British prisoner-of-war camp in India, became a friend to the young Dalai Lama, teaching him English and answering his many questions about the outside world. As it was, events beyond the cloistered life of Tenzin Gyatso would soon end this phase of the Dalai Lama's education.[427]

The Tibetan government was determined to maintain a neutral stance during the Second World War. The Chinese Nationalist government, allied with the British and faced with the uncertainties of the Burma Road as a supply route, announced their intention to push a road through south-eastern Tibet into India. Tibet responded with troops at her border, and the situation was eased when Britain persuaded Tibet to allow non-military supplies to move through the country by pack animals, greatly increasing trade in general and contacts with the outside world in particular.[428] Western influences, which had been gaining favour with the nobility, slowly increased. None the less, the monasteries continued stubbornly to resist Western ways, as exemplified by the closing of the English language schools, keeping Tibetans ignorant of the changes going on around them.[429]

Tibet, constantly trying to show the world it was an independent country, sent goodwill missions to China and India in 1946. The

427. Goodman, *The Last . . .*, pp. 109-17. See, Levenson, *The Dalai Lama*, pp. 61-2. Also, the Fourteenth Dalai Lama, *My Land . . .*, pp. 55-7. See also, John Avedon, *In Exile from the Land of Snows*, 1986, who says Harrer also taught mathematics, geography, natural sciences, and an assortment of other topics to the Dalai Lama, pp. 23-5.

428. Richardson, *Tibet and Its History*, pp. 159-64. See, Shakabpa, *Tibet: A Political History*, p. 286.

429. Snellgrove & Richardson, *A Cultural History . . .*, pp. 260-5.

Chinese, wishing to show Tibet as part of China, contrived to have the Tibetans attend the National Assembly of China. Then they publicized the event as if the Tibetans were members. In 1947, against Chinese wishes, Tibet attended the Asian Relations Conference in India, which was then independent of British rule.[430] Indian policy towards China, while initially pro-Tibet, changed somewhat in 1949, with Nehru tacitly acknowledging a vague Chinese suzerainty over Tibet. By this time the Tibetans had already expelled all Chinese officials from Tibet. The Communists, under Mao Tse-tung, took over the Chinese government and announced their plans to liberate Tibet, a plan supposedly endorsed by the twelve-year-old Panchen Lama.[431]

Earlier, in 1944, the staff of the deceased Panchen Lama, who were still in exile, had announced the discovery of his reincarnation in Amdo, which was part of Chinese-controlled Tibet. Ten candidates had been declared in 1942 but none were sent to Lhasa for examination. Lhasa did not immediately recognise the Seventh Panchen Lama, Chokyi Gyaltsen. However, he was confirmed without the usual tests, by the Nationalist government in China, just before it fell to Mao's Communist party. The Dalai Lama recognized the Seventh Panchen Lama in 1951.[432]

Tibet had already endured another controversy with one of its high lamas when, in 1947, an attempt to kill the regent Taktra Rinpoche, during a *coup d'etat* led by the ex-regent Reting Rinpoche and his followers, failed. Reting Rinpoche had tried to enlist Chinese assistance and he was supported by the monks of Che, his college at Sera. Before it was over the army bombarded the college, Reting Monastery was destroyed, the ex-regent and his followers were arrested and jailed, and hundreds had died in the fighting. Shortly after he

---

430. Richardson, *Tibet and Its History*, pp. 166-8.

431. *Ibid.*, pp. 173-7. See, Shakabpa, *Tibet: A Political History*, pp. 297-9. Also, Goodman, *The Last . . .*, pp. 151-2.

432. Richardson, *Tibet and Its History*, pp. 172-3. See, Doboom Tulku, "the lineage of the panchen lamas", p. 9. See also, Shakabpa, *Tibet: A Political History*, who says the Panchen Lama was recognized by a Tibetan delegation in Beijing as part of the Sino-Tibetan agreement which the Tibetans were forced to sign, pp. 306-7. See also, the Fourteenth Dalai Lama, *My Land . . .*, who says he received a telegram from the Tibetan delegation saying refusal to recognize the Panchen Lama would hinder the negotiations, p. 103.

was jailed, Reting Rinpoche died in prison, likely due to poisoning. The Dalai Lama freed the other conspirators, who had been jailed for life, when he assumed temporal power in 1950.[433]

In August of 1950 a violent earthquake, accompanied by unusual atmospheric phenomena, shook all of Tibet. Many, including the Dalai Lama, saw in this devastating event 'a harbinger of their nation's fate'.[434] In October of 1950 the Communist Chinese invaded Tibet from the east and the west, quickly gaining control of those areas. India protested weakly and, later, with Britain led the move to have any discussion of Tibet at the United Nations deferred, which it was for nine years. Tibet, having ignored the warnings of the Thirteenth Dalai Lama in his last testament, was woefully unprepared to meet the onslaught of China. Once China had succeeded in occupying much of Tibet, it announced that Tibet was an integral part of China.[435] The Tibetan government, after consulting the Nechung oracle, decided to invest temporal authority in the sixteen-year-old (fifteen by Western standards) Dalai Lama.

Just before he was enthroned, the Dalai Lama's brother, Thubten Jigme Norbu, who was the Takster Rinpoche and abbot of Kumbum monastery, arrived from Amdo. He told of brutal persecutions of the monasteries by the Chinese prior to the invasion, of killings and destruction of sacred books, and of his own constant harassment until he resigned his position as abbot of Kumbum. In order to escape, he agreed to a thinly veiled plot to convince his brother to accept Chinese rule and, failing that, to kill him. The Taktser Rinpoche then apprised

---

433. Richardson, *Tibet and Its History*, pp. 169-73. See, Shakabpa, *Tibet: A Political History*, who says no evidence of foul play in the regent's death was found, pp. 292-4. See, Rato Khyongla Nawang Losang, *My Life and Lives*, 1977, who says that the attending physician, a friend and teacher of the author, told him Reting Rinpoche died of illness, brought on by extreme mental stress, pp. 144-6. See also, the Fourteenth Dalai Lama, *Freedom . . .* , who calls the whole affair silly but adds that he still retained "a deep personal respect for Reting Rinpoche as my first tutor and guru", pp. 30-1.

434. Avedon, *In Exile . . .* , p. 25. Also, the Fourteenth Dalai Lama, *Freedom . . .* , pp. 50-1. See also, Goodman, *The Last . . .* , p. 147.

435. Richardson, *Tibet and Its History*, pp. 183-7. See, Shakabpa, *Tibet: A Political History*, pp. 301-3. Also, the Fourteenth Dalai Lama, *Freedom . . .* , pp. 52-3. See also, Goodman, *The Last . . .* , pp. 151-63.

the government of the full scope and true intentions of the Chinese before leaving for India and America in the party of the Dalai Lama.[436]

Tenzin Gyatso initially hesitated to assume power, citing his youth and incomplete religious education. However, he knew the country had become fragmented during the regency, with the administration deteriorating overall. He felt that unity was paramount and he was "the only person whom everybody in the country would unanimously follow".[437] On 17 November 1950, the Dalai Lama assumed temporal power. Shortly thereafter he and the government left in secret for the Chumbi valley close to the Indian border to prevent his falling into Chinese hands. There was a problem almost immediately when the party's advance was blocked by hundreds of monks pleading with the Dalai Lama not to leave them. It was only when the young Dalai Lama himself took control of the situation and promised he would return that the party was permitted to continue.[438]

While the Dalai Lama and the government were at Yatung, in the Chumbi valley, a Tibetan delegation headed by the captured governor of Chamdo, which was in eastern Tibet, was forced to sign a Seventeen-Point Agreement. The Chinese held the members of the delegation virtual prisoners. The Chinese also forged the Dalai Lama's seals of office to validate the agreement. Essentially the agreement stated that Tibet was part of China, and it would work to drive out foreign elements. It also called for absorption of Tibetan forces into the Chinese army, and it deprived Tibet of authority in its external affairs. The Chinese promised to respect the status and function of the Dalai Lama, respect religion, not interfere with the monasteries, not compel people to accept reforms, and improve the standard of living.[439] All of these promises would be broken.

---

436. The Fourteenth Dalai Lama, *Freedom . . .* , pp. 54-5. See, Shakabpa, *Tibet: A Political History*, p. 301. Also, Avedon, *In Exile . . .* , p. 36.

437. The Fourteenth Dalai Lama, *My Land . . .* , p. 83.

438. Goodman, *The Last . . .* , pp. 165-8. See, Heinrich Harrer, *Seven Year in Tibet*, 1957, p. 313. Also, the Fourteenth Dalai Lama, *Freedom . . .*, pp. 55-9.

439. The Fourteenth Dalai Lama, *My Land . . .* , pp. 87-9.

In 1951 the Dalai Lama returned to Lhasa.[440] Shortly thereafter Lhasa was inundated by several thousand Chinese troops. Land was confiscated for military camps, and the food reserves were soon depleted to the point that famine was immanent. Protests from the Tibetans brought demands from the Chinese for immediate integration of the Tibetan army into the People's Liberation Army (PLA). The two prime ministers, refusing to co-operate with the Chinese, were forced to resign. The Dalai Lama soon felt he was "the sole buffer between his people and China's armies", and in order to avoid provoking the Chinese pursued a path of accommodation, largely due to his non-violent religious convictions.[441]

The Dalai Lama also established his own office for social reform, ending some long-standing practices such as unpaid transport for government officials by the local populace. He cancelled agricultural debts and proposed a land re-distribution policy all of which "took the wind out of the Communists' sails" according to Richardson.[442] The Chinese introduced other, more concrete reforms, such as schools, hospitals, and roads, which were initially well received by the Tibetans. The Chinese had hoped to win popularity and the support of the Tibetans, but they soon became much more repressive in reaction to the Tibetan resentment towards interference with traditional customs, religion, and institutions.[443]

During this period the Dalai Lama twice met the Panchen Lama, who had gone to Tashi Lhunpo to assume his position. The Chinese tried to elevate the position of the Panchen Lama in order to diminish that of the Dalai Lama. The Dalai Lama personally got along well with the Panchen Lama feeling that, if left to himself, the Panchen

---

440. Avedon, *In Exile . . .* , says a secret plan between India and the United States was drawn up for the Dalai Lama to escape into exile to India and repudiate the Seventeen-Point Agreement. However, he returned to Lhasa under pressure from the abbots of Drepung, Sera, and Ganden as well as proclamations from the Nechung oracle, p. 36.

441. Avedon, *In Exile . . .* , p. 38.

442. Richardson, *Tibet and Its History*, pp. 192-3.

443. *Ibid.*, pp. 193-5. See, Shakabpa, *Tibet: A Political History*, p. 307. See also, Snellgrove & Richardson, *A Cultural History*, who note that "like all unwanted occupying powers, the Chinese were driven to sterner and more cruel repression", p. 267.

Lama "would have whole-heartedly supported Tibet".[444] In spite of all the burdens placed on his young shoulders, the Dalai Lama was able to continue his religious education. Ling Rinpoche initiated him into the Kalachakra Tantra and gave the Dalai Lama his full ordination in 1954. Always aware of his spiritual position, Tenzin Gyatso continued his regimen of personal prayer and meditation, with periodic retreats and regular teachings.[445]

In 1954 the Dalai Lama and Panchen Lama travelled to Beijing where they met with Mao Tse-tung. The Dalai Lama also met with the Russian leader Khrushchev and Prime Minister Nehru of India, but he was prevented from speaking freely to them. After a lengthy stay and thousands of requests for his return from the Tibetan people, the Dalai Lama proceeded slowly to Lhasa, visiting towns and monasteries along his route. The end result of this trip was the Preparatory Committee for the Autonomous Region of Tibet headed by the Dalai Lama with the Panchen Lama as vice-chairman. In reality this committee was controlled by the Chinese and further diminished the Dalai Lama's political effectiveness.[446]

Once the Chinese had completed their roads to Lhasa in 1954, they started a policy of severe repression in eastern Tibet in order to completely take over the country and impose their communist ideas. Taxation was increased, lands were confiscated, and religion was outlawed. All resistance was met with brutal punishment, including the destruction of monasteries and whole villages, and public executions. The independently minded Khampas and Amdowas organised an effective guerilla movement, which brought even fiercer Chinese repression. Children and even infants were taken from their parents to be educated in China. Children were forced to kill their parents. The Tibetan people were forced to humiliate and even kill monks and nuns. There were also forced sterilizations. All these were flagrant violations of China's agreements with Tibet. The Chinese also began moving in thousands of Han Chinese settlers. These actions

444. The Fourteenth Dalai Lama, *My Land . . .* , pp. 103, 113-14. See, Goodman, *The Last . . .* , pp. 185-6.

445. The Fourteenth Dalai Lama, *Freedom . . .* , pp. 80-1.

446. Shakabpa, *Tibet: A Political History*, pp. 307-11. See, Richardson, *Tibet and Its History*, pp. 200, 204.

combined with Chinese brutality drove many activists and refugees into central Tibet and Lhasa. Before long they had the effect of raising resistance in and around Lhasa in spite of the Dalai Lama's appeals for non-violence. Realizing his own ineffectiveness, the Dalai Lama was contemplating his resignation from temporal office.[447]

The 2,5000th anniversary of the Buddha's birth fell in 1956 and with it an invitation for the Dalai Lama to attend celebrations marking the event in India. After initial Chinese opposition was removed through Nehru's intervention, the Dalai Lama travelled to India where he was a leading participant in the ceremonies. He also gave many talks during his stay and made a pilgrimage to the sites sacred to Buddhism. While in India he approached Nehru about asylum but the Indian prime minister strongly suggested that the Dalai Lama return and work peacefully with the Chinese. Nehru's discussions on the topic with Chou En-lai, the Chinese prime minister, resulted in announcements from Beijing that Tibet was not ready for reforms and that Chinese efforts in this direction would be scaled back significantly. Bolstered by these developments the Dalai Lama returned to Tibet in 1957.[448]

Contrary to Chinese promises, their repression in eastern Tibet continued, as did the growing guerilla movement of the Tibetans. Under the leadership of Gompo Tashi Andrugtsang, an organized resistance movement quickly developed in central Tibet. Clandestine aid, arranged in India by Gyalo Thondup, the Dalai Lama's elder brother, came from Taiwan and the Central Intelligence Agency of the United States.[449] Before long, up to 80,000 Khampa fighters were in central Tibet and the Chinese brought in 150,000 men to counter the Tibetan forces. All requests by the Chinese to the Tibetan government and leading abbots to stop the fighting were met with resistance. The Dalai Lama continued to urge non-violence but the people knew he only had their welfare in mind.[450]

---

447. Richardson, *Tibet and Its History*, pp. 200-2. See, Avedon, *In Exile . . .*, pp. 44-5. Also, Goodman, *The Last . . .*, pp. 228-7.

448. Shakabpa, *Tibet: A Political History*, pp. 311-14. See, Avedon, *In Exile . . .*, pp. 45-7. Also, Richardson, *Tibet and Its History*, pp. 202-4. See also, the Fourteenth Dalai Lama, *My Land . . .*, pp. 139-54.

449. Goodman, *The Last . . .*, pp. 259-64. See, Avedon, *In Exile . . .*, p. 47.

450. *Ibid.*, p. 164. See, *Ibid.*, pp. 48-9.

As tensions mounted, concerns for the Dalai Lama's safety prompted the Tibetan National Assembly to position themselves between His Holiness and the Chinese by declaring that all dealings with the Dalai Lama should be channeled through them. An invitation for the Dalai Lama to visit Beijing in 1959 was viewed as an attempt to gain physical control over Tenzin Gyatso. That invitation was avoided on the pretext of the Dalai Lama's upcoming *geshe lharampa* exams. (This was the highest level of Tibetan religious education, equivalent to a doctoral degree in religious studies.) In the midst of these preparations, which were going on during the Great Prayer Festival, the Dalai Lama was requested to attend a theatrical performance at the Chinese command post. It was later stipulated he should come alone or with few unarmed bodyguards. It seemed to the Tibetans that the Chinese were intent on abducting the Dalai Lama.[451]

The Dalai Lama successfully completed his final exams over a period of several days. Meanwhile he opposed plans for his escape, not wishing to give up hope of a peaceful solution or to leave his people. About 30,000 people, having learned of the Chinese invitation, surrounded the Norbulingka to prevent the Dalai Lama from being taken by the Chinese. When the Chinese fired two shells into the Norbulingka on 17 March 1959, the Dalai Lama agreed to flee.[452]

The Dalai Lama and his party slipped out of the Norbulingka in disguise and made a harrowing escape to India where asylum was granted immediately. Over the next several months he was followed by upwards of 100,000 refugees escaping the Chinese who, once they heard of the escape, shelled the Norbulingka and massacred thousands of Lhasa's rebellious citizens. The Chinese quickly secured the country by rooting out guerilla resistance and abolishing the government. They immediately set to work to destroy the religious

---

451. Levenson, *The Dalai Lama*, pp. 82-5. See, Richardson, *Tibet and Its History*, who adds that throughout these events Nehru continued to condone the Chinese initiatives in Tibet while denying the excessive use of Chinese force, pp. 206-8. See also, Shakabpa, *Tibet: A Political History*, p. 318.

452. Richardson, *Tibet and Its History*, pp. 208-9. See, Avedon, *In Exile . . .*, who notes the Dalai Lama's performance at his exams was considered all the more remarkable in light of the burdens of political office, pp. 49-53.

institutions by killing thousands of monks and destroying monasteries and sacred images. The lands of the aristocracy were confiscated and agricultural collectives were organized. The populace was forced into labour, building roads, and many other tasks. Thousands were imprisoned. Chinese propaganda went to work to conceal from the world their rape of Tibet, as that country fell into a state of despair.[453]

The Dalai Lama and his entourage were taken by special train to Mussoorie, a Himalayan hill station north-west of New Delhi. They remained there for a year before moving to a more permanent location at Dharamsala. At the outset the Dalai Lama clearly outlined to the world press the atrocities committed in Tibet by the Chinese, bringing furious denunciations from China. He also declared that a temporary Tibetan government in exile had been set-up, stating "wherever I am, accompanied by my government, the Tibetan people will recognise us as the government of Tibet".[454] The Indian government, still wedded to its policy of *Panch Shila* (a non-alignment stance taken to maintain peaceful co-existence with China), would not recognize the Tibetan government in exile but did offer material assistance and moral support.[455] The Dalai Lama, before the end of his first year in exile, managed to have a resolution passed through the United Nations, which condemned the massive human rights abuses in Tibet. His more immediate concern, however, was the thousands of refugees who, against staggering odds, had survived the journey to India.[456] He also realised nothing could be the same[457] and must also

---

453. Richardson, *Tibet and Its History*, pp. 209-14. See, Shakabpa, *Tibet: A Political History*, who says that on the second day after the Dalai Lama's escape the Norbulingka was bombarded and in the ensuing massacre 12,000 people were killed by the Chinese. The Chinese only discovered the Dalai Lama's escape on the third day, pp. 318-20. See also, Avedon, *In Exile . . .* , who says there was "a wholesale effort on the part of China to uproot Tibetan society and culture", pp. 71-2. See also, the Fourteenth Dalai Lama, *My Land . . .* , pp. 221-3.

454. Goodman, *The Last . . .* , p. 322. See, Richardson, *Tibet and Its History*, who mentions the Dalai Lama rested at Tawang the birthplace of the Sixth Dalai Lama, (see p. 72 above) after crossing the Indian frontier, pp. 210-17.

455. Richardson, *Tibet and Its History*, p. 217.

456. The Fourteenth Dalai Lama, *My Land . . .* , pp. 224-30.

457. *Ibid.*, p. 231.

have certainly known that the Dalai Lama was at the centre of a desperate struggle for the survival of Tibetan culture.

The institution of the Dalai Lama came into being as a result of historical and cultural forces. Tibet, following its people's wholesale acceptance of Buddhist values, became a land dominated by religious concerns. This gave rise to religious schools, which vied with one another and the lay nobility for predominance. The *bodhisattva* Chenrezig (Avalokiteshvara), Tibet's patron deity and the progenitor of its peoples according to Tibetan creation mythology, became identified with the lineage of Gedun Truppa, the First Dalai Lama. The Dalai Lama came to be regarded, through a line of spiritual succession, as the father of Tibet's peoples and its most powerful protector.[458] Each Dalai Lama was revered by the Tibetan people not only as their divine protector but also for his actions, generally believed to be for their benefit.

Tibetans believe that all the Dalai Lamas were chosen because their particular qualities were needed at a particular time. The First Dalai Lama, Gedun Truppa, spread the teachings of Tsongkhapa and strengthened the Gelugpa order. The Second incarnation, Gedun Gyatso, furthered this growth throughout central Tibet. The Third Dalai Lama, Sonam Gyatso, brought the faith to Mongolia and further into eastern Tibet. The Fourth, Yonten Gyatso, brought Mongolia firmly into the fold. The Great Fifth, Ngawang Lobsang Gyatso, unified Tibet and established the temporal rule of the Dalai Lama. Tsangyang Gyatso, the Sixth Dalai Lama, tested the sincerity of Tibetan's faith, becoming one of the most beloved of his people. The Seventh, Kelsang Gyatso, became known for his high spiritual attainment. The Eighth, Jampal Gyatso, was known for his spirituality and the building of the Norbulingka. The next four Dalai Lamas, Lungtok Gyatso, Tsultrim Gyatso, Khedrup Gyatso, and Trinley Gyatso, all died too early to fulfil their promise. The Great Thirteenth Dalai Lama, Thubten Gyatso, restored Tibetan independence, brought more accountability into its highest institutions, and championed Buddhist virtues. The

---

458. P. Christiaan Klieger, "The Institution of the Dalai Lama as a Symbolic Matrix", *The Tibet Journal*, vol. XVI, no. 1, Spring 1991, pp. 98-9.

Fourteenth Dalai Lama, Tenzin Gyatso, faces the greatest challenge yet as he brings his exceptional spiritual qualities to the task of preserving Tibet's cultural and spiritual heritage during its darkest hour.[459]

---

459. Goodman, *The Last* . . . p. 85.

3

How the Institution of the Dalai Lama Works

BEFORE continuing with the narrative of the Fourteenth Dalai Lama and the fate of the Tibetan people and their culture, a review of the actual workings of the institution of the Dalai Lama as it existed prior to the Communist Chinese takeover of Tibet is of use. The institution of the Dalai Lama was, and still is, rooted in and built upon the person of the Dalai Lama himself. This section looks at how the Dalai Lama is discovered and educated, the household and daily life of the Dalai Lama, his duties both temporal and religious, and the position of the Dalai Lama within the structures of government and religious hierarchy.

Discovery and recognition

When a Dalai Lama passed away the government of Tibet would consult the leading lamas of the country, primarily those of the three state monasteries, the Panchen Lama, if of age, and the state oracles, in order to locate his reincarnation. The first clues were often given by the previous Dalai Lamas as in the case of the Sixth, through verse (p. 79 above), or the Twelfth and Thirteenth in death (p. 108, p. 121 above), and by specific directives from the oracles at Nechung and Samye Monasteries. From these monasteries, search parties were sent out in greatest secrecy. Suitable candidates may have already been indicated through the clues given, the extraordinary circumstances surrounding their births and early years, as with the First and Sixth Dalai Lamas (p. 31, pp. 72-3 above), and their intelligence and precociousness, as with the Fourteenth Dalai Lama (p. 121 above).[1]

1. Bell, *The Religion of Tibet*, p. 160. See, Norbu & Turnbull, *Tibet*, pp. 228-9. See also, R. Rahul, "The Institution of Dalai Lama", *International Studies*, vol. 10, no. 4, April 1969, pp. 498-9.

The successful candidate would show some or all of the body markings associated with the Dalai Lama. These included: large ears, an extra piece of flesh near each shoulder blade indicating Chenrezig's additional set of arms, wide eyes with long upward curving eyebrows, streaks like those of a tiger skin on the legs and an imprint resembling a conch-shell on the palm of one hand.[2] The young Dalai Lama was expected to correctly identify several of his predecessor's personal articles from amongst similar ones or replicas.[3] Once a candidate was selected, further confirmation was usually sought from the state oracles. Thubten Jigme Norbu, the present Dalai Lama's elder brother, says all these tests and their successful outcome depended on the prayers of the priests and people, "offered to secure the spiritual guidance necessary to make the correct choice".[4] Once that choice was clear, the announcement of the discovery was made, and the Dalai Lama and his family were brought to Lhasa when he reached an appropriate age.[5]

Education

Once at Lhasa, the Dalai Lama was admitted as a novice monk into Namgyal, his personal monastery, located in the Potala. He was shortly thereafter enthroned as the spiritual leader of Tibet, his full temporal and spiritual authority usually being conferred at the age of eighteen.[6] To prepare for that eventuality he was given the best religious education available in Tibet. A senior and junior tutor were appointed, as well as several other tutors. These tutors were drawn from the ranks of the Gelug sect, the most prominent being the Panchen Lamas, with whom the Dalai Lamas have developed a reciprocal *guru*-disciple relationship over several incarnations of each. As a member of the Gelug sect, the Dalai Lama's first responsibility was to master its doctrines. However, as Norbu points out, the Dalai Lama generally

2. Avedon, *In Exile . . .* , says the current Dalai Lama displayed three of these markings on his body, p. 7. See, Bell, *The Religion of Tibet*, pp. 160-1.
3. Rahul "The Institution . . . ," p. 499. See, Norbu & Turnbull, *Tibet*, p. 230. Also, the Fourteenth Dalai Lama, *My Land . . .* , pp. 23-4.
4. Norbu & Turnbull, *Tibet*, pp. 230-1.
5. Rahul, "The Institution . . . ," p. 499. See, Norbu & Turnbull, *Tibet*, p. 233.
6. Rahul, "The Institution . . . ," p. 499.

took instructions and initiations from the other schools, once his Gelug training was complete. Then he could better understand and lead all the religious communities within the country, since all the sects recognized the Dalai Lama as the spiritual and temporal leader of Tibet.[7]

The Gelug tradition, we may recall, is an amalgam of the teachings of the major sects of Tibetan Buddhism. In the Gelug school, the religious training a Dalai Lama was expected to master can be divided into four broad categories. The first, the teaching of which was adopted from the Sakya order, is his philosophical training. This is mainly comprised of the five subject areas of: *prajnaparamita*, *madhyamaka*, *pramana*, *abhidharma* and *vinaya* (perfection of wisdom, emptiness theory, higher logic, metaphysics, and ethics). The second category, adopted from the Kadam tradition, is the oral transmission teachings dealing with Sutrayana meditations (the path outlining the teachings attributed to the historical Buddha), using texts known as Lam Rim and Lo Jong. The third category, as adapted from the Kagyud, Sakya, Kadam, and Nyingma schools, is the Vajrayana (diamond way), or tantric (esoteric) tradition. The fourth category involves subjects such as grammar, prose, poetry, art, medicine, history, and so forth. In addition to these he received some training in government administration by selected tutors.[8]

In the Tibetan system of religious education, the student, after learning to read and write, started memorizing the scriptures by heart. To facilitate a proper understanding, concentration and meditation on the teachings and their meanings were emphasized, as were the student's thoughts on the subject. Also, by engaging in dialectical debating sessions with progressively more advanced students and scholars, the Dalai Lama's memory and understanding were further tested. The Dalai Lamas were expected to attain to the level of *geshe* (spiritual guide), a mark of superior scholarship. Some of the Dalai Lamas, the present included, have also passed their *geshe*

7. Norbu & Turnbull, *Tibet*, pp. 233-4.
8. Mullin, *Path of the Bodhisattva Warrior*, p. 40. See, Bell, *Portrait of the Dalai Lama*, pp. 47-8. See also, Goodman, *The Last . . .*, who says the summation of the five branches of philosophical training are contained in the *Kangyur*, which is 108 volumes of the Buddha's teachings and the *Tengyur*, which is 225 volumes of commentary on those teachings, p. 106.

lharampa degree (see p. 131 above), which is considered a recognition of superior scholarship and debating skills.[9] Finally and concurrently with these studies the Dalai Lamas would be initiated into various types and ever-deepening levels of meditation practice in order to further their spiritual development.[10]

The household and daily life of the Dalai Lama

After their discovery and recognition the Dalai Lamas were brought to Lhasa, their families accompanying them. The father of the Dalai Lama received a title, large grants of land, and he could, if he chose to do so, enter the ranks of lay officials. The mother was given the honorific title, "Great Royal Mother". Brothers were not allowed to hold government posts, but could hold a private position in the Dalai Lama's household. The younger brother of the Thirteenth Dalai Lama, for instance, was his chief comptroller.[11]

The Dalai Lama lived in the Potala, his winter palace, and in the summer, the Norbulingka. His family resided outside these compounds and saw him less frequently as the Dalai Lama grew older. The Fourteenth Dalai Lama says the regent forbade him to visit his parents' home from the age of twelve.[12] The Dalai Lama had his own apartment within the Potala and his needs were seen to by a number of male monks who essentially raised him.[13] Apart from his bodyguards, sweepers, and cooks, three monk attendants saw to his specific needs. These were the Master of Tea (food and drink), the Master of Robes (clothing and dressing), and the Master of Religious Ceremony (his religious objects and rituals). The Dalai Lama's chief of staff, the Lord Chamberlain, oversaw the entire household. He was also in charge of both the Dalai Lama's personal treasury and the Potala treasury. The Lord Chamberlain had direct access to the Dalai Lama and was often involved in discussions of national interest.[14]

---

9. Powers, *Introduction to Tibetan Buddhism*, pp. 413-14. See, Goodman, *The Last* . . . , pp. 107-8.
10. Goodman, *The Last* . . . , p. 109. See, Mullin, *Path*. . . , pp. 42-3.
11. Rahul, "The Institution . . . ," pp. 449-500.
12. The Fourteenth Dalai Lama, *Freedom* . . . , p. 37.
13. Avedon, *In Exile* . . . , p. 21.
14. Goodman, *The Last* . . . , pp. 82-3, 93-4.

When young, the Dalai Lama's schedule was taken up with his education. Nevertheless, even at a young age the Dalai Lama was expected to give blessings,[15] receive visitors of all classes, and to preside over major religious occasions such as the Great Prayer Festival. As he attained his majority temporal affairs would take up more of his time, as would the ordination of monks and other religious duties such as teaching and writing. Each of the Dalai Lamas, according to circumstances and temperament, adjusted their schedules according to the needs at hand. However, no matter what the circumstances, the daily schedule of the Dalai Lama was grounded in his own spiritual practices, generally including several hours of prayer and meditation.[16]

A typical day in the life of a Dalai Lama, in this case the Thirteenth, started with him rising long before sunrise. Like any other Buddhist monk he would engage in a few hours of prayer and meditation before breakfast. The morning would likely be taken up with correspondence. It is said the Thirteenth Dalai Lama personally dealt with each letter sent to him. After lunch and an hour or so to paint or meditate, the Dalai Lama would meet with his ministers and committee heads and give audiences to groups, large and small, who usually sought teachings and blessings. He might garden for an hour or so in the early evening, perhaps followed by a walk before retiring to his chambers to write or meditate. Or instead, he might join the monks in Namgyal, his private monastery, for prayers and rituals. It would usually be midnight before he retired for sleep. Often, in the midst of a long ritual or teaching, which could take weeks, he was known to sit all night in meditation.[17] If we were to look at the daily schedule of the Fourteenth Dalai Lama, we would discover a typical day in his life was remarkably similar to that of his predecessor.[18]

15. Rahul, "The Institution . . . ," p. 500. See, Mullin, *Path* . . . , who says the giving of group blessings could be quite exhausting as upwards of 10,000 people would expect to receive an individual blessing as they passed before the Dalai Lama in single file, pp. 90-1.

16. Rahul, "The Institution . . . ," who notes "there is immense centralisation of power in the person of the Dalai Lama. Every conceivable problem . . . is brought before him", and generally the Dalai Lama would be asked to make the final decision in any matter of importance, pp. 500-1.

17. Mullin, *Path* . . . , p. 90.

18. Levenson, *The Dalai Lama*, pp. 101-24.

The role of the Dalai Lama in the governance of Tibet

The Dalai Lama assumed the dual role of secular and spiritual leader of Tibet. Being a Buddhist monk and the embodiment of Chenrezig, Tibet's patron deity, the Dalai Lama's principle role is that of protector of his people and his country. He is primarily concerned with their spiritual welfare. Prior to the Communist Chinese takeover of Tibet (and even to a certain extent today) the government headed by the Dalai Lama was, in essence, religious in character. It had secular and religious branches with an approximately equal number of monks and lay officials in these respective branches.[19]

During the minority of the Dalai Lama, a regent, appointed by the National (or General) Assembly, headed the administration. When the Dalai Lama turned eighteen he theoretically assumed full and absolute power. In reality, except for strong personalities such as the Fifth and Thirteenth Dalai Lamas, his power was often held in check by the high authorities surrounding him, especially the high ecclesiastical figures.[20] When the Dalai Lama was in full power he would appoint a prime minister, a layman, who acted as a liaison between the Dalai Lama and the cabinet, or council of ministers. If a second prime minister were appointed he would be a monk. The prime minister held no real authority, as all final decisions were the Dalai Lama's. Nevertheless, the position carried considerable influence.[21]

The secular officials were drawn from the ranks of the aristocracy who supplied at least one family member for government service in exchange for grants of land from the state, which were held hereditarily.[22] The most important of these officials were in the Kashag,

---

19. Norbu & Turnbull, *Tibet*, p. 325. See, Goodman, *The Last . . .* , p. 81.
20. Tucci, *Tibet Land of Snows*, p. 203. See, Ram Rahul, *The Government and Politics of Tibet*, 1969, who says the Thirteenth Dalai Lama reduced the power of the monasteries, pp. 11-12 (see my text above, pp. 116, 117). See also, Shakabpa, *Tibet: A Political History*, who says, "In theory, the power of the Dalai Lama is absolute, but in practice he does not exercise his authority without consultation to aid his judgement", p. 21.
21. Michael, *Rule by Incarnation*, 1982, pp. 60-1. See, Goodman, *The Last . . .* , who says the post of prime minister was abolished in 1940 and briefly resurrected by the Fourteenth Dalai Lama in 1950, p. 81.
22. Goodman, *The Last . . .* , p. 81.

or council of ministers, which included three laymen and one monk, all appointed by the Dalai Lama. All work was done collectively by the four ministers. This cabinet received decisions and recommendations from the administrative departments below them such as finance, justice, foreign affairs, military, agriculture, and district administration. The cabinet was also the highest court of appeal for lay Tibetans except in matters of the highest importance (usually those involving families of superior status), in which case the appeal could go directly before the Dalai Lama. The cabinet's decisions were subject to approval by the Dalai Lama.[23]

The highest ecclesiastical figure, appointed by the Dalai Lama, was the Lord Chamberlain who, besides running the Dalai Lama's household and treasury, also took care of the Norbulingka, oversaw government parks, and supervised the stables of the government and the mounted courier service. He attended meetings of the cabinet if important matters were to be discussed and was the liaison between the Dalai Lama and the *Yiktsang*, a council of monks. The Lord Chamberlain could decide appeals referred to him by the *Yiktsang* except for the most important, which went before the Dalai Lama. His direct access on a daily basis, as a personal secretary and counsellor to the Dalai Lama, conferred great influence on the post of Lord Chamberlain.[24]

The monastic council administered religious affairs and the monastic civil service. Its authority did not extend to the Three Pillars (the monasteries of Drepung, Sera, and Ganden). The executive of the monastic council, also appointed by the Dalai Lama, were four secretaries known as *Drunyik Chenmo*, who also made their decisions collectively as with the Kashag. These secretaries were the Dalai Lama's chief executives in religious matters but also, according to Michael, dominated the secular government. The secretaries of the *Yiktsang* adjudicated any civil disputes between monasteries. In conjunction with the four heads of the finance department, the most important of the secular administration, the *Yiktsang* secretariat chaired the General, or National, Assembly and its smaller working committee.[25]

---

23. Rahul, *The Government*. . . , pp. 25-7. See, Goodman, *The Last*. . . , p. 82. Also, Michael, *Rule*. . . , pp. 61-3.
24. *Ibid.*, p. 27. See, *ibid.*, pp. 82-3. Also, *ibid.*, p. 51.
25. Michael, *Rule*. . . , pp. 52-3. See, Rahul, *The Government*. . . , p. 28.

The General Assembly (*Tsongdu*) only met to consider matters of national importance, but its decisions were binding, even upon the Dalai Lama. Its smaller working committee would be called to meet on orders of the cabinet, but the cabinet members did not take part. The members of the General Assembly included all the monk and lay officials, military officers, the abbots and representatives of the Three Pillars, and representatives of professional and secular groups — in all totalling about 700. The Tsongdu represented the nation, any of its members being allowed to voice their concerns. In practice the representatives of the three great monasteries tended to have the most influence. The General Assembly would choose the regent as well as making other national decisions. Its smaller working committee met more often, usually to consider important decisions such as the conflict with the Panchen Lama, the investigation of a regent, border troubles with China, or the reaffirmation of Tibet's independent status. Its members, drawn from the same groups as the General Assembly, except for the professional and secular organisations (and also dominated by the three state Gelugpa monasteries), forwarded their recommendations to the cabinet and the Dalai Lama. This working committee was primarily weighted towards ecclesiastical opinion, and its decisions carried great influence with the cabinet and the Dalai Lama.[26]

The government, while divided between secular and religious administration, leaned towards religious considerations, which is not so surprising in a country where all life is held to be subservient to spiritual priorities. Thus, in Tibet, it is not so strange to find the government in consultation with the oracles and high lamas on matters of national and international importance. Of these the Nechung oracle was the chief state oracle. Though the oracles held no position of official authority, their pronouncements affected government decisions very profoundly.[27]

It is also clear that all authority in Tibet devolved from the hands of the Dalai Lama. He made the principal government appointments. In him rested the final decision in most matters and all matters of any significance. While it is true that political circumstance and forceful personalities have often limited the power of the Dalai Lama, the

---

26. Michael, *Rule* . . . , pp. 63-4. See, Rahul, *The Government* . . . , pp. 31-2.
27. Rahul, *The Government* . . . , p. 25.

structure of power in Tibet was such that the Dalai Lama was at its apex. The Dalai Lama, as the supreme head of Buddhism in Tibet, exercised enormous influence throughout central Asia. No power in Tibet or outside of it would try to interact with Tibet or inside its borders without considering the influence and authority of the Dalai Lama.[28]

The spiritual role of the Dalai Lama

The Dalai Lama is a Buddhist monk and, as such, is obligated to a life of prayer and meditation. He is a special Buddhist monk, one of approximately 1000 tulkus, or incarnate lamas, in Tibet.[29] He is also an emanation of Chenrezig (Avalokiteshvara), the *bodhisattva* of compassion and protector deity of Tibet. The Dalai Lama thus works in a compassionate way for the protection and welfare of Tibet and her people. The religious authority invested in the Dalai Lama is extended outside the borders of Tibet to adherents of Tibetan Buddhism. A review of the historical section above shows this to be the case.

The Dalai Lama has many spiritual or religious duties other than his personal obligations, within which he prays for the benefit of all sentient beings.[30] He is called upon to perform ordinations of monks, especially those of high incarnations. The Thirteenth Dalai Lama was known to have performed thousands of ordinations.[31] The Dalai Lamas often participated in the discovery and recognition of newly reincarnated lamas either by giving clues as to the whereabouts of their rebirth or later, confirming the chosen candidate.[32] Another duty of the Dalai Lamas, as regards the monks and monasteries, was that that of final arbitration in religious disputes.

---

28. *Ibid.*, p. 15.
29. Mullin, *Essence of Refined Gold*, p. 248. See, Tucci, *The Religions of Tibet*, pp. 134-5.
30. The Fourteenth Dalai Lama, *Tibet, China and the World*, 1989, p. 4.
31. Mullin, *Path . . .* , p. 92.
32. *Ibid.*, p. 91. See, Norbu & Turnbull, *Tibet*, who describe how the Thirteenth Dalai Lama repeatedly rejected the lists of candidates for Taktser Rinpoche until Thubten Jigme Norbu's name was placed on it, pp. 236-7.

The Dalai Lamas were called upon to confer blessings on individuals and groups who asked for them, either in person or through correspondence. In the same way the Dalai Lamas would give teachings and advice. Giving teachings to groups and individual students often meant composing verses or interpreting religious texts, an extension of the Dalai Lamas scholarship, as were their writings. Presiding over rituals such as the Great Prayer Festival in Lhasa or the Kalachakra initiation, one of the most important in the tantric tradition, were part of the Dalai Lama's duties.[33] The Dalai Lamas also were builders of monasteries and temples. The efforts of the First Dalai Lama in building Tashi Lhunpo Monastery come to mind, as do his, and his immediate successor's, efforts in the construction of sacred images.[34]

These creative pursuits were part of the contributions of the Dalai Lamas to the cultural life of Tibet, which was almost exclusively a religious culture.[35] The creation of religious buildings, paintings, images, music, drama, and writings provided a wide field of endeavour for many artists and artisans. The Dalai Lamas generally patronised these artists.[36] In some cases the Dalai Lamas themselves were highly skilled in these areas. The Thirteenth was a painter and the Sixth a master of operatic dance and also a great poet.[37]

One final note regarding the Dalai Lama's role within the religious hierarchy of Tibet needs to be added. While a member of the Gelug sect, the Dalai Lama, according to Norbu, was "above sectarianism".[38] The Dalai Lama is not the head of the Gelugpa order. The abbot of Ganden, who is known as the Tri Rinpoche, holds that position. As mentioned earlier in this section, the Dalai Lama's training, while in the Gelug tradition, was an amalgam of the teachings of all the sects

33. The Fourteenth Dalai Lama, *Freedom . . .*, says the Kalachakra initiation has great significance for world peace and he has given this initiation many times in all parts of the world, pp. 80-1.
34. See my text above, pp. 34-5, 45.
35. Mullin, *Path . . .*, p. 107.
36. *Ibid.*, pp. 107-8.
37. See my text above, pp. 139, 74, 76.
38. Norbu & Turnbull, *Tibet*, p. 324. See, Mullin, *Essence . . .*, p. 248.

of Tibetan Buddhism. All the Dalai Lamas, except for the Seventh, have leaned to some degree towards the Nyingma tradition as well.[39]

The institution of the Dalai Lama has been at the centre of Tibetan culture and society for over 400 years. With the Communist Chinese invasion of Tibet in 1950 that culture has been irrevocably altered within Tibet, almost to the point of extinction. The escape of the present Dalai Lama along with thousands of his countrymen has created the possibility that Tibetan Buddhist culture and values will survive. The story of that struggle for survival and its aftermath, as presented in the following section, concludes this exploration of the institution of the Dalai Lama.

39. See footnote 277 above, p. 87. See Norbu & Turnbull, *Tibet*, p. 324.

4

Tibetan Identity and Culture and the Dalai Lama Since 1959

FOLLOWING the Dalai Lama's flight into exile, Chinese repression in Tibet continued unabated. During the period of the Cultural Revolution in China, these repressive measures became intensified, followed by a period of moderation. In recent years the suppression of Tibet has once again been intensified.

In India, the Dalai Lama led a desperate effort to settle the thousands of refugees who managed to escape the Chinese occupation of Tibet. Tibetan culture was in danger of dying, but the persistent endeavours of the Tibetans in exile led to the creation of several successful resettlement colonies in India and abroad. The re-establishment of some of Tibet's leading monasteries and the salvaging of much of the Buddhist literature have enabled Tibetan Buddhist culture to not only resurrect itself but also find favour in many Western countries. The Dalai Lama has been at the forefront of this movement. In the process, and because of his tireless efforts on behalf of Tibet and the greater issues of world peace, the Fourteenth Dalai Lama has become a well-known and much respected figure on the world stage.

The struggle for Tibetan identity and culture

As the Chinese consolidated their position in Tibet through severe repression, thousands of Tibetans followed the Dalai Lama into exile. After much hardship most of the Tibetan refugees arrived in India penniless and in failing health. Many were unaccustomed to the warmer climates of India and Nepal and died of illnesses not present in the higher altitudes of Tibet. To alleviate this problem and provide some source of income for the Tibetan refugees they were gradually moved from the transit camps set-up by the Indian government to jobs in road construction in the Himalayan region. The Dalai Lama and the Indian government jointly planned this move.[1]

With help from the Indian government and international relief agencies in the way of food, medical supplies, and money, the refugee crisis became one of resettlement rather than survival. The Dalai Lama and most of the leading Tibetans who had survived were joined at Dharamsala by many more refugees. A Tibetan settlement soon grew up at Dharamsala becoming, in the process, the centre of the Tibetan community in exile. The majority of Tibetan exiles literally cleared large tracts of jungle on large plots of donated land in the southern Indian state of Karnataka. Communities such as Bylakuppe and Mundgod eventually became prosperous through farming and crafts. In all, about twenty Tibetan resettlement communities were established in India housing about 100,000 people. The Dalai Lama's financial help to these communities has lessened over the years, with some of the communities themselves now being able to send funds to Dharamsala. The Dalai Lama also established craft centres, which led to much trade by and amongst the Tibetans in exile. Many have opened private businesses and become successful. As well, by the early 1980s, about 13,000 Tibetans were in Nepal, 1,500 in Bhutan, and another 10,000 scattered in small groups and communities throughout Western countries.[2]

Near the end of his first year in exile the Dalai Lama made a pilgrimage to Bodh Gaya, the site of the Buddha's enlightenment. He ordained his first group of monks while there. He also gave a number of teachings and held informal sessions where he gave advice, a practice he has continued throughout his life. On this occasion and again on the anniversary of the Lhasa uprising the Dalai Lama outlined a long-range plan for the resettlement of his people and their struggle for independence. At that time he stressed that the utmost need was to preserve Tibetan religion and culture.[3]

---

1. Powers, Introduction to Tibetan Buddhism, p. 176. See, Avedon, *In Exile . . .* , pp. 72-3. Also, the Fourteenth Dalai Lama, *Freedom . . .* , pp. 148-9.
2. Richardson, *Tibet and Its History*, pp. 252-3. See, Powers, *Introduction . . .* , pp. 176-7. Also, the Fourteenth Dalai Lama, *Freedom . . .* , pp. 170-2.
3. Avedon, *In Exile . . .* , pp. 81-2. See, the Fourteenth Dalai Lama, *Freedom . . .* , pp. 157-9.

The Dalai Lama managed to convince the Indian government to fund a scholastic community of 1,500 monks, selected from the 6,000 who had escaped Tibet. The refugee transit camp, Buxa Duar, became Buxa Lama Ashram. All sects of Tibetan Buddhism were represented, but the majority of the monks were Gelugpa. Many monks of the other sects had been able to find refuge in monasteries in Sikkim, Bhutan, and Nepal, where these sects were already well established, and they continued their work in these places. Working under severe hardships — many contracted tuberculosis — the Buxa monks soon were able to resume examinations for the *geshe* degree. They also started the work of reproducing the scriptures from the works that had been smuggled out of Tibet.[4]

In 1963 the Dalai Lama brought together the heads of all the different Tibetan Buddhist traditions, as well as those of the Bon religion, in order to find common ground for preserving their Tibetan culture. Soon thereafter the Dalai Lama re-established his own monastery, Namgyal, at Dharamsala. By 1968 the monasteries of Ganden, Drepung, and Sera had been re-established in Karnataka with the 1,300 surviving monks of Buxa Lama Ashram. Gradually about 150 of the leading monastic institutions of Tibet have been rebuilt in India and the Himalayan countries with over 6,000 monks practising within them by 1990.[5] The Dalai Lama tries to visit these monastic centres every year, especially the re-established Three Pillars. The Dalai Lama gives teachings, oversees examinations, and ordains monks during these visits.[6]

Important centres of Tibetan culture soon established themselves at Dharamsala; the first was the Tibetan Dance and Drama Society. The Buddhist School of Dialectics helps keep the art of debating in the monastic communities vibrant. The Tibetan Medical Centre, starting with three doctors who managed to escape Tibet, had, by

---

4. The Fourteenth Dalai Lama, *Freedom . . .* , p. 167. See, Avedon, *In Exile . . .* , pp. 92-3.

5. The Fourteenth Dalai Lama, *Freedom . . .* , pp. 183-4. See, Powers, *Introduction . . .* , p. 178. Also, Avedon, *In Exile . . .* , p. 93. See also, Richardson, *Tibet and Its History*, who points out important lamas of the Sakyapa, the Karmapa, the Nyingmapa, and the Bonpo have successful establishments at Dhera Dun, Gangtok, Kalimpong, and Simla respectively, p. 253.

6. Levenson, *The Dalai Lama*, p. 196.

the early 1970s, graduated enough practitioners of traditional Tibetan medicine to staff the settlement communities. One of the more significant cultural institutions, begun in 1971, was the Library of Tibetan Works and Archives, which has attracted Tibetan scholars worldwide. By 1984 the library had amassed over 50,000 volumes of Tibet's literature, about 40 per cent of the total, the rest lost to the ravages of the Chinese troops. The library has also published many works on Tibet's religion, history, and culture in both Tibetan and English.[7]

From the very outset of the Tibetans life in exile the Dalai Lama made a number of moves to provide protection and education for the refugee children. Very early on Prime Minister Nehru agreed that schools must be established in order to preserve the Tibetan identity and to introduce the Tibetans to the modern world.[8] The Dalai Lama had established the first Tibetan school within two weeks of arriving at Mussoorie in 1959. The Indian government created the Tibetan Schools Society as a separate branch of the Indian Ministry of Education. Tibetan children would receive a Tibetan education in their own schools, and the curriculum also included subjects that would prepare them to live in modern society. By the early 1980s over 15,000 Tibetan children were studying in more than fifty schools throughout the Tibetan settlements in India. The expenses for this system have been born by the Indian government to this day.[9]

Initially the Dalai Lama felt that education should be directed towards vocational training, but within a few years many Tibetan children were qualifying for higher academic studies, a trend which increases as time goes on. To provide further opportunities towards this aim, the Institute of Higher Tibetan Studies was established in Sarnath near Benares in 1968. Many of the university-trained Tibetans have been absorbed into the Dalai Lama's administrative service.

---

7. Avedon, *In Exile . . .* , p. 93. See, Richardson, *Tibet and Its History*, p. 253. See also, the Fourteenth Dalai Lama, *Freedom . . .* , who says much of the Library of Tibetan Works and Archives collection comes from manuscripts, *thankas* (religious paintings), and religious artefacts presented to the Dalai Lama by those who fled Tibet, which he turned over to the library, pp. 183-4.

8. The Fourteenth Dalai Lama, *Freedom . . .* , pp. 149-50.

9. Avedon, *In Exile . . .* , pp. 94-7. See, the Fourteenth Dalai Lama, *Freedom . . .* , pp. 149-50. Also, Richardson, *Tibet and Its History*, p. 254.

Opportunities for study abroad for several hundred Tibetans have helped to broaden the outlook of the Tibetan exile community. One such initiative, funded by the Rockefeller Foundation, has allowed learned monks, lamas, and laymen to work at universities in several Western countries to the mutual benefit of all involved.[10]

The Dalai Lama did much to restructure the government, with a return to Tibet clearly in mind. In 1963, using socialist principles as guidelines, the Dalai Lama oversaw the drafting of a new constitution for the Tibetan government.[11] It provided for a popularly elected legislature, which included men and women from each province and one cleric from each of the major sects including Bon. The Dalai Lama appointed one member who had distinguished himself in the Tibetan community. The Dalai Lama, who stood at the head of the government, appointed the cabinet under whom a number of departments worked. Another way to balance the power of the Dalai Lama and cabinet other than through an elected legislature was to establish a Supreme Court. The constitution also renounced war, provided for universal suffrage, equality before the law, freedoms of religion, speech and assembly, the state ownership of land, and a prohibition against the amassing of wealth. The Dalai Lama could also be impeached by a two-thirds vote of the legislature in the new Constitution of Tibet. All Tibetans in the exile community vigorously opposed this clause, but the Dalai Lama insisted that no one should be above the law. The Dalai Lama has also publicly stated that, should he return to a free Tibet, he would not exercise temporal authority but remain the spiritual leader.[12]

Tibet under Chinese rule

According to Snellgrove and Richardson, China's claim to Tibet, based on rights of possession, ceased to have any validity in 1912. They further note that Tibet and China, over the last 1,000 years, have developed quite differently. Each had a separate language and literature, distinct forms of Buddhism, different forms of art and architecture, separate economies, and different forms of government.

---

10. Richardson, *Tibet and Its History*, pp. 255-6.
11. Avedon, *In Exile . . .* , who notes this constitution remains in draft form, pending approval of the six million Tibetans within Tibet, p. 106.
12. Avedon, *In Exile . . .* , pp. 106-9. See, Powers, *Introduction . . .* , pp. 178-9. Also, Goodman, *The Last Dalai Lama*, pp. 322-3.

For China to concretize their assertion that Tibet was an integral part of China, the Chinese policy had to become one of effacing those differences.[13] The Communist Chinese regime inherited and upheld the "five races" doctrine, first espoused by Sun Yat-sen, which laid claim to, not only Tibet, but also Manchuria, Mongolia and Xinjiang (Turkestan).[14] Furthermore, according to Avedon, Chinese occupation troops were "unremittingly racist" in their attitudes towards Tibetans, regarding them as barbarians.[15]

After consolidating their hold on Tibet, the Chinese systematically demolished much of Tibet's religious culture, plundering the monasteries of their valuables before razing them or turning them into stables and granaries. Of 6,254 monasteries in Tibet, eventually only thirteen remained and those were used as propaganda museums. The monks were tortured, imprisoned, forced into labour or forced to marry. The religious literature was destroyed until the Chinese realized it could be sold for profit. The lay population did not fare much better and were subjected to the same treatment. The Tibetans were re-educated in Chinese Communist ideology, their level of compliance to that ideology determining their subsequent treatment. The education system became such that Tibetan children could not learn their own language or culture; most teachers were Chinese; and facilities were primitive or non-existent. Much of Tibet's harvests were sent to China resulting in widespread famine within Tibet. Destructive forestry practices caused flooding. The poor treatment of the people resulted in approximately 1.2 million Tibetan deaths in the first decade of the occupation.[16]

These excesses only intensified during the period of the Cultural Revolution in China, a programme instituted by Mao to speed up the transition to a full Communist society. Mao believed that by destroying the symbols of the old culture, Marxism could move in to fill the cultural vacuum.[17] In Tibet gangs of Red Guards moved across the

---

13. Snellgrove & Richardson, *A Cultural History of Tibet*, p. 273.
14. Avedon, *In Exile* . . . , p. 19.
15. *Ibid.*, p.228. See also, Powers, *Introduction* . . . , pp. 179, 185.
16. Powers, *Introduction* . . . , pp. 179-81. See, Richardson, *Tibet and Its History*, pp. 244-5. Also, Avedon, *In Exile* . . . , pp. 231-8. See also, Jetsun Pema, *Tibet: My Story*, 1997, pp. 156-9.
17. Powers, *Introduction* . . . , p. 181.

country inflicting severe punishments including torture, gangs rapes, and wholesale executions. China's activities in Tibet were condemned by numerous international human rights organizations. After the Cultural Revolution had run its course, the new leader, Deng Xiaoping, who took over after Mao's death in 1976, admitted that mistakes had been made. A more pointed comment came from the Russian writer, Alexander Solzhenitsyn, a Nobel laureate and himself a victim of Soviet repression, who wrote that China's rule in Tibet was "more brutal and inhumane than any other communist regime in the world".[18]

In the aftermath of the Cultural Revolution, Chinese policy in Tibet became more conciliatory. Tibet was proving to be expensive to hold securely, and Chinese indoctrination policies had not produced the desired effects. Also, China, becoming concerned about world opinion, likely viewed the Dalai Lama and his Tibetan government in exile as an embarrassment.[19] China hoped for the return of the exiles and the Dalai Lama, perhaps thinking his active participation would speed up by many years their plans to rehabilitate Tibet.[20] Travel restrictions were relaxed, prisoners were released and fact-finding missions sent by the Dalai Lama were allowed to tour Tibet. These missions, headed by the brother and sister of the Dalai Lama respectively, found Tibetans living in the most appalling conditions, the country's cultural institutions in ruins, and the Tibetan people still fervently loyal to the Dalai Lama and the Buddhist faith. These findings, coupled with similar reports from foreigners allowed into Tibet, induced the Chinese to further relax their policies while denouncing the abuses of power since 1959, laying the ultimate blame on the leaders of the Cultural Revolution.[21]

---

18. Powers, *Introduction . . .*, pp. 181-2.
19. The Fourteenth Dalai Lama, *Freedom . . .*, pp. 229-30. See, Richardson, *Tibet and Its History*, pp. 257-8.
20. Goodman, *The Last . . .*, p. 334.
21. Richardson, *Tibet and Its History*, pp. 247-51. See, the Fourteenth Dalai Lama, *Freedom . . .*, who says the fact-finding missions revealed "the full extent of China's rape of Tibet". He also states that most of the destruction in Tibet occurred before the Cultural Revolution, pp. 229-39, 243. Jetsun Pema, *Tibet: My Story*, who is the sister of the Fourteenth Dalai Lama and was the head of the third fact-finding expedition into Tibet in 1980 writes, "the greater part of Tibet's cultural and religious heritage was destroyed between 1956 and 1961, and not during the famous Cultural Revolution of 1966 to 1976", p. 166.

The Seventh (10th) Panchen Lama, Chokyi Gyaltsen, who had been imprisoned and confined since 1966, was rehabilitated at this time as well. He had originally co-operated with the Chinese in the 1950s but had become less compliant after the Tibetan revolt in 1959. In 1960 the People's Liberation Army (PLA) destroyed much of Tashi Lhunpo Monastery, and its monks were put into forced labour. From this time the Panchen Lama openly did what he could to preserve the religion of Tibet, and he repeatedly told the people that the Dalai Lama was Tibet's true leader. In 1961 the Panchen Lama, openly defying China, gave a 70,000-character memorandum to Mao, which denounced China's harsh treatment of Tibet and demanded better conditions and freedom of religion. Mao's promise to rectify the situation went unheeded and the Panchen Lama was told he must publicly condemn the Dalai Lama. At the Great Prayer Festival in 1962 the Panchen Lama did the opposite. Subsequently he and his family disappeared. The Panchen Lama, it was later discovered, had been imprisoned and tortured over a long period in China. Chinese officials released him in 1978, hoping he would persuade the Dalai Lama to return to Tibet. The Panchen Lama continued to advise the Tibetans to co-operate with the Chinese but also to "be for the Tibetan Cause", according to Doboom Tulku. In 1989, he died suddenly at Tashi Lhunpo Monastery.[22]

When China admitted its mistakes in Tibet and allowed some freedoms, one of the first spontaneous acts of the Tibetan people was to rebuild their monasteries all over Tibet.[23] Young men and women, who had been raised within thirty years of communist indoctrination, began to renounce their lay status and seek ordination as monks and nuns, totally astonishing the Chinese overlords. The Chinese also only allowed such religious practices as would impress tourists who were now allowed into Tibet. No practice of any substance or control over religious institutions by Tibetans was allowed.[24] Yet

22. Avedon, *In Exile . . .* , pp. 271-6, 324-5. See, Doboom Tulku, "the lineage of the panchen lamas", pp. 9-10. See also, the Fourteenth Dalai Lama, *Freedom . . .* , who notes that just before his death the Panchen Lama made a speech criticising China's Tibet policy and stating that the Panchen Lama's death in his own monastery was "symbolic, the deliberate gesture of a true spiritual master", pp. 225, 232-3, 259-60.

23. Robert Thurman, "Tibetan Buddhist Monastic and Intellectual Culture", *White Lotus*, 1990, pp. 108-9.

24. Powers, *Introduction . . .* , p. 183.

the people's devotion to the Dalai Lama and their Buddhist faith made it clear to the Chinese that their policies were not working. A new policy of moving in thousands of Han Chinese into Tibet was begun in 1984 and continues to this day. The Chinese in Tibet now outnumber the Tibetans by many millions, all "part of a process through which, according to China's Central Institute of Nationalities, 'minorities will amalgamate and disappear'".[25] In addition Chinese repression in Tibet has intensified since the early 1980s. Demonstrations in 1987, 1988, and 1989 by the Tibetan people resulted in the loss of life as they were brutally put down. This "strike hard" policy against Tibetan religion and nationalism "amounts to a deliberate policy of cultural genocide in Tibet", according to the Dalai Lama.[26] To this day the repression of Tibet by China continues. Torture is endemic according to Amnesty International. Asia Watch reports that any in Tibet who have participated in "illegal separatist activity" are "punished with escalating force and severity".[27]

The Fourteenth Dalai Lama emerges as a global figure

The present Dalai Lama has consistently advanced a peaceful and non-violent approach towards regaining Tibetan independence. He has pointed out that as a follower of Madhyamaka (the middle-way philosophy of Buddhism) he always tries to find the middle path. For this reason he has tried to establish a compromise position between the Tibetan insistence on independence and Chinese unwillingness to even consider such an option.[28] The Dalai Lama has done everything

---

25. Powers, *Introduction . . .*, pp. 183-5. See, the Fourteenth Dalai Lama, *Freedom . . .*, pp. 245. 250-1. See also, Pema, *Tibet: My Story*, who puts the number of Chinese settlers in Tibet in 1997 as 7.5 million, p. 159.
26. The Fourteenth Dalai Lama, "Statement of His Holiness the Dalai Lama On the 39th Anniversary of Tibetan National Uprising Day", *Snow Lion Newsletter*, vol. 13, no. 2, Spring 1998, p. 24. See, the Fourteenth Dalai Lama, *Freedom . . .*, who notes that the demonstrations in 1987 were widely reported by the foreign press, following which foreign journalists were expelled from Tibet. The 1988 and 1989 events were reported by foreigners present in Lhasa at the time. All these events were widely criticised by human rights organisations worldwide, and the events of 1989 were condemned by many countries, including France, the United States, and the European Parliament, pp. 254-62.
27. Powers, *Introduction . . .*, pp. 182-3.
28. Levenson, *The Dalai Lama*, p. 265.

in his power to not antagonise the Chinese leadership so as to keep channels of dialogue and communication open. At the same time he has firmly reiterated the position of the Tibetan people that Tibet is a separate country from China. Another position he holds firmly is refusing to accept the Chinese view that the Dalai Lama is the only problem. The present Dalai Lama has made it clear he will not return to Tibet until the situation inside the country is such that the Tibetan people can be happy and satisfied.[29]

Perhaps the central platform in the Dalai Lama's efforts towards reconciliation with China is his Five-Point Peace Plan, which he first outlined in an address to the United States Congress in 1987. It is comprised of the following: (1.) the transformation of Tibet into a zone of peace, (2.) abandonment of China's population transfer policy, (3.) respect for human rights and democratic freedom in Tibet, (4.) the restoration and protection of Tibet's environment, including the removal of China's nuclear weapons programme and nuclear waste facilities from Tibet, and (5.) negotiations on Tibet's status and relations between the peoples of China and Tibet. In explaining this plan the Dalai Lama said it was his desire "to restore to Tibet her invaluable role (as a buffer between India and China), by converting the entire country . . . into a place of stability, peace and harmony".[30] The following year, in a speech to the European Parliament in Strasbourg, the Dalai Lama offered Beijing the option of retaining control over foreign affairs and defense in Tibet in exchange for Tibetan autonomy in matters of civil administration, religion, education, trade, culture, tourism, and science.[31] While the Chinese response to these overtures was to denounce them, which in turn triggered the 1987 and 1989 demonstrations in Lhasa, the world's response was more positive. In 1989 the Dalai Lama was awarded the Nobel Peace Prize.

Not all of the Tibetan exile community has agreed with the Dalai

---

29. The Fourteenth Dalai Lama, *Tibet, China and the World*, 1989, pp. 36-7. See, Levenson, *The Dalai Lama*, who reports the present Dalai Lama as saying the Chinese believed their indoctrination of the Tibetan people would lead to their being disloyal to the Dalai Lama thus making the Dalai Lama easier to manipulate, p. 257.
30. The Fourteenth Dalai Lama, *Freedom . . .* , pp. 247-8. See, Catherine Ingram, "The Dalai Lama in Depth", *Yoga Journal*, no. 90, January-February 1990, p. 51.
31. Levenson, *The Dalai Lama*, p. 265. See, *Freedom . . .* , pp. 258-9.

Lama regarding his conciliatory approach to China. In the early years of their exile many younger members supported guerilla activities within Tibet and organized themselves to join such efforts. But with the maturation of the Dalai Lama's peaceful efforts towards reconstruction of Tibetan diaspora society the clamour for violent resistance died away. The Dalai Lama's stance, as a Buddhist, was that violence would only be condoned if the motivation were purely to benefit the majority of the people and only if it were used as a last resort for self-defense. The Dalai Lama maintained that, while a militant attitude amongst Tibetan youth might be good for morale, a military movement in the face of Chinese aggression would be suicidal.[32]

However, the current situation in Tibet, according to Professor Ron Schwartz, is that there is "no accommodation whatever" from the Chinese who now view Tibetan religion, cultural developments, and language as "a fundamental threat" to their power.[33] Schwartz goes on to say that since 1984, Chinese policy has been total eradication of the Tibetan language, religion, economy, and culture. Moves towards these ends are being implemented, and any negative reaction or criticism from the Tibetan population is severely punished. This is creating an explosive situation within Tibet, as there seems to be a viable underground reform movement within the country.[34] Frustration is also mounting amongst some Tibetans outside the country concerning the Dalai Lama's moderate approach and his refusal "to endorse a detailed plan for Gandhi-like non-violent resistance to Chinese authority in Tibet, as proposed by Prof. Samdhong Rinpoche", speaker of the legislature in the Tibetan government in exile.[35] Some of the more radical Tibetans in exile are even talking of an armed guerilla movement within Tibet. A number of Tibetan

32. Avedon, *In Exile . . .* , pp. 130-3. See, the Fourteenth Dalai Lama, *Tibet, China and the World*, pp. 60-2.

33. Ron Schwartz (interview with), "Potential for Catastrophe", *Shambhala Sun*, vol. 5, no. 2, November 1996, p. 32.

34. Schwartz, "Potential . . . ," pp. 32-4. See, "Frustrated Tibetans Vow Action", *The Record*, 29 May 1998, (no pg. # available). See also from the *Daily Telegraph*, "Monks forced to denounce Dalai Lama", *The Record*, 2 August 1997, which also says that riots, protests, and bomb attacks attributed to Tibetan separatists demonstrate China has yet to achieve its aims, p. A10.

35. Associated Press, "Frustrated Tibetans Vow Action", *The Record*, 29 May 1998 (no pg. # available).

support groups worldwide are also taking various political positions. They either fully support the Dalai Lama or insist on complete independence.[36] Perhaps the most noticeable voice in this regard is the Dalai Lama's elder brother, Thubten Jigme Norbu, who is pushing for full Tibetan independence, although he fully supports the Dalai Lama's non-violent philosophy.[37]

The Dalai Lama defends his stance by saying that asking for genuine self-rule through dialogue with China is the most practical and realistic approach to save and protect Tibetan culture. Since Tibetan culture includes Buddhist spirituality, he maintains that all of historical Tibet, including Amdo and Kham, and its four million Tibetans, who are already absorbed into China, must be considered as part of Tibet in the negotiations. Simply insisting on the political independence of Tibet might mean only the current Tibet Autonomous Region would be considered. This would exclude Amdo and Kham. In any case the Dalai Lama makes it clear his main concern is Tibet's special cultural heritage, its spirituality.[38]

Perhaps it is because the Dalai Lama is, first of all, the Buddhist monk Tenzin Gyatso that his actions in the secular sphere are informed by his spiritual understanding. In a recent statement the present Dalai Lama said,

> I feel personally that the Tibetan issue in which I am involved is actually a struggle for the survival of spirituality, of human values. . . . The preservation of Tibetan Buddhist culture, and Buddhism itself, is not only for the benefit of six million Tibetans; . . . humanity itself is benefited by this tradition and culture. . . .[39]

In support of Tibetan cultural and spiritual values and Tibet's plight as a nation under duress, and also as leading spokesperson for Tibet and its culture, the Dalai Lama has travelled extensively

---

36. John Ackerly, "Tibetan Cause at the Crossroads", *Shambhala Sun*, vol. 5, no. 2, November 1996, p. 38.
37. Tsoltim N. Shakabpa, "Free Tibet, one way or the other", *Los Angeles Times*, August 1996 (no pg. # available).
38. Robert Thurman (in an interview with the Dalai Lama), "The Realpolitik of Spirituality", *Shambhala Sun*, vol. 5, no. 2, November 1996, pp. 43-4.
39. Brother Wayne Teasdale, "Catholic. Buddhist Relations and Dialogue", *The Roll*, vol. XIV, no. 51, March 1998, p. 35.

throughout the world. The Dalai Lama has maintained close contacts with those regions of central Asia where Tibetan Buddhism is still practised. In places like Kinnaur, Ladakh, or Mongolia "tens of thousands of enthusiasts" will come to receive his blessings and teachings.[40] Mongolia, especially, having regained its independence, has not only welcomed the Dalai Lama repeatedly but reclaimed its status as a "linchpin of the Tibetan religious world" by recognizing Tibet's independence from China.[41]

The Dalai Lama's attention to spiritual issues has been at the forefront during his world travels. One of his main activities has been to exchange views with scholars, religious heads, and leaders in the arts.[42] The Dalai Lama is the most visible representative of a number of Tibetan scholars and eminent lamas who, as a result of the Chinese invasion of Tibet, travel widely spreading the Buddhist teachings, or the Dharma.[43] As a result of these efforts a number of Western universities offer programmes in Tibetan Buddhist studies.[44] A large number of books on Tibetan Buddhism and Tibetan culture have been published, to which the Dalai Lama has himself contributed a considerable number of titles. The Dalai Lama has also responded to the many invitations he receives and has given talks and teachings to the growing numbers of Buddhist centres worldwide that have flourished in the wake of the Tibetan diaspora. His oft-repeated message of universal love, responsibility, compassion, and kindness has made him a leading figure in promoting human rights and an internationally respected religious leader.[45]

Even as a young man the Fourteenth Dalai Lama clearly displayed his predecessor's penchant for reform. One of the first things he did, once in exile, was to lessen the degree of protocol surrounding the position of Dalai Lama and make himself much more accessible to

---

40. Mullin, *Mystical Verses of a Mad Dalai Lama*, p. 149.
41. From the Baltimore Sun, "Buddhism finds new homeland", *The Record*, 10 August, 1993, p. A10. See also, Roger Hicks & Ngakpa Chogyam, *Great Ocean*, 1990, pp. 165-6.
42. Malik, *Dalai Lamas of Tibet*, p. 83.
43. Powers, *Introduction . . .* , p. 186.
44. Hicks & Chogyam, *Great Ocean*, p. 168.
45. Malik, *Dalai Lamas of Tibet*, p. 83. See, Powers, *Introduction . . .* , pp. 185-6. Also, Richardson, *Tibet and Its History*, pp. 256-7.

his people.[46] He followed this with a more democratic constitution for Tibet. He also teaches in a manner responsive to the times, emphasising the underlying similarity of religions.[47] But perhaps one area in which he is having some profound influence in effecting change is that of the status of women in Tibetan Buddhism. The *bhikshuni* lineage (fully ordained nun) was never transmitted to Tibet. With many Western women expressing their desire to practice Tibetan Buddhism and receive full ordination as nuns this has become an issue to which the Dalai Lama, along with the late Gyalwa Karmapa (the head of the Kargupa sect), have lent their full support.[48] The Dalai Lama has also supported the full education of nuns towards the geshe degree in the Tibetan Buddhist tradition. One way of demonstrating that was to have nuns debate before him and other leading scholars at Dharamsala in October of 1996.[49] The Dalai Lama emphasized the role women should be taking when he later said "It is heartening to observe . . . that Buddhist women are casting off traditional and outmoded restraints."[50]

One restraint to the fair and free practice of religion with which the Dalai Lama and Tibetans in exile must deal is the controversy over the protector deity, Dorje Shugden. Briefly, Dorje Shugden is said to be the reincarnation of a prominent Gelugpa lama who had been a candidate for Fifth Dalai Lama. He was, according to legend, later found dead after defeating the Fifth Dalai Lama in debate. Dorje Shugden is exclusively associated with the Gelugpa sect as a protector but is regarded as dangerous to Gelugpa monks who engage in Nyingmapa practices, as did most of the Dalai Lamas, including the current Dalai Lama. The Thirteenth Dalai Lama ordered the practice of Dorje Shugden worship stopped on the grounds it was damaging Buddhism. The present Dalai Lama, on the advice of the Nechung oracle, has publicly discouraged Shugden worship on similar

---

46. Levenson, *The Dalai Lama*, pp. 118-19. See, the Fourteenth Dalai Lama, *Freedom . . .*, p. 152.
47. Hicks & Chogyam, *Great Ocean*, p. 158.
48. China Galland, *Longing for Darkness*, 1990, pp. 114-15.
49. Thubten Chodron, "Tibetan Nuns Debate for Dalai Lama", *Snow Lion Newsletter*, vol. 11, no. 1, Winter 1996, pp. 1, 12.
50. Thubten Chodron, "Life as a Western Buddhist Nun", *Snow Lion Newsletter*, vol. 11, no. 3, Summer 1996, p. 5.

grounds, claiming that it is dangerous to him personally.[51] According to Canadian scholar Gareth Sparham,

> Shugden is today a political symbol representing . . . an emerging political party, . . . wedded to the idea that the final arbiters of Tibet's destiny should be monks and, . . . that it should champion a fundamentalist version of Tibetan Buddhism as a state religion in which the dogmas of the Nyingmapa, Kargyupa and Sakyapa schools are heterodox and discredited, . . . in short a religious fundamentalist party which wants to make its religious dogma into the sole political ideology acceptable to the state.[52]

The Dalai Lama, and by extension the Tibetan government in exile, reject Shugden propitiation in order to ensure that the Dalai Lama and his government are fair and seen to be fair to as wide a spectrum of Tibetan society as possible.[53] The unfortunate result of this dispute has seen the proponents of Shugden worship picketing the Dalai Lama at some of his appearances in different parts of the world.[54] Geshe Lobsang Gyatso, head of the Institute of Buddhist Dialectics and an outspoken supporter of the Dalai Lama over the Shugden issue, and two of his disciples were murdered, supposedly by Shugden followers.[55] Another development was the expulsion from Sera Monastery of Geshe Kelsang Gyatso, the most visible proponent of Shugden worship.[56]

Another controversy with the Dalai Lama at its centre is his recent recognition of Gedhun Choekyi Nyima as the Eleventh Panchen Lama. (The Tibetan government in exile and the Dalai Lama have in recent

---

51. Stephen Batchelor, "Letting Daylight Into Magic. The Life And times of Dorje Shugden", *Tricycle*, vol. VII, no. 3, Spring 1998, pp. 60-6.
52. Gareth Sparham, "Why the Dalai Lama rejects Shugden", *Tibetan Review*, June 1996, p. 12.
53. Sparham, "Why the Dalai Lama rejects Shugden", p. 13.
54. Don Lattin, "Feud Divides Tibetan Buddhists", *San Francisco Chronicle*, 6 June 1997, pp. A1, A16.
55. "Deity or Demon", *Tricycle*, vol. VII, no. 3, Spring 1998, p. 59.
56. Geshe Gendun Gyatso and David Patt, translators, "Declaration of Expulsion of Kelsang Gyatso from Sera Je Monastery", *Snow Lion Newsletter*, vol. 11, no. 4, Fall 1996, p. 3.

years referred to the late Seventh Panchen Lama as the Tenth).[57] This action has infuriated the Chinese leadership who, wishing to maintain complete control over the selection of the Panchen Lamas, have proclaimed their own candidate and taken the candidate recognised by the Dalai Lama into custody. Since the Panchen Lama is considered the ultimate authority in choosing a new Dalai Lama these moves may have serious repercussions at a later date. Within Tibet and without, the Chinese action has been widely condemned, even at the level of the United Nations.[58] In another controversial case of recognition it was hoped the Dalai Lama's confirmation of Ugyen Thinley as the reincarnation of the Sixteenth Gyalwa Karmapa (head of the Kagyupa order) would end the disagreement over the matter.[59] Ugyen Thinley's recent escape from Tibet (much to the embarrassment of China), and his subsequent visit to Dharamsala, highlighted the important role the Dalai Lama plays as an arbiter of religious affairs within the world of Tibetan Buddhism.

Even as he exercises his traditional responsibilities on the home front, the Dalai Lama has also made extensive contacts with religious leaders around the world. He has met with, amongst others, the popes in Rome, the Archbishop of Canterbury, Orthodox archimandrites, and Muslim leaders from Ladakh and the former Soviet Union.[60] The Dalai Lama also participated in interfaith dialogue during his involvement at the Second Parliament of World Religions.[61]

An intriguing and on-going dialogue, which has developed in recent years, involving the Dalai Lama and other Tibetan lamas, is with the Native American community, particularly the Hopi nation. In the ninth century Padmasambhava prophesised "when the iron bird flies and horses run on wheels, the Dharma will come to the land of the red man".[62] The Hopis have a corresponding prophecy that

57. Doboom Tulku, "the lineage of the panchen lamas", p. 6.

58. International Campaign for Tibet, "The Panchen Lama Controversy", *Tibetan Review*, December 1995, pp. 13-14. See, Anthony Spaeth, "What Child is This", *Time*, 27 November 1995.

59. "Dharamsala seeks to end Karmapa controversy", *Tibetan Review*, May 1994, p. 6.

60. Levenson, *The Dalai Lama*, pp. 206-7.

61. William Metzger, "Toward a New Spiritual World Order", *Quest*, vol. 6, no. 4, Winter 1993, p. 16.

62. Galland, *Longing for Darkness*, pp. 328-9. See, Steven McFadden. "Ancestral Voices", *Yoga Journal*, no. 80, May-June 1988, pp. 38-9.

says, "men will come with red hats and reveal themselves to be the friends of the Hopi", which was revealed during visits by the heads of the Kagyupa and Nyingmapa orders (Red Hat sects) to the Hopi.[63] Yet another Hopi prophecy says that a true spiritual being, whose name is linked to a large body of salt water (the Dalai Lama is known as Ocean of Wisdom), will come to the Hopi when the earth is threatened. Another interesting coincidence is that an axis drawn through the earth directly connects Tibet and the land of the Hopi. It is also noted that Tibetan and Hopi dances and rituals are very similar, and both cultures have a remarkably similar fire *puja* (ritual offering or worship).[64] The Dalai Lama, who has now met with the Hopi elders and those of other Native American nations several times, is content to note the analogies and common concern for the health of the planet shared by the Hopi and Tibetans.[65]

When asked recently if he would return to Tibet in his lifetime, the Dalai Lama replied affirmatively, even going so far as to suggest it might be only another two or three years.[66] Just what role he will play is something the Dalai Lama has spoken about on many occasions. He sometimes says he might be the last Dalai Lama but quickly qualifies that by saying it is up to the Tibetan people to decide whether or not the institution of the Dalai Lama is useful to Tibetan culture. At any rate, he has also said he would prefer to see the Dalai Lama serve only as the spiritual head in Tibet and remain free of politics.[67]

As for the future of the institution of the Dalai Lama, Tenzin Gyatso has gone on record to say it may not exist in the future but for now the Dalai Lama is an important symbol of Tibet. He adds that a new Dalai Lama would certainly be sought if he were to die and that the choice would likely be according to tradition. He has also suggested that in several years time it could be possible for a departing Dalai Lama to designate a successor, or for the Dalai Lama to be chosen in

---

63. Galland, *Longing for Darkness*, p. 329.
64. McFadden, "Ancestral Voices", p. 39. See, Levenson, *The Dalai Lama*, pp. 207-8. Also, Hicks & Chogyam, *Great Ocean*, pp. 168-9.
65. Levenson, *The Dalai Lama*, p. 208. See, McFadden, "Ancestral Voices", p. 39.
66. Thurman, "The Realpolitik of Spirituality", p. 47.
67. The Fourteenth Dalai Lama, *Tibet, China and the World*, pp. 3-4.

the same manner as the popes.[68] The Dalai Lama is clearly trying to force Tibetans to consider all the alternatives for their future. But it is also clear that, while many may not agree with the Dalai Lama's approach to solving the problems of Tibetan aspirations for freedom, there is no disputing the almost "unanimous view that the Dalai Lama is Tibet".[69]

Since fleeing Tibet in 1959 the Fourteenth Dalai Lama has worked to ensure the survival of Tibetan identity and culture. He has also proposed reforms in the governing of Tibet and even the institution of the Dalai Lama itself. As a result of these efforts the Dalai Lama has taken on an international profile becoming in his own words "a global spiritual guide", whose responsibility is to see to the purity of the Buddhist religious institutions and make sure "none of the great lines of descent is lost".[70] He has acted without rancor towards those who are oppressing him and his people. He continually stresses the need for the practice of altruism and kindness in the world. To Tibetans everywhere and to a growing number of admirers worldwide the Dalai Lama truly is the embodiment of compassion.

Concluding remarks

The lineage of the Dalai Lamas directly benefited from the ascendancy of the Gelugpa hierarchy. Great prestige became attached to this lineage through the spiritual attainments and proselytizing efforts of the early Dalai Lamas. This prestige took on trans-cultural proportions when the lineage of the Dalai Lamas became associated with Tibet's protector deity Avalokiteshvara. The lineage became institutionalized about the same time as the rise to secular power of the Fifth Dalai Lama. As the Gelugpa sect, to which the Dalai Lama lineage was attached, solidified its pre-eminent position within Tibetan Buddhism, the institution of the Dalai Lama grew in spiritual authority and political significance. The institution of the Dalai Lama was first and foremost a religious institution in a culture where religion and politics were inexorably intertwined. Invested with the status of a protector deity,

---

68. Levenson, *The Dalai Lama*, pp. 267-70. See, the Fourteenth Dalai Lama, *Tibet, China and the World*, p. 5. See also, Ingram, "The Dalai Lama in Depth", p. 87.
69. Levenson, *The Dalai Lama*, p. 271.
70. *Ibid.*, pp. 268-9.

the Dalai Lamas commanded the full devotion and support of the Tibetan people. Thus it was, when conquering forces intent on destroying its culture overran Tibet, Tibetan culture was able to hang on by the slimmest of threads. This was due, in great measure, to the overwhelming love for and prestige of the Dalai Lama as a cohesive and protective force in the lives of the Tibetan people. This prestige, while attached to the institution of the Dalai Lama, is also invested in the person of the Dalai Lama himself. For these reasons, and by forcefully adhering to the values of the religious culture which he personifies, the present Dalai Lama has successfully led the struggle to preserve Tibetan Buddhist culture. That this success has grown into a worldwide dissemination of Tibetan Buddhist spirituality and concurrent concern for the fate of Tibet itself is largely due to the personality and prestige of the Dalai Lama and, by extension, the institution he personifies. As the institution of the Dalai Lama is representative of one of the great wisdom traditions bequeathed to human society we can all hope it continues to serve the growing constituency it represents.

Glossary

Abhidharma: the teachings of the Buddha on manifest knowledge or metaphysics.

Akshobhya: the Buddha corresponding to the perfected state of our faculty of consciousness.

Amban: a representative of the Emperor of China (stationed in Tibet).

Amdo: the north-eastern part of Tibet and one of the three traditional provinces.

Amitabha: the Buddha corresponding to the perfected state of our faculty of perception/discrimination.

Arhat: the ideal disciple (Worthy One), in the Theravada tradition, who has renounced all desire and seeks the final goal of *nirvana* with complete concentration.

Bardo: an intermediate state between death and rebirth.

Bhikshu: a fully ordained monk.

Bhikshuni: a fully ordained nun.

Bodhimind (*Bodhicitta*): the mind of enlightenment or altruistic attitude of working for the enlightenment of all sentient beings.

Bodhisattva: one, who having attained *bodhicitta*, renounces final liberation to remain in the world of suffering and work compassionately for the liberation of all sentient beings.

Bon: the native religion of Tibet before the coming of Buddhism, which has, over the years, assimilated many of the Buddhist teachings.

Brugpa: a faction of the "Red Hat" Karmapa sect.

Cham: a form of sacred dance or the Tibetan monastic opera.

Ch'an: the branch of Mahayana Buddhism influenced by Taoism and known as Zen.

Chenrezig (*Avalokiteshvara*): the embodiment of the compassion of the Buddhas. The patron deity of Tibet.

Ch'ing: or Manchu Dynasty of China from 1644-1912.

Cho-Yon: the priest or lama/patron relationship.

Completion Stage Yogas: (or perfection stage) in which techniques for controlling the winds and seminal fluids within the energy channels of the *yogin*'s transmuted body are employed.

Dalai Lama: (Great) Ocean (of Wisdom) Lama.

Depa: a chief administrator.

Desi: the Regent or (later) the Prime Minister.

Dharma: the Buddha's teachings. The way or the path.

Dhyani: meditation.

Drepung: one of the principal Gelug monasteries known as the Three Pillars.

Drunyik Chenmo: the executive branch of the monastic council. The Dalai Lama's chief executives in religious matters.

Dukkha: suffering.

Emptiness: lack of inherent existence and self-identity with respect to all phenomena. The ultimate nature of reality.

Ganden: one of the principal Gelug monasteries known as the Three Pillars.

Ganden Phodrang: The name of the Tibetan government taken from the name of the Dalai Lama's residence at Drepung monastery.

Ganden Tripa: the throne holder of Ganden Monastery who is head of the Gelug order. He is also referred to as the *Tri Rinpoche*.

Gelug(*pa*): (one of) the "virtuous order" school of Tibetan Buddhism.

Geshe: a scholar with the equivalent of a doctorate in traditional Buddhist studies.

Geshe Lharampa: the highest geshe designation or title.

Getsul: a novice monk.

Gongma: a king.

Guptas: peoples of northern India from whose language the first script in Tibet came.

Guru: spiritual preceptor or teacher.

Gyalwa Karmapa: (lit. conqueror or victor) the head of the Karma Kagyud school.

Hinayana: (lit. the Lesser Vehicle) one of the two main branches of Buddhism. Also, generally referred to as Theravada.

Jokang: the central cathedral of Lhasa and Tibet's holiest shrine.

Jonang: a small sect within Tibetan Buddhism disenfranchised by the Fifth Dalai Lama.

Kadam(pa): (one of) the "bound by command" school of Tibetan Buddhism. The forerunner of the Gelug school.

Kagyud(pa): (one of) the "transmission of oral teachings" school of Tibetan Buddhism. Often referred to as the Karma Kagyud.

Kailas: the mountain in south-western Tibet sacred to Buddhists and Hindus.

Kham: the south-eastern region of Tibet and one of the three traditional provinces.

Kalachakra (Tantra): one of the most popular Tibetan meditational deities, who is associated with the Shambhala salvation mythology. (The commentaries or teachings concerning Kalachakra).

Kangyur: 108-volume set of the Buddha's teachings

Karma: the process of cause and effect, action and reaction, which shapes our destiny.

Karma Kagyud (Karmapa): See Kagyud. The Karmapa are the most prominent sect within the Karma Kagyud.

Kashag: the cabinet of the Tibetan government.

Kow-tow: to bow low. A sign of subservience.

Kushob: "Mister". The name given derisively by the people to Lhazang Kahn's nominee for Dalai Lama after the Sixth was deposed.

Lama: (from bla-ma: a potency of highest significance) A monk who is a master or teacher.

Lamaism: the name given to Tibetan Buddhism by early Western observers.

Lamo oracle: one of Tibet's most important oracles.

Lineage: oral instructions on texts and practices transmitted through an unbroken line of successive masters. An unbroken line of masters.

Lojong: practices related to training the mind in the generation of *bodhicitta*.

Madhyamaka: the Middle way philosophy of Buddhism. Emptiness theory.

Mahakala: the wrathful protective form of Chenrezig.

Maitreya: The Buddha to come.

Mahayana: (lit. the Greater Vehicle) one of the two main branches of Buddhism.

Mandala: visual icon representing the sacred.

Manichaean: relating to the teachings of Manes or Manichaeus, which combined Zoroastrian, Gnostic, Christian and pagan elements, and based on the doctrines of the two contending principles of good and evil.

Manjushri: the fully enlightened mind embodied as a meditational deity.

Mantra: sacred symbol or formula, which is spoken or chanted.

Ming: Chinese dynasty from 1368-1644.

Monlam Chenmo: the Great Prayer Festival.

Mudra: hand gesture or sacred dance.

Namgyal Monastery: the Dalai Lama's personal monastery.

Nechung oracle: the channel for one of Tibet's principal protector deities.

Nirvana: inner bliss, the end of suffering, which leads to freedom from rebirth.

Norbulingka: (Jewel Park) the summer residence in Lhasa of the Dalai Lamas.

Nyam Gur: mystical verse.

Nyingma(pa): (one of) the Ancient Ones, the oldest school of Tibetan Buddhism based on the original teachings brought from India by Padmasambhava.

Om mani padme hum: (Hail to the Jewel in the Lotus) the archetypal *mantra* of Tibet. In praise of Avalokiteshvara or Chenrezig.

Ongghon: the Mongolian deity whose worship was banned by the Third Dalai Lama.

Pali: a literary language of Buddhism developed in Sri Lanka and based on the orally transmitted literature of the monastic Buddhist scriptures since the Buddha's time in a language resembling that of the Magadha region of India.

Panchen Lama: (lit. Great Scholar Lama) an emanation of Amitabha Buddha, the highest ecclesiastical figure in Tibet after the Dalai Lama.

Panch Shila: a non-alignment stance taken by the Indian government to maintain a peaceful co-existence with China.

Phamo Drupa (or *Phagmotru*): monastic order that came to power in the mid-fourteenth century.

Potala: the winter palace of the Dalai Lamas, also housing Namgyal Monastery and some government offices.

Prajnaparamita: perfection of wisdom teachings and practices.

Pramana: higher logic.

Puja: ritual offering or worship.

Pure Land: pure environments, devoid of true suffering, in which enlightened Buddhas continuously teach for the benefit of all sentient beings. A form of Buddhism.

Ringpung: a leading aristocratic family which held secular power in Tibet during the time of the Second Dalai Lama.

Sakya: (Lit. Grey Earth) school of Tibetan Buddhism named after the place where its first monastery was built.

Sangha: community of followers.

Saravastivadin: pertaining to Hinayana teachings.

Sera: one of the principal Gelug monasteries known as the Three Pillars.

Shakyamuni: (lit. silent sage of the Shakya clan) the historical Buddha.

Shastras: commentaries on the Buddha's teachings.

Shunyata: emptiness.

Sung bum: collected works.

Sutrayana: (Sutra Vehicle) the path outlining the teachings attributed to the Buddha.

Tara (*Tantra*): female Buddha, goddess or *bodhisattva* (the teachings regarding).

Tanha: desire or clinging.

Tantra: writings and teaching about and practices, which utilise all energies latent in the human condition, the body included, in service of the spiritual quest.

Tashi Lama: the Panchen Lama, referring to his monastic seat of Tashi Lhunpo.

Tashi Lhunpo: the monastic seat of the Panchen Lamas at Shigatse.

Tengyur: 225 volumes of commentaries on the Buddha's teachings.

Terma: (treasure) in the Nyingmapa tradition, previously hidden texts to be found for the benefit of future generations.

Terton: a treasure (terma) finder.

Thanka: religious paintings, usually a wall hanging.

Theravada: (way of the elders), Hinayana, one of two major branches of Buddhism.

Tsongdu: the Tibetan General Assembly.

Tukdam: a mystical state between life and death wherein consciousness is withdrawn to the heart and the body is preserved intact by the powers of meditation.

Tulku: an incarnate lama, a manifestation of enlightened awareness.

Tushita Pure Land: pure realm of the Buddha Maitreya.

Upaseka: pre-novice monastic vows.

U-Tsang: one of the three traditional provinces of Tibet, western and central Tibet.

Vajrayana: (the Diamond Way) Tibetan Buddhism.

Vinaya: the Buddha's teachings on moral and ethical conduct.

Yana: a way or path.

Yuan: the dynasty of the Mongols, which ruled China from 1271 to 1368.

Yiktsang: a council of monks overseeing religious matters in Tibetan governance.

Appendix I

The Dalai Lamas of Tibet

I Gedun Truppa (1391-1475)

II Gendun Gyatso (1475 -1542)

III Sonam Gyatso (1543-88)

IV Yonten Gyatso (1589-1617)

V Ngawang Lobsang Gyatso (1617-82)

VI Tsangyang Gyatso (1683-1706)

VII Kelsang Gyatso (1708-57)

VIII Jampal Gyatso (1758-1804)

IX Lungtok Gyatso (1806-15)

X Tsultrim Gyatso (1816-37)

XI Khedrup Gyatso (1838-56)

XII Trinley Gyatso (1856-75)

XIII Thubten Gyatso (1876-1933)

XIV Tenzin Gyatso (1935-)

Appendix II

Chronological Table

AD

627	Songtsen Gampo (first religious king) succeeds.
754	Trisong Detsen (second religious king) succeeds.
759	Shantirakshita and Padmasambhava in Tibet. Samye Monastery founded.
815	Ralpachan (third religious king) succeeds.
838	Lang Dharma (*d.* 842). Suppression of Buddhism in Tibet. Break-up of Tibetan kingdom.
978	Nyingmapa school forms.
1042	Atisha comes to Tibet. Founding of Kadampa school (sometime later by Atisha's disciple Dromton). Marpa active.
1073	Sakya Monastery built.
1110	Gampopa; founding of Kargyupa school.
1207	Tibet submits to Ghengis Khan.
1249	Sakya Pandita appointed viceroy of Tibet by Mongols.
1253	Phagpa succeeds as viceroy.
1357	Birth of Tsongkhapa, founder of Gelugpa sect.
1368	Fall of Yuan dynasty in China. Resumption of Tibetan independence.
1391	First Dalai Lama, Gedun Truppa, born.
1409	First Gelugpa Monastery, Ganden, founded.
1475	Second Dalai Lama, Gendun Gyatso, born.

1543 Third Dalai Lama, Sonam Gyatso, born.

1565 Karma Tseten of Tsang takes power.

1570 First Panchen Lama, Chokyi Gyaltsen, born.

1589 Fourth Dalai Lama, Yonten Gyatso, born.

1617 Fifth Dalai Lama, Ngawang Lobsang Gyatso, born.

1623 Karma Tenkyang becomes king of Tibet.

1642 Gushri Khan defeats Karma Tenkyang. Fifth Dalai Lama assumes temporal rule of Tibet.

1644 Beginning of Manchu dynasty in China.

1653 Fifth Dalai Lama visits Beijing.

1679 Sangye Gyatso becomes regent.

1683 Sixth Dalai Lama, Tsangyang Gyatso, born.

1697 Lhazang Khan becomes king of Tibet.

1708 Seventh Dalai Lama, Kelsang Gyatso, born.

1717 Dzungar Mongol occupation of Lhasa.

1720 Beginnings of Chinese protectorate in Tibet.

1728 Pholanas' rule begins in Tibet.

1750 Seventh Dalai Lama assumes temporal authority.

1758 Eighth Dalai Lama, Jampal Gyatso, born.

1792 Gurkha invasion of Tibet.

1806 Ninth Dalai Lama, Lungtok Gyatso, born.

1816 Tenth Dalai Lama, Tsultrim Gyatso, born.

1838 Eleventh Dalai Lama, Khedrup Gyatso, born.

1856 Twelfth Dalai Lama, Trinley Gyatso, born.

1876 Thirteenth Dalai Lama, Thubten Gyatso, born.

1888 First clash between Tibet and British.

1904 Younghusband expedition. Treaty between Tibet and Britain. Dalai Lama flees to Mongolia and China.

1910 Chinese occupy Lhasa. Dalai Lama flees to India.

1911 End of Manchu dynasty in China.

1912 Tibet resumes independence.

1914 Simla Conference. Treaty with Britain. Hostilities with China.

1935 Fourteenth Dalai Lama, Tenzin Gyatso, born.

1950 Communist Chinese attack Tibet.

1951 China annexes Tibet.

1959 Lhasa revolt. Dalai Lama flees into exile in India, followed by thousands of refugees. Tibetan government in exile formed. Tibetan government dissolved by China.

1967 Completion of destruction of holy places by Red Guards.

1989 Fourteenth Dalai Lama receives Nobel Peace Prize.

Bibliography

Ackerly, John, "Tibetan Cause at the Crossroads", *Shambhala Sun*, vol. 5, no. 2, November 1996.

Anuruddha, R.P., *An Introduction into Lamaism*, Hoshigrapur: Vishveshvananda Vedic Research Institute, 1975.

Apri, Claude, "In the footsteps of the 6th Dalai Lama", *Tibetan Review*, August 1996.

Avedon, John, *An Interview with the Dalai Lama*, New York: Littlebird, 1980.

———, *In Exile from the Land of Snows*, New York: Random House, 1986.

Batchelor, Stephen, "Letting Daylight Into Magic. The Life And Times of Dorje Shugden". *Tricycle*, vol. VII, no. 3, Spring 1998.

Bell, Sir Charles, *Portrait of the Dalai Lama*, London: Collins, 1946.

———, *The Religion of Tibet*, London: Oxford University Press, 1968.

———, *Tibet: Past and Present*, London: Oxford University Press, 1968.

Blofeld, John, *The Tantric Mysticism of Tibet*, New York: Dutton, 1970.

Burman, Bina Roy, *Religion and Politics in Tibet*, New Delhi: Vikas, 1979.

Chodron, Thubten, "Life as a Western Buddhist Nun", *Snow Lion Newsletter*, vol. 11, no. 3, Summer 1996.

———, "Tibetan Nuns Debate for Dalai Lama", *Snow Lion Newsletter*, vol. 11, no. 1, Winter 1996.

Coleman, Graham, (ed.), *A Handbook of Tibetan Culture*, Boston: Shambhala, 1984.

Craig, Mary, *Tears of Blood*, London: Harper Collins, 1992.

Dalai Lama, The Fourteenth, 'Inner Guru, Outer Guru, Secret Guru". *Quest*, vol. 1, no. 1, 1988.

———, "Statement from His Holiness the Dalai Lama on the Reincarnation of the Panchen Lama", *Snow Lion Newsletter*, vol. 10, no. 3, Summer 1995.

———, "Statement of His Holiness the Dalai Lama on the Occasion of the 36th Anniversary of the Tibetan National Uprising of 1959", *Snow Lion Newsletter*, vol. 10. no. 2, Spring 1995.

———, "Statement of His Holiness the Dalai Lama on the 39th Anniversary of the Tibetan National Uprising Day", *Snow Lion Newsletter*, vol. 13, no. 2, Spring 1998.

———, *Freedom in Exile*, New York: Harper Collins, 1990.

———, *Kindness, Clarity, and Insight* (tr. & ed. by Jeffrey Hopkins), Ithaca: Snow Lion, 1985.

———, *My Land and My People*, New York: McGraw Hill, 1962.

———, *The Buddhism of Tibet* (tr. & ed. by Jeffrey Hopkins), Ithaca: Snow Lion, 1978.

———, *Tibet, China and the World*, Dharamsala: Narthang, 1989.

Das, Sarat Chandra, *Tibetan Studies*. Calcutta: K.P. Bagchi, 1984.

Das, Surya, *The Snow Lion's Turquoise Mane*, San Francisco: Harper, 1982.

David-Neel, Alexandra, *Initiates and Initiations in Tibet*, London: Rider, 1975.

———, *Magic and Mystery in Tibet*, New York: Dover, 1971.

"Deity Or Demon", *Tricycle*, vol. VII, no. 3, Spring 1998.

"Dharamsala seeks to end Karmapa controversy", *Tibetan Review*, May 1994.

Dhondup, K. *Songs of the Sixth Dalai Lama*, Dharamsala: Library of Tibetan Works and Archives, 1981.

———, *The Water-Horse and Other Years*, Dharamsala: Library of Tibetan Works and Archives, 1984.

Doboom Tulku, "the lineage of the panchen lamas", *lungta*, no. 10, Winter 1996.

Druppa, Gyalwa Gendun, the First Dalai Lama (tr. Glenn Mullin). *Training the Mind in the Great Way*, Ithaca: Snow Lion, 1993.

Elchert, Carole, (ed.), *White Lotus: An Introduction to Tibetan Culture*. Ithaca: Snow Lion, 1990.

Eliade, Mircea, (editor in chief), *The Encyclopedia of Religion* (vols. 2, 4, 14), New York: MacMillan, 1987.

Evans-Wentz, W.Y., *The Tibetan Book of the Dead*, London: Oxford University Press, 1960.

From the Associated Press, "Frustrated Tibetans Vow Action", *The Record*, May 29, 1998.

From the Baltimore Sun, "Buddhism finds new homeland", *The Record*, 10 August 1996.

From the Daily Telegraph, "Monks forced to denounce Dalai Lama", *The Record*, 2 August 1997.

From the International Campaign for Tibet, "The Panchen Lama controversy", *Tibetan Review*, December 1885.

Galland, China, *Longing for Darkness*, New York: Penguin, 1990.

Goodman, Michael H., *The Last Dalai Lama*, Boston: Shambhala, 1986.

Govinda, Lama Anagarika, *Foundations of Tibetan Mysticism*, New York: Samuel Weiser, 1974.

———, *The Way of the White Cloud*, Berkeley: Shambhala, 1970.

Guenther, H.V., *Tibetan Buddhism in Western Perspective*, Emeryville: Dharma

Publishing, 1977.

Guide to Places of the World, London: Readers Digest Association Ltd., 1987.

Gyatso, Geshe Gendun and David Patt, (tr.) "Declaration of Expulsion of Kelsang Gyatso from Sere Je Monastery", *Snow Lion Newsletter*, vol. 11, no.4, Fall 1996.

Gyatso, Geshe Kelsang, *Introduction to Buddhism*, London: Tharpa, 1992.

Haraldsson, Erlender, *Modern Miracles: An Investigative Report on Psychic Phenomena Associated with Sathya Sai Baba*, New York: Fawcett Columbine, 1987.

Harrer, Heinrich, *Seven Years in Tibet*, London: Rupert Hart-Davis, 1957.

Harvey, Andrew, *A Journey in Ladhak*, London: Flamingo. Harper Collins, 1984.

Hicks, Roger and Ngakpa Chogyam, *Great Ocean*, London: Penguin, 1990.

Hoffmann, Helmut, *The Religions of Tibet*. London: Allen & Unwin, 1961.

Hopkirk, Peter, *Trespassers on the Roof of the World*, New York: Kodansha America, 1995.

Ingram, Catherine (in interview with the Dalai Lama), "The Dalai Lama In Depth", *Yoga Journal*, no. 90, January, February 1990.

Karan, Pradyumna, *The Changing Face of Tibet*, Lexington: The University Press of Kentucky, 1976.

Klieger, P. Christiaan, "The Institution of the Dalai Lama as a Symbolic Matrix", *The Tibet Journal*, vol. XVI, no. 1, Spring 1991.

Kornfield, Jack, *Living Buddhist Masters*, Santa Cruz: Unity Press, 1977.

Lattin, Don, "Feud Divides Tibetan Buddhists", *San Francisco Chronicle*, June 6, 1997.

Levenson, Claude, *The Dalai Lama*, London: Unwin Hyman, 1988.

Losang, Rato Khyongla Nawang, *My Life and Lives*, New York: Dutton, 1977.

Malik, Inder L., *Dalai Lamas of Tibet*, New Delhi: Uppal, 1984.

McFadden, Steven, "Ancestral Voices", *Yoga Journal*, no.80, May-June 1998.

Merton, Thomas, *Asian Journal*, New York: New Directions, 1975.

Metzger, William, "Toward a New Spiritual World Order", *Quest*, vol. 6, no. 4, Winter 1993.

Michael, Franz, *Rule by Incarnation*, Boulder: Westview, 1982.

Moore, Peter, "A Thunderstorm in the Open Sky: An Interview with Catherine Ingram", *Quest*, vol. 8, no. 3, Autumn 1995.

Morreale, Don, (ed.), *Buddhist America*, Santa Fe: John Muir Publications, 1988.

Mullin, Glenn, "Faces of the Dalai Lama: Reflections on the Man and the Tradition", *Quest*, vol. 6, no. 3, Autumn 1993.

———, "The Passing of the Second Dalai Lama", *Quest*, vol. 7, no. 2, Summer 1994.

———, *Essence of Refined Gold*, Ithaca: Snow Lion, 1985.

———, *Mystical Verses of a Mad Dalai Lama*, Wheaton: Quest Books, 1994.

———, *Path of the Bodhisattva Warrior*, Ithaca: Snow Lion, 1988.

———, *Selected Works of the Dalai Lama I*, Ithaca: Snow Lion, 1990.

———, *Selected Works of the Dalai Lama II*, Ithaca: Snow Lion, 1985.

———, *Songs of Spiritual Change*, Ithaca: Snow Lion, 1981.

Norbu, Dawa, *Tibet: The Road Ahead*, New Delhi: HarperCollins, 1997.

Norbu, Thubten Jigme & Colin Turnbull, *Tibet*, New York: Simon & Shuster, 1968.

Pallis, Marco, *Peaks and Lamas*, London: Woburn, 1974.

Pema, Jetsun, *Tibet, My Story*, Rockport Ma.: Element Books, 1997.

Petech, Luciano, "The Dalai Lamas and Regents of Tibet: A Chronological Study", *T'oung Pao*, no. 47, 1959.

———, *China and Tibet in the Early Eighteenth Century*, Leiden: E.J. Brill, 1950.

Powers, John, *Introduction to Tibetan Buddhism*, Ithaca: Snow Lion, 1995.

Price, Joan, "The Life and Teachings of the Buddha", *Quest*, vol. 8, no. 1, Spring 1995.

Rahul, Ram, "The Institution of Dalai Lama", *International Studies*, vol. 10, no. 4, April 1969.

———, *The Government and Politics of Tibet*, Delhi: Vikas, 1969.

Richardson, H.E., *Tibet and Its History*, London: Oxford University Press, 1962.

Rockhill, W.W., *The Dalai Lamas of Lhasa and their Relations with the Manchu Emperors of China, 1644-1908*, Leyden: E.J. Brill, 1910.

Schulemann, Gunther, *Geschichte Der Dalai-Lamas*, Leipzig: Veb Otto Harrassowitz, 1958.

Schwartz, Ron (interview with), "Potential for Catastrophe", *Shambhala Sun*, vol. 5, no. 2, November 1996.

Shakabpa, Tsoltim N, "Free Tibet, one way or the other", *Los Angeles Times,* August, 1996.

Shakabpa, W. D., *Tibet: A Political History*, New Haven: Yale University Press, 1967.

Shen, Tsung-Lien and Shen-Chi Liu, *Tibet and the Tibetans*, New York: Farrar, Straus & Giroux, 1973.

Smith, Huston, *The World's Religions*, San Francisco: Harper, 1991.

Smith Jr., Warren W., *Tibetan Nation*, Boulder: Westwiew Press, 1996.

Snellgrove, David and Hugh Richardson, *A Cultural History of Tibet*, New York: Frederick A. Praeger, 1968.

Snellgrove, David, *Indo-Tibetan Buddhism*, London: Serinda, 1987.

Spaeth, Anthony, "What Child Is This", *Time*, 27 November 1995.

Sparham, Gareth, "Why the Dalai Lama Rejects Shugden", *Tibetan Review*, June 1996.

Stein, R.A., *Tibetan Civilization*, Stanford: Stanford University Press, 1972.

Teasdale, Brother Wayne, "Catholic.Buddhist Relations and Dialogue", *The Roll*, vol. XIV, no. 51, March 1998.

Thondup Rinpoche, Tulku, *Buddhist Civilization in Tibet*, New York: Routledge, Kegan & Paul, 1987.

Thurman, Robert, *Essential Tibetan Buddhism*, Edison N.J.: Castle Books, 1997.

———, (in interview with the Dalai Lama), "The Realpolitik of Spirituality", *Shambhala Sun*, vol. 5, no. 2, November 1996.

Tieh-Tseng, Li, *Dalai Lamas of Tibet*, New York: Bookman Associates, 1960.

Trungpa, Chogyam, *Born in Tibet*, Boston: Shambhala, 1995.

Tucci, Giuseppe, *The Religions of Tibet*, Berkeley: University of California Press, 1988.

———, *Tibet, Land of Snows*, New York: Stein and Day, 1967, also London: Elek, 1967.

Waddell, L.A., *Tibetan Buddhism*, New York: Dover, 1972.

Walters, Frank, *Book of the Hopi*, New York: Viking, 1963.

Wilber, Ken, *Up from Eden*, Boulder: Shambhala, 1983.

Wylie, Turrell, "Lama Tribute In The Ming Dynasty", *Tibetan Studies in Honour of Hugh Richardson* (Michael Aris & Aung San Suu Kyi, editors), Warminster: Aris & Phillips, 1980.

Yongden, Lama, *Mipam*, San Francisco: Mudra, 1971.

INDEX

A page number followed by a footnote number in brackets refers to both the text and footnote on that page. No brackets indicate a reference to the footnote only.